Effective Business Presentations

JUDY JONES TISDALE, PH.D.

NETEFFECT SERIES

PEARSON
Prentice
Hall

Upper Saddle River, New Jersey
Columbus, Ohio

Library of Congress Cataloging-in-Publication Data

Tisdale, Judy Jones.
  Effective business presentations / Judy Jones Tisdale.- 1st ed.
    p. cm. - (NetEffect series)
  Includes bibliographical references and index.
  ISBN 0-13-097735-7
  1. Business presentations. 1. Title. II. Series.

  HF5718.22.T57 2005
  658.4'52-dc22

                    2004006321

Pearson Education Ltd.
Pearson Education Singapore Pte. Ltd.
Pearson Education Canada, Ltd.
Pearson Education—Japan

Pearson Education Australia Pty. Limited
Pearson Education North Asia Ltd.
Pearson Educación de Mexico, S.A. de C.V.
Pearson Education Malaysias Pte. Ltd.

10 9 8 7 6 5 4 3
ISBN 0-13-097735-7

Dedication

To John—
my husband,
my friend,
my co-adventurer in life

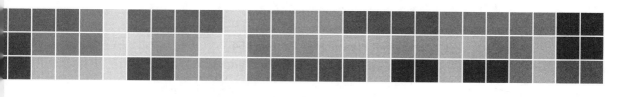

Contents

9

Preface

PURPOSE OF THIS BOOK

Effective Business Presentations offers strategies and tools to plan, develop, and deliver dynamic business presentations. Equally important, it provides tactics to analyze performance for effectiveness. This practical book includes the following key topics: audience analysis, message development, delivery techniques, strategic PowerPoint® use, anxiety management, question-and-answer sessions, and team presentations.

HOW TO USE THIS BOOK

Whether you've presented many times or you're someone new to presentations, this book is for you! Individuals who haven't presented before or who present infrequently will find the organization of the book offers structure in planning and building presentations. Additionally, it provides specific details for honing delivery skills and creating visuals to be as effective as possible in promoting a message. Other presenters may desire to reassess or refine the way that they generate and deliver presentations; these readers can review the chapters in the order they're presented or go straight to the chapters relevant to the areas on which they want to work. Experienced presenters can selectively skim various chapters at any stage of their presentation development to find useful tips and tools to assist them in developing their presentation methods. *Effective Business Presentations* is a resource for presenters to learn how to identify strengths and challenges and then develop action plans at each presentation stage in order to hone the skills necessary to accomplish presentation goals.

Questions and suggestions about *Effective Business Presentations* are welcomed. You may email me at Judy_Tisdale@unc.edu. Best wishes for successful presentations!

ACKNOWLEDGMENTS

Many people contributed in various ways to *Effective Business Presentations*. I thank Laura Rogers, a former book representative now editor for Prentice Hall, for her encouragement to start this project. Special thanks to my editor Elizabeth Sugg, my production editor Gay Pauley, and my copyeditor, the eagle-eyed Susan Higgins. Their patience and suggestions have been appreciated more than I can express to them! I also thank UNC's Kenan-Flagler Business School and my colleagues Heidi Schultz and Susan Irons for the support and resources that enabled me to research and write about business presentations, and David Ernsthausen, Kenan-Flagler Faculty Teaching and Support Librarian, for his expertise and guidance concerning business resource databases. Additionally, the UNC Graduate School, specifically Michael Poock and Sandra Hoeflich, gave me the opportunity to apply my research by working with the Professional Development Program and the Roysters Fellows Program. Of course, this book would not have been possible without my students; they inspire me every day. In particular, I'd like to acknowledge David Watson, an accomplished cartoonist, for the original artwork in this text. I so much appreciate his creativity in bringing presentation concepts to life in his illustrations. Last, but never least, I thank my husband, John, for his boundless enthusiasm for this project and his enduring patience throughout the process of writing this book.

ABOUT THE AUTHOR

Judy Jones Tisdale, Ph.D., is an Adjunct Associate Professor and Associate Director of the Management Communication Program at the University of North Carolina Kenan-Flagler Business School. She teaches oral and written management communication for the undergraduate and M.B.A. programs, and she is the director of the Kenan-Flagler Business Communication Center. Additionally, Judy is a member of UNC's Graduate Faculty and teaches presentation courses for graduate students across all disciplines at UNC-Chapel Hill. A former vice president with Nations-Bank (now Bank of America), Judy joined the Kenan-Flagler faculty in August 1998 after 13 years in sales and sales management in Bank of America's consumer/small business division. She earned her B.A. in English and Spanish from High Point University, her M.A. in English from Appalachian State University, and her Ph.D. in English from the University of North Carolina at Greensboro. Her current research, presentations, and publications involve academic service-learning, business presentations, and accounting communication.

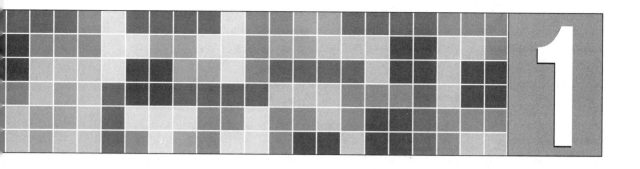

Developing Presentations and Presenters

PERFORMANCE GOALS

After completing this chapter, readers will be able to:

■ identify the presentation stages: plan, prepare, polish, perform, and assess performance

■ understand the organization of this book and its content highlights

The purpose of this book is simple: to give you strategies to develop, deliver, and then analyze effective presentations. Professionals in all industries consistently rank solid oral communication as one of the key factors for success. In many fields, in fact, research shows that business practitioners believe it's almost impossible to rise through the career ranks without polished presentation skills (Curtis, Winsor, Stephens, 1989).

Indeed, it's difficult these days to go through a career without strong oral communication skills. You may need to (1) share with general management your department's recommendation on a cost-savings initiative, (2) explain new annual goals to your regional sales team, (3) brief a department on policy changes, (4) promote your company's progress on diversity issues within your industry to an outside review board, or (5) pitch a service, a product, or even your company to a potential client. Whatever the level of presentation you might make—internal, external, to peers, to direct reports, to upper management—you should convey yourself, your company, and your information as professionally as possible. The practical strategies that this book offers will support you in refining and polishing your presentation skills.

FORMAL PRESENTATION TRAINING

Though you may have made numerous presentations in school and in your career, take a moment to consider how much formal training you've had to actually create and deliver these presentations. You've probably given presentations in school about a topic you had been studying. You've likely had considerable experience and practice making presentations in the workplace. And chances are you've attended workshop sessions on presentation skills. Mark the appropriate boxes in Exhibit 1.1 to gauge your comfort level with the presentation skills training you've received. If you feel that you didn't receive in school the training you needed to develop effective business presentation skills, you're not alone. The National Communication Association (1998) conducted a study that showed only 20 percent of Americans surveyed believed that their school experiences prepared them to create and deliver strong presentations. Further, the same study found that less than one quarter of the American public felt comfortable speaking in front of others.

EXHIBIT 1.1 Skills assessment.

I've received formal training in the following areas:	Yes	No
Analyzing an audience		
Structuring a message to accomplish a particular purpose (to inform, to persuade, etc.)		
Creating professional notes		
Developing a dynamic delivery style		
Creating appropriate visuals and knowing how and when to use each type of visual		
Working on and delivering a team presentation		
Handling the question-and-answer session		
Assessing performance after a presentation		

One of the greatest myths in our society about speaking in front of people is that some individuals are "born presenters." Yes, it's true that some people are more comfortable speaking to groups of people than others. These individuals seem to have a gift that makes them appear poised, comfortable, and confident no matter what might happen during a presentation. However, presenters who aren't as confident about their oral communication skills can benefit from developing strategies for their presentations; they *can* plan to promote themselves and their concept(s) effectively. Even those who love being in front of an audience need to develop similar strategies to achieve their desired results. Simply enjoying public speaking doesn't necessarily translate into an effective presentation. This book offers presenters techniques to analyze an audience, develop a message designed to accomplish a specific purpose, refine delivery style, present in a team format, manage the Q&A session, and assess performance.

PRESENTATION STAGES

Delivering a presentation is but one step in a series of stages that make up a presentation. Exhibit 1.2 shows these steps within each stage. Presenters may well look at this exhibit and despair of being able to master all of these steps. Or, they may try to identify which steps appear to be more important and focus attention on these, neglecting the others. Furthermore, this diagram doesn't include research or work that a presenter may already have completed on the topic itself or strategies that presenters may use at any stage of the presentation process to calm or channel anxieties! However, it's

EXHIBIT 1.2 Steps to an effective presentation.

5. Post-Presentation Stage

Follow Up on Any Unanswered Questions	Assess Performance

⬆

4. Presentation Stage

Use Effective Delivery Techniques	Present Visuals	Handle Q&A

⬆

3. Polishing Stage

Practice	Solicit Feedback

⬆

2. Preparation Stage

Develop and Organize the Message	Develop Visuals	Plan for Potential Questions

⬆

1. Planning Stage

Determine Presentation Purpose	Analyze Audience Characteristics	Assess Presenter's Situation

important to think about each step within the stages as an integral part of the whole.

Consider how we learn to play a sport or a musical instrument. We don't—we can't—begin with a performance itself. Instead, we must master each step that will ultimately lead to a performance. Let's look as an example at some basic stages a tennis player must go through in order to learn the game and play competitively. First, the tennis player must *plan* which racquet to purchase, when and where to take lessons, and how much time to invest in learning the game. Second, the tennis player must *prepare* by learning how to play. The player needs information such as how to hold the racquet, how to move on the court, how to perform the various swings, and how to keep score. Third, the tennis player must *polish* performance by practicing, perfecting swings, and volleying with another player. Fourth, the tennis player must *perform* in a match-type scenario; without this critical step, it's difficult for a player to improve style, accuracy, and performance—basically, the player "tests" the learned skills. And, finally, the tennis player must *assess* performance in order to know which features of his or her game need additional work. Just because tennis players learn the game doesn't mean that they don't need to practice any longer before playing matches. Instead, planning, preparing, practicing, and assessing performance become even more important for players to work on if they wish to excel in their game.

Let's now transfer this example back to making a presentation. Just as athletes (or musicians, for that matter) focus on "the basics" of their craft—preparation and practice—before performing and then assess their performance afterward for improvement purposes, so presenters should hone the steps they need to work on as well. It's not reasonable to expect a presentation to be as polished and professional as possible if a presenter hasn't put time and effort into the planning, preparation, polishing, and assessment stages. Some experienced presenters might be able to "wing it" and survive unscathed, but most of us need to pay attention to the pre-presentation work and the post-presentation assessment to help us be as confident and prepared as possible.

Effective presenters are methodical in planning for, crafting, honing, and delivering presentations. In addition, they're honest with themselves in analyzing how well they performed. Effective presenters consistently work hard to complete each step in the presentation process, always keeping in mind the particular goal(s) they wish to achieve from the presentation session. For individuals who present regularly, the presentation stages discussed in this book may appear to be time consuming and somewhat unnecessary. After all, if you make numerous presentations, why would you need to practice what you'll say out loud before each presentation? Why write out notes for a message before you design visuals? Why make time to learn as much as possible about the audience if the presentation purpose appears fairly simple? Why try to determine what questions an audience might have and then plan for answering them? Why assess performance after each presentation? The answer to these questions is simple: No matter how many presentations you make, each one is unique.

To be truly effective, it is important to customize each presentation to the situation and for the audience. Audiences know when they're experiencing a "canned presentation." The differences between dynamic presenters and average presenters lie in how well the presenter understands his or her goal(s) and then tailors, prepares for, and delivers a presentation to a specific audience.

HOW THIS BOOK IS ORGANIZED

This book devotes a chapter to each of the key elements of dynamic presentations:

- *Chapter 1, Developing Presentations and Presenters.* Introduces the concepts that we'll examine in this text.
- *Chapter 2, Getting Started.* Addresses the following pre-presentation planning strategies: presentation purpose, audience analysis principles, and presenter considerations. The chapter covers the importance of clarifying each presentation's purpose and desired outcome to best achieve the desired goal(s). And it explains how presenters can identify audience characteristics to customize a presentation. Additionally, presenters can inventory their current presentation skills to recognize their strengths and identify the areas that they wish to improve.

- *Chapter 3, Developing an Effective Message.* Demonstrates how presenters might organize typical presentations to accomplish a particular purpose. The chapter examines rhetorical strategies to develop several presentation patterns and problem-solving messages.

- *Chapter 4, Delivering with Impact.* Gives readers strategies to present themselves effectively to audiences. Describes and analyzes various delivery techniques to help presenters enhance credibility during a presentation. Encourages presenters to understand their own communication style, as they learn how and when to use other communication styles. This chapter focuses on the following delivery areas: speaking voice, nonverbal communication cues, and presentation notes.

- *Chapter 5, Using PowerPoint Wisely.* Explains how to use PowerPoint® wisely. The PowerPoint program can be an important presentation tool; however, this tool should support the presenter's message—not become the presentation itself. This chapter addresses effective slide design techniques, organized information structure, and slide enhancements.

- *Chapter 6, Using Other Visuals.* Addresses how presenters can support their messages using visuals other than PowerPoint. Although it's almost expected for most presentations, PowerPoint isn't the only visuals tool available. The chapter addresses the following alternative visuals and examines the effectiveness of each in various presentation situations: overhead transparencies, flip charts and whiteboards, and handouts.

- *Chapter 7, Overcoming Presentation Anxieties.* Offers ways for readers to minimize or control presentation jitters. The chapter defines types of presentation anxieties so that speakers can learn how to diagnose their nervousness and make plans to compensate for it. Additionally, the chapter addresses several methods for presenters to use in combating presentation anxiety.

- *Chapter 8, Handling Q&A.* Gives readers a context to help them prepare for question-and-answer sessions. The chapter explains how to prepare for questions, how to anticipate specific types of questions, how to address questions during the Q&A, and how to present confidently during the session.

- *Chapter 9, Presenting as a Team.* Addresses team presentation strategies, explaining techniques in developing stronger teams and then delivering the presentation.

As you can see from this outline, the design of *Effective Business Presentations* allows readers to dip into any one chapter or combination of chapters to address various stages of the presentation process.

EXERCISES　Developing Presentations and Presenters

EXERCISE 1　Taking Stock of My Situation

Complete Exhibit 1.3 by checking "Yes" or "No" in the appropriate box beside each statement:

EXHIBIT 1.3　Taking stock.

Statement	Yes	No
I feel varying levels of anxiety before making presentations.		
I feel more nervous during the presentation than the audience probably realizes.		
I'd like to make my presentations more dynamic.		
I've "frozen up" during a previous presentation.		
I'd like my audience to view me as a credible, accomplished professional.		
I'd like to refine my performance in team presentations.		
I'd like to be more confident in my ability to motivate or persuade an audience.		
I'd like to learn how to better deal with a presentation habit that I need to break (e.g., saying "uhm" frequently, talking too rapidly, not making enough eye contact).		
I'd like to develop more interesting visuals (e.g., PowerPoint, handouts)		
I'd like to be more concise and "on topic" in my presentations.		
I'd like to learn how to better analyze my audience to get the results that I want from my presentations.		
I'd like to refine my team presentation skills.		
I want to better handle question-and-answer sessions in presentations.		

EXERCISE 2   Analyzing Myself as a Presenter

What would you list as your top three presentation strengths and challenges?

Strengths	*Challenges*
1.	1.
2.	2.
3.	3.

Ask a colleague who has seen you present to identify your top three presentation strengths and challenges. Does your colleague's list match up with your own assessment?

EXERCISE 3   Analyzing Others' Presentations

Attend a presentation and answer the following questions as soon after the session as possible:

1. What did the presenter do well?
2. What could the presenter do to strengthen performance?
3. What was the presenter's key message?
4. What visuals did the presenter use to support and enhance the message? Were they effective?
5. How did the presenter handle the Q&A?
6. How did the audience respond to the presenter?
7. What was your impression of the presenter? What did the presenter do or say to give you that impression?

Using what you've learned from this presentation, write a one-page critique outlining what you believe to be the presenter's strengths and challenges.

EXERCISE 4   Learning from Accomplished Presenters

Interview two people you believe to be accomplished presenters. Ask them the following questions:

A. What types of presentations do you typically make?

B. How do you prepare for a presentation?

C. What is the most difficult part of presentations for you? The most rewarding?

D. What do you believe to be your presentation strengths? Weaknesses?

E. What have you done to polish the areas you believe to be your weaknesses?

F. How do you manage presentation anxiety?

Compare their answers to see how individual presenters vary their approach to the presentation process.

EXERCISE 5 Considering How to Handle Those Tough Situations

As you're interviewing the presenters you selected for Exercise 4, ask them how they would handle any of the situations in Exhibit 1.4.

EXHIBIT 1.4 Handling tough situations.

Presentation Situation	Action Question
PowerPoint Issues	
■ The audience is "trapped" in a session while a presenter reads line by line through what seems like endless PowerPoint slides—and many of them have such small text or graphics on them that people can't see them anyway.	■ How would you design your slides differently? Be specific here—what slide design techniques would you use to make the slides more attractive from the audience's viewpoint?
■ An audience is waiting for a presentation to start, and the presenter doesn't know what to do because the computer server won't allow access to the PowerPoint program.	■ What would have been your back-up plan if you were this presenter?
■ Audience members walk out of a presentation with a handout of the PowerPoint slides wishing that the presenter would have saved their time by just sending the handouts through interoffice mail so that they could read them for themselves.	■ How would you have designed your slides and your handout differently to maximize use of the presentation time and audience patience?

EXHIBIT 1.4 Continued.

Presentation Situation	Action Question
Delivery Styles ■ Audience members start doodling to try to stay awake as a presenter drones on in a monotone and avoids looking at anyone directly. ■ The audience is nervously anticipating when the presenter, who's been practically bouncing off the walls, might jump onto the conference room table and start shouting.	■ What delivery techniques would you use to avoid losing the audience? ■ What movements would you plan to show enthusiasm and energy during your presentation—without making the audience nervous?
Nervous Presenters ■ Audience members feel sorry for a presenter who is sweating profusely and seems to be gasping for air at the end of each sentence. ■ Most of the audience members watch without envy as someone challenges the presenter's credentials or intentions in the Q&A session. ■ The audience watches the back of the presenter's head through most of the presentation as he talks to the screen where his PowerPoint slides are displayed.	■ What can you do to minimize the amount of nervousness that you feel during a presentation? ■ How can you prepare yourself to anticipate challenge questions during the Q&A session? ■ How would you maintain eye contact with the audience during a PowerPoint presentation?
Message Strategies ■ The audience believes the presentation started off interestingly enough, but they just can't seem to figure out where the presenter is going with the topic. ■ A presenter waits her turn to present to a group, but the presenter who has the floor is eating into her time . . . and the presenter who is waiting knows that she's up last on the agenda before lunch break begins.	■ How will you structure your message to accomplish the goal you've set for the presentation? ■ How would you handle having less time to deliver your message than you'd anticipated?

References

Curtis, D. B., Winsor, J. L., & Stephens, R. D. (1989). National preferences in business and communication education. *Communication Education, 38*(1), 6–14.

National Communication Association. (1998). How americans communicate. Retrieved April 1, 2002, from www.natcom.org/research/Rober/how_americans_communicate_htm

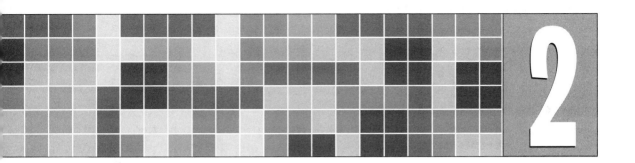

Getting Started

PERFORMANCE GOALS

After completing this chapter, readers will be able to:

- craft and articulate specific purpose and goal for each presentation session
- analyze audience to customize each presentation

It's tempting when assigned a presentation to open up Microsoft PowerPoint and begin creating a dynamic multimedia presentation with all the program's bells and whistles. However, close attention to a few critical planning stages— before PowerPoint—helps presenters avoid spending precious time backtracking or revamping an entire presentation because groundwork wasn't laid efficiently. Additionally, early attention to details can alleviate a speaker's nervousness about being in front of a group of people and result in enhanced speaker credibility during a presentation.

Think about the preliminary work for a presentation as "homework." You know from school that completing homework prepares students to anticipate and master topics for upcoming tests or class discussions. Likewise, early presentation planning readies presenters because it helps them craft content and structure to meet a specific audience's expectations and needs. With this knowledge, presenters can customize a unique message for each situation and deliver it with confidence.

Presentation sessions will vary in content, purpose, audience composition, and speaker-audience interaction, just to name a few variables. Some situations might not need much in-depth planning because the presenter might already know the audience well and is an expert on the topic. Others may require more planning because the presenter might not have built-in credibility with the audience, or the topic might be one that the audience will be resistant to hearing. This chapter addresses two issues common to all presentations that presenters should consider before preparing a message and visuals:

- Purpose and goal
- Audience analysis

Close attention to details in these areas will pay off by contributing to a well-planned message tailored to a specific audience. Additionally, this planning will enhance credibility, result in a strong performance, and aid in minimizing nervousness.

PURPOSE AND GOAL

Each time you begin creating a presentation, consider the following questions:

1. What is the purpose of the presentation?
2. What should be the outcome of the presentation?

Communication experts J. V. Thill and C. L. Bovée (2002) call these same questions the "general purpose" and the "specific purpose," respectively (p. 74). Articulating the answers to these questions helps to define a purpose and focus on structure.

Presentation Purpose

Businesspeople have many reasons to deliver a presentation. Some of these might include the following (Locker & Kaczmarek, 2001; Thill & Bovée, 2002):

- Inform
- Persuade
- Motivate
- Entertain
- Build goodwill

Of course, most presentations will have some combination of these purposes. For example, to persuade, a speaker may need to inform as well as to motivate. Or, to build goodwill, a speaker needs to persuade the audience that the topic is relevant and the speaker is credible.

Typically, the primary purposes for most business presentations are to inform and to persuade. Managers may need to inform an audience about a particular issue, product, service, or process. Trainers might need to offer information for audience members to understand a new product line. More than simply informing, a team leader might need to persuade a group of people to act on a recommendation, contract for a firm's services, or adopt a specific attitude about a new procedure. Division heads may need to encourage a group of managers to adopt cost-saving recommendations or a new training method. Executives may need to convince an audience to support an unpopular business decision or accept unwelcome news about less-than-expected earnings. Whether the purpose is to inform or to persuade, however, presenters must clearly identify a presentation purpose before beginning to develop the message that they wish to convey. Without a sense of the presentation's "bottom line," presenters may struggle to generate an organized message and, as a result, deliver an unfocused presentation.

To determine a presentation purpose, first write out a simple sentence or phrase stating exactly what your task is. In a presentation to *inform* a group of bankers about proposed federal lending guidelines, for example, here's how the presentation purpose might read:

> "My purpose for this presentation is to inform the audience about proposed equal credit lending guidelines."

Bankers who attended the session would take the information back to their legal and credit departments to determine how they would implement new policies. The purpose statement would be different if the presenter instead met with a group of bankers to *convince* them to support proposed new federal regulations on equal credit lending opportunities. The presentation purpose statement might then read:

> "My purpose for this presentation is to persuade the audience to act on my recommendation."

More than informing the group of bankers about the proposed regulations, the purpose indicates that the presenter intends to convince the session participants to support the new rules.

Presenters who can clearly summarize the purpose of the presentation in one sentence will stay on track while developing message content and designing supporting visuals. The purpose serves as a constant reminder of the presentation's focus—to inform, to persuade, to motivate, and so forth.

Presentation Goal

Once you've identified the purpose of a presentation, what's the next step? Decide what the presentation outcome should be. Put simply, you're articulating what you want the audience members to know or to do when they leave the presentation session (Guffey, 2003). Presenters who take time during the presentation planning process to determine—specifically—what they want to accomplish will focus their efforts on structuring a presentation to meet their goal. As a result, audiences won't leave a session wondering why they just spent the past 45 minutes or so listening to a presentation with a vague point; they'll know exactly what the presenter needs them to know or wants them to do.

Let me elaborate a bit more about goal statements in two examples of presentations I recently gave. I often talk with various groups about dynamic presentation skills and tailor my discussion depending on who my audience members are and why I was asked to speak to that particular group. In one workshop, I spoke with a group of international students who wanted to learn more about presentation proficiency as defined by U.S. business conventions. Here are the purpose and goal statements I wrote for that presentation:

1. *Purpose:* to inform these students about basic presentation skills
2. *Goal:* to have them understand the typical U.S. presentation styles and to give them practice using these styles in front of a small group

Notice how much more specific the goal statement is—more tailored to the students' specific situation and learning needs than simply a general session on presentations. Because these students were concerned primarily with learning how U.S. presentation styles compared to presentation styles from their native countries, I focused the session on delivery skills, with a segment reserved for organizational patterns used in the United States.

I had a very different agenda with a session that I conducted for a group of advanced graduate students. Here are the purpose and goal statements I wrote for this group:

1. *Purpose:* to inform them about basic presentation skills
2. *Goal:* to explain how they could use effective presentation skills to communicate their doctoral research to the general public

Steeped in their academic specializations, these graduate students wanted to know how they could efficiently and clearly convey their research to civic or government groups (lay audiences). Therefore, I focused the session on organizational patterns to give them a framework within which to place their information, depending on the purpose of their own presentations. I also addressed the importance of couching language and findings in terms that laypeople would understand.

Notice that in both workshops (the international student session and the graduate student session) the purpose was the same: to inform the audience about basic presentation skills. However, my goal—and thus what I discussed and how I organized my message—was strikingly different for the two groups.

To further illustrate the distinction between a presentation purpose and a presentation goal, Exhibit 2.1 outlines some examples from a few presentations that I've delivered. As you can see in this exhibit, the outcome statements are

EXHIBIT 2.1 Presentation purpose and goal.

Presentation Purpose	Presentation Outcome Goal
Inform audience about my recent research on accounting education practices	When audience members leave the session, I want them to understand what selected college and university accounting programs across the country are doing to refine accounting students' communication skills.
Inform audience about business proposals	When audience members leave the session, I want them to better understand how to create an effective business proposal based on the model that we discussed in the session.
Persuade audience to view me as an expert	When audience members leave the session, I want them to consider me a resource for their sales training program.
Persuade audience to adopt sales technique changes	When audience members leave the session, I want them to implement the sales training methods that we discussed in the session.

more detailed than the purpose statements. For example, in the first presentation scenario listed, the purpose statement says that the presentation should *inform* the audience about a particular topic: recent research on accounting education practices. But the outcome statement spells out what I want the audience to know or understand, specifically, when they leave the session: know what college and university accounting programs across the country are doing to refine accounting students' communication skills. The outcome statement includes the purpose statement and details that I want the audience to know about accounting education practices.

In the first scenario in Exhibit 2.1, my explicit purpose was to inform. I didn't necessarily need the audience (a group of communication educators) to do anything other than learn about the research I'd completed. I didn't ask them to adopt the material in their own programs, to contract with me for consulting projects, or to follow up on the research. Admittedly, however, I did have what Kitty Locker (2000) calls a "secondary purpose" (p. 222)—a desire to create a positive image of myself and my academic institution. I wanted the audience to view me as a credible, professional researcher. To this end, I developed a clear message based on my findings, created dynamic visuals, and polished my delivery skills.

Consider the following examples of goal statements when planning a presentation outcome:

- ❑ I want my audience to commit to doing business with my firm *(purpose: to inform and to persuade)*
- ❑ I want your associates to understand a new operational process *(purpose: to inform)*
- ❑ I want our marketing group to map out a new strategy *(purpose: to inform and to persuade)*
- ❑ I want to inform senior management about the sales results for the past fiscal year *(purpose: to inform)*
- ❑ I want the audience to have a better appreciation of the company's efforts to improve performance in a particular segment during the past year *(purpose: to inform and to persuade)*
- ❑ I want to share our company's community development efforts with concerned citizens *(purpose: to inform and to persuade)*

You can see how much more specific the goal statements are when compared to the purpose (in italics at the end of each example). Visualize during the planning stages your desired outcome after each presentation session; in one or two sentences, what should audience members know or do when they leave the session?

To hone your focus on identifying presentation purpose and goals, type them in either the header of each of your note pages or on the first and last page of the notes. The constant reminder will keep you focused on the outcome each time you practice the presentation. And during a session, it can keep you motivated to accomplish your goal.

AUDIENCE ANALYSIS

A thoughtful audience analysis is one of the most crucial steps in the presentation process. Presenters need to understand as much as possible about a presentation situation and the people who will attend a session in order to shape "strategy, organization, style, document design, and visuals" (Locker & Kaczmarek, 2001, p. 33). Additionally, a thorough analysis can provide a measure of security for anxious presenters. If they learn as much as possible about an audience *before* a presentation, they can minimize the chance of surprises *during* the presentation—they'll feel more prepared. Essentially, audience analysis drives the presentation.

If presenters are already familiar with a company and/or the people who will attend the session, an audience analysis can be fairly simple. For example, a team leader who needs to explain a new government regulation to his project team wouldn't need to spend much time learning about the audience; he likely works closely with the team and understands how much they know about the topic, what motivates them, and what their attitudes are toward it. Likewise, he probably also knows the room and the technology he'll

use during the presentation. Conversely, presenters who don't know much about an audience should spend more time learning about audience characteristics and the presentation environment to prepare efficiently. Key categories of information that presenters need to know to develop a comprehensive audience analysis include the following:

- Demographic factors
- Corporate factors
- Knowledge and attitude factors
- Miscellaneous factors

You can learn details about many of these categories simply by talking in depth with the individual(s) who arranged for you to make a presentation.* Don't hesitate to ask questions to learn as much as possible in the initial conversation so that you don't waste time or lose credibility with follow-up telephone calls or e-mails. At the end of this chapter, you'll find a presentation preparation worksheet that you can use to prepare for upcoming presentations.

Demographic Factors

Corporate marketers divide consumers into various segments based on common characteristics shared by groups. In his textbook *Marketing Management* (2003), Philip Kotler points to demographics as one of the most common methods to target specific consumer groups. Demographics include the following segments: age, gender, income, occupation, education, relation, race, and nationality. Understanding the needs and desires of these segment groups helps marketers position products and services to meet consumer demands and appeal to specific audiences.

Though it's important to avoid sweeping generalizations and stereotypes, presenters can use demographics to learn about commonalities among audience members, thus allowing for informed assumptions about those who attend a presentation. This knowledge supports presenters in preparing messages customized to each audience and structured to support each unique presentation goal.

Exhibit 2.2 lists the most common audience demographic groupings that presenters may explore prior to presentations, depending, of course, on how well they already know an audience. "Doing their homework" in these categories enables presenters to tailor presentations to each group.

The following example shows how this customization can boost the presenter's credibility and enrich message content: I recently saw a corporate re-

---

*Locker and Kaczmarek (2001) title these people the *initial audience* (the individual who assigns the message) and the gatekeeper (the individual who sets up the message).

EXHIBIT 2.2 Demographic groupings.

- Gender
- Age
- Income level
- Position within company
- Educational background
- Ethnicity
- Occupation or level of job within company
- Relationships among audience members

cruiter discuss job interviewing skills with a group of college students who attended his presentation as part of a job search assignment in a business communication course. The presenter's content and visuals indicated he had clearly customized his presentation to this audience at this particular university. When he was asked to make the presentation, he talked at length with the individual who scheduled him to facilitate the session and to communication instructors who taught the related course. He learned that the students already had a solid grounding in writing cover letters from the course assignment, and so he knew he didn't need to explain how to write a strong cover letter during his presentation. He did, however, reference in his talk the cover letter that the students had been working on in the context of how that document complemented interviewing strategies. Additionally, the recruiter discovered in his audience analysis that the majority of the students had not yet worked in career-level positions.

With what he learned about the audience in planning for the presentation, the presenter explained his interview strategies with illustrations that the students could readily identify with: he structured the content level to address students who were just beginning their search for an entry-level career position. He also used the university's logo and mascot as a graphic on each of his PowerPoint slides. An accomplished speaker, this recruiter had obviously made this presentation to many different student groups. However, he gained instant credibility in referring to the communication course assignment because the students recognized that he understood their more immediate goal (the assignment), over and beyond the higher goal (getting a job). And when asked later to reflect on the recruiter's presentation, virtually all of the students mentioned that they liked the logo and mascot graphic the recruiter used on his visuals. They felt that it showed he was closely connected with their university. As a result of his efforts to learn about this audience and then customize the material for them, the recruiter came across as a likeable and credible presenter. His thorough discussions with the presentation planners clearly helped him shape the message content to achieve his goal: to inform students about effective interview strategies.

Depending on the presentation purpose and goal, presenters don't necessarily need to explore all the demographic categories in Exhibit 2.2. In a presentation to a group of managers informing them about the implementation plan for a new computer networking system in their company, for example, a presenter really would have no reason to know an individual manager's income level. Instead, the presenter should know the corporate needs for a new system and the impact that the implementation would have on each manager's department; this is more relevant information to best explain the plan to these particular managers. On the other hand, an insurance agent who holds a seminar for potential clients should learn about the audience's income levels before the presentation in order to effectively select products and investment plans for the session. As you can see, knowing the income level is nonessential in the first scenario and crucial in the second.

One particular audience demographic category to highlight is culture or ethnicity. Because today's workforce is significantly more diverse than in the past and has access to vast amounts of information via the Internet, presenters need to learn as much as possible about this demographic factor for most presentations. Not only are companies and the U. S. workforce more diverse, but also technology and international mergers give businesspeople the opportunity to communicate more frequently with people in other cultures. Presenters can't assume that the standards they use in delivering presentations in their own culture will be the same across cultures. If they're unaware of various societal expectations, speakers could run the risk of offending their audiences without even knowing that they're doing so. Or, worse, they may appear intentionally arrogant or insensitive by not taking time to learn basic cultural or ethnic distinctions.

Audiences want to know that a speaker is credible, that the evidence the speaker uses clearly supports the recommendations or information, and that the speaker will address all necessary information (Locker & Kaczmarek, 2001, pp. 25–26). Presenters who demonstrate an understanding that all cultures don't interact or conduct business in the same fashion will enhance both presenter and message credibility—and audiences will be more receptive to their ideas.

To illustrate different cultural expectations of presentations, note these brief examples. First, consider audience impressions of *presenter status and competence.* Someone presenting to audiences composed primarily of Germans, Scandinavians, or North Americans would do well to remember that these particular cultures tend to value competence over social status and position in the corporate hierarchy. As a result, a presenter could demonstrate competence by allotting substantial time in the presentation for hard facts and statistics to support the message and by incorporating graphics and chart data to show mastery of the material. On the other hand, Arab, Chinese, and Japanese cultures, among others, tend to place as much emphasis on the presenter's status as on the presenter's competence. Therefore, a presenter speaking to groups composed of individuals from these cultures would need to establish corporate ranking and credentials early in the session, solicit support from senior management both before and during the session, and primarily address the highest-ranking people in the room (Thill & Bovée, 2002, p. 53).

Another key cultural difference is varying expectations of *acceptable delivery techniques.* Eye contact, space, gesture, volume, and nonverbal communication signify vastly different meanings to members of various cultures. In the U.S. business culture, for example, presenters use direct eye contact with most, if not all, members of an audience to demonstrate confidence and credibility—and audience members in this culture expect this behavior. Conversely, in many Asian countries such direct eye contact with audience members could be considered rude or overly aggressive (Beamer & Varner, 2001, pp. 163–164). Presenters should be aware of their audiences' cultural backgrounds so that they can plan their delivery pattern accordingly. Chapter 4 gives more specific information on intercultural differences relating to delivery skills.

One more example of a significant cultural difference is *how directly audiences expect the presenter to get to the point of the session.* In some European and North American countries, audiences demand that presenters start immediately with the key points. This technique won't work well in Asian and Muslim societies; presenters who do so could be considered too aggressive or too brusque (Beamer & Varner, 2001, pp. 130–133).

Learn as much as you can about the cultural background of those in your audience to enhance your credibility and possibilities for success with each audience.*

Corporate Factors

When developing a presentation session to a group outside your own organization, make time to learn about that company. And if you're in a large corporation and presenting outside your division or line of business, find out what's happening with the target audience. For example, what are the organization's corporate values? Its culture? How has it performed lately? What has been in the media about it? Understanding current corporate situations and the way that companies promote themselves as distinctive work environments can help presenters customize message content, visuals, and delivery. Here are three aspects of corporate factors to investigate:

■ Corporate values
■ Corporate expectations
■ Corporate hierarchy

*For a good introduction to intercultural business practices, see Beamer & Varner, 2001.

By learning about these aspects, presenters can avoid political quagmires and corporate cultural land mines.

Corporate Values

Corporate values are the basic principles that companies espouse and adhere to in business practices. Some organizations, for example, may be focused on employee development, believing that they can't be successful without trained employees who desire to excel. Others may be more customer driven; if they don't delight their customers, their culture maintains, they won't be successful. Still others may concentrate on the bottom line, adhering to a belief that success lies in an efficient operation. Some companies may place more emphasis on future success while others give attention to streamlining current best practices. Some believe in stoking employee competition by continually challenging them and rewarding only the most productive; others feel more strongly that job security will stoke employee initiative. Depending on the industry and the management leadership, any (or any combination) of these corporate values may drive companies—there's no one right way to do business.

Presenter knowledge of corporate values is as important to a presentation as knowledge of audience demographics. If presenting your company's services to a potential client that values employee security, you obviously should couch your services in the context of how these services will help the client support that particular corporate value. Or, if you've come up with a cost-saving proposal for your department and know that senior management values grooming employees to succeed, underscore in a presentation how the proposal ultimately will play into the corporate push to reward employees who excel. Customize each presentation to corporate values so that the message complements and supports the audience's needs and goals.

To obtain a quick overview of company information, start with the individual who contacted you about making a presentation. Alternatively, you could interview various people within the company. Another easy place to begin researching, of course, is the Internet. Corporate websites are an obvious place to learn key information. Each company's website typically has links describing the company mission, history, and areas of business.

Corporate annual reports are another particularly helpful source of information about the company's culture, lines of business, and growth plans. Studying a CEO's annual letter to shareholders, for example, offers a high level overview of a company's performance during the previous year and what investors can expect in the coming year. Additionally, the language the CEO uses and the style design of the letter and the annual report itself reveal a taste of the company's "personality," or corporate culture. Exhibit 2.3 shows a page from The Body Shop International's 2001 annual report. The company (www.thebodyshop.com) prides itself on its activism

EXHIBIT 2.3   Body Shop International Plc. 2001 annual report.

Reproduced with permission of The Body Shop International, Plc., copyright owner.

and includes several pages of information and pictures in the annual report about its activities with human rights.

When planning an extensive Internet search on a company to learn about corporate values or traditions, be careful to screen for sites with credible and comprehensive information. Some websites may exist simply because a disgruntled customer or former employee set them up to promote negative press about the company or its method of business. Additionally, some sites may slant information in a particular way that doesn't provide you with a balanced view of the information that you need. For example, corporate websites, while they're a wealth of information about the company's performance and mission, don't share all company information. Realistically, companies use their websites to provide basic corporate information and to promote the company; typically, corporations won't post information that they'd prefer the public not know. Many dot-com corporations, for example, may not want Internet visitors to know how investment banking analysts have rated their companies—unless the analysts have positive forecasts! You likely will have to dig a bit deeper than a company's website if you want to learn objective information about a particular company. Exhibit 2.4 gives you a few of the many resources that you can use to research most publicly held companies. Some of these

EXHIBIT 2.4   Research resources.

Helpful to locate financial information
- Edgar: www.sec.gov/edgar.shtml
- Zack's Investment Research: http://my.Zacks.com
- Yahoo Business: www.yahoo.com

Helpful for news about businesses and industries
- Factiva (a Dow Jones & Reuters Company): www.factiva.com
- Business Source Elite: www.ebscoweb.com
- *Fortune*
- *Wall Street Journal*
- *New York Times*

Helpful for ranking and lists
- Price's List of Lists: www.specialissues.com/lol/
- J.D. Power & Associates: www.jdpower.com/

Internet resources offer free access; however, others charge fees to subscribe. If you don't have access to the fee-based electronic databases, check out public libraries; they often hold subscriptions to electronic and print business resources.

Corporate Expectations

Anticipating corporate expectations for typical presentation formats will be helpful in structuring both the message and the physical interaction in sessions. Some companies may prefer presentations to run specific time lengths. Some may hold presentations in small conference rooms; others might want them in larger forums for many employees to attend. Some expect teams to present, and others prefer only one presenter. Some want presenters to use PowerPoint, and others may discourage use of the technology because of past overuse. Additionally, key executives may prefer to get information quickly, while others might want break-out groups to discuss concepts, enact role plays to practice new techniques, or view skits that illustrate ideas.

Take time to learn corporate expectations for presentations in order to customize the sessions and meet each group's anticipation of a particular presentation pattern. To illustrate, if key decision makers in an audience are known to want the bottom line within the first couple of sentences, presenters will know to give them the main point of the discussion up front. Advance knowledge of this audience preference would help a speaker avoid being surprised by a demand for the bottom line recommendation shortly after beginning. This doesn't mean, of course, that presenters should structure their message only in the format that a company expects. Just because a department is used to role-playing to help them practice sales techniques, for example, doesn't mean that another demonstration—watching an excerpt from a sales scenario on a videotape—might not work as effectively. Therefore, if you break from the expectations, do so intentionally; just be sure to set a context for audiences if you vary from the format they're used to.

Presenters should set clear expectations during the session explaining how they've organized the discussion; this cues the audience to know how to respond. If presenters want participation during a presentation to companies that are more used to the "lecture style," they'll find it difficult to get the audience to participate. As a result, they'll wonder how well they're conveying the message when the audience doesn't appear involved—unless they let the audience members know how the session will run. Conversely, companies that traditionally prefer a more participatory presentation style will be unused to the "lecture" style if they're not forewarned. Audience members may "interrupt" throughout a lecture-style presentation to interject their ideas, and they might not understand why presenter responses to their comments and questions are deferred. Likewise, a presenter will be frustrated with these "interruptions" if unable to talk through prepared remarks before opening the floor for questions, comments, or discussion.

EXHIBIT 2.5 Presenter roles.

Role	Advantages	Disadvantages
Lecturer	Give information concisely. Lay out case before soliciting feedback.	Lack opportunity for audience interaction. Run the risk of losing audience.
Facilitator	Give audience chance to interact with presenter. Allow for audience buy-in or opportunity to address objections.	Risk possibility of losing control of presentation timing. Risk challenges from audience.
Moderator	Offer balanced perspective on group or team discussion.	Risk not accomplishing goal because of audience involvement.
Assurer	Help audience deal with anxiety about critical information. Support company policies.	Risk challenges from audience.

Beyond audience expectations are the various roles a presenter can take. Exhibit 2.5 shows four roles that speakers may use in leading presentations. These roles will vary depending on the presentation purpose and the corporate expectations.

As you can see in this table, presenters need to map out the presentation purpose and take time limitations into consideration before deciding their role in a presentation. How presenters plan to interact with the audience and what role they take is directly related to the outcome they wish to achieve.

Corporate Hierarchy

Once you've considered corporate expectations, turn attention next to the individuals who will attend the presentation. Will the participants be directly affected by the information you give? Will they be making decisions for the company or division based on what they learn (or learn how to do) in your presentation? Are they trainers who will apply to other sessions the information that you're presenting? Does the audience comprise senior management, midlevel managers, colleagues, or employees who work for you, or perhaps a mixture of all levels?

Knowledge of the various job levels of individuals who attend a presentation helps speakers determine how much information to provide in a message and what information they need to target. If giving a presentation, for example, about a new job process to employees who will then use what they learn on their jobs, a presenter should focus more on applied, concrete details. The presentation goal, after all, is to give them the information they need to efficiently manage the change to this new process. If presenting the same material to management, a presenter should offer similar details, but this level of audience might not need as much of the hands-on information. Supervisors of the employees who are performing the new job process will need enough details to gain a sense of how to manage the new process. To supervisors, information about how the new process benefits individual departments or the company as a whole will be more useful.

The following example details the importance of tailoring the material to specific audience levels.

Let's say a presenter is asked to explain to a group of employees why their company is closing operations in a particular state. The presenter will need to know the employment level of those attending the presentation to be able to appropriately tailor the message. For employees who work in that state, the presenter obviously would need to include information about why the decision was made, but she also needs to explain severance packages (if any) and how the company plans to support displaced employees in transitioning to new jobs—information this particular audience wants and needs to hear. A presentation on the same topic to senior managers who won't lose their positions would need to include basic information about the reasons for the decision and how the company is helping workers in that state. However, it probably needs to focus more on what impact this business decision will have on the company operations as a whole.

These brief examples show the importance of knowing the employment levels of participants at a presentation session so that presenters can structure the message to clearly address the needs of each group. The audience in front of you, however, probably isn't the only audience your message will have an impact on. Communication expert M. E. Guffey (2003) views audience analysis as a way for presenters to learn whether the message will have a secondary audience—a group of people who need to hear the message but who aren't present at the session. Individuals who attend the session will be responsible for taking the message to this secondary audience, so presenters may need to incorporate more background information or instructional techniques to enable audience members to later deliver a concise and accurate message to the secondary audience (p. 137).

Knowledge and Attitude Factors

Level of Knowledge About the Topic

What does your audience already know about the topic you'll discuss? Presenters must answer this question to ensure that they develop appropriate content and message structure. They shouldn't spend too much time (and the audience's goodwill) covering material that audience members already know. And, if the majority of those attending a session are unfamiliar with background or a "big picture" perspective of the topic, a presenter must familiarize them with information they need to know or understand before the main part of a presentation.

More than likely, presenters have been working on projects for days, weeks, or even months before they're asked to present results, findings, and recommendations. They know the material and why it is important. Audiences, however, may come to presentations with varying levels of knowledge about session topics. They may have expertise in that area, they may have received written briefings on the topic that will be discussed, they may have heard through the corporate grapevine about the upcoming session content, or (less likely, but still possible) they may not really know why they're getting together for a presentation.

Ask the individual who scheduled you for a presentation what the audience already knows about the topic. Then, consider the material from the perspective of that audience. How much do they need to know? Is it important, for example, to give exhaustive details that show a progression of steps leading up to the conclusion you wish to draw? Or, would they really need to know a few key steps and then hear more about why that conclusion will benefit their department or their company?

Another reason presenters should discover what an audience already knows about the topic is *clarity*. Use the language and jargon appropriate for each audience. To illustrate, an insurance executive speaking to a group outside the insurance industry should avoid technical phrases such as, "Last year, we spent considerable resources investigating replacing our PMS system," or, "Our target LAE should be 28 percent of the CORE." Conversely, if the audience comprises insurance industry analysts or veterans of the insurance industry, they will probably know the terms "PMS system," "LAE," and "CORE"; the phrases are standard jargon in the insurance business.

It's tempting to use professional language and terminology to evidence credentials and boost credibility, but audience members will become frustrated if they're not familiar with field-specific terms that they hear. Therefore, unless a presentation purpose is to inform or educate, avoid using overly specific terms and spending precious time explaining phrases or words peculiar to an industry. Presenters who do need to be specific should reserve a segment of presentation time to define terms and, perhaps, even develop a handout explaining the most complex ideas.

What an Audience Thinks or Feels About the Topic and Presenter

Equally important as knowing an audience's level of familiarity with a topic is learning what they think or feel about the topic and the presenter's credibility on the topic.

If you'll be speaking on an issue that an audience is skeptical or negative about, they'll be less likely to be receptive to recommendations about that issue. Let's use the example of sales goals. Most salespeople expect sales goals to rise each year. Yet, most salespeople also believe that they worked very hard in the prior year to reach, what at the time, appeared to be challenging goals. When they attend an annual meeting about new goals, they typically hear that their goals will be even higher than the year before. For those who believe the goals were challenging enough or too high the previous year, increased goals will seem daunting; audience members in this scenario likely would be emotional and anxious that their goals are going up. Knowing in advance the anxiety that these salespersons are feeling, a presenter should avoid giving a factual presentation focusing solely on the new goals themselves. Instead, the message should incorporate content showing audience members how they can attack these new goals and encouragement about how their performance in the past can act as a predictor for success in achieving these new targets. Additionally, the speaker should emphasize the rewards system so that those in the audience clearly understand the tangible rewards for reaching these goals.

Here's another example illustrating why presenters need to learn as much as possible about what audience members feel about the material being presented. A speaker may discover that word of a division's new initiatives leaked to associates in that division, and they've already come to a consensus that they're not pleased with the initiative. Armed with this advance knowledge, the presenter can plan appropriate content and tone before "introducing" the information in a kickoff session to an already skeptical group.

Presenters also need to learn about audiences' attitudes about the speaker, the speaker's position within the company, and the speaker's company because audience members may come to a presentation session with preconceived biases. A speaker pitching a product should know, for example, that some of the decision makers in an audience may have rejected a bid from his firm several years ago because of personality conflicts—these audience members may have a slight bias against his firm even before he begins his presentation. In situations like this, a speaker should plan time and presentation content to rebuild credibility and even acknowledge knowing about the past relationship.

Presenter credibility is the audience's impression of the speaker's expertise, background, and trustworthiness. Mary Munter (2000) identifies five factors that drive audience's impression of credibility: "rank, goodwill, expertise, image, and common ground" (p. 8).* Similarly, Jay Conger (2000) stresses the importance of building a relationship between the presenter and the audience members to enhance credibility. If a presenter already knows individuals in the audience, the presenter has an established reputation that can be drawn upon. For example, audiences view presenters as trustworthy and reliable if they've made thoughtful recommendations in the past and followed up on requests for information. On the other hand, if audience members are unfamiliar with a presenter, she may need to rely on audience analysis and any possible pre-presentation conversations with that audience to begin to establish common ground that will lend itself to building credibility.

Let's now consider some questions to assess your own credibility. What are your credentials to present material? What is your position in relation to an audience in an upcoming presentation? What does the audience already know about you, your product/service, and your company? If you're presenting to a group of people you don't know, plan to spend more time early in the presentation building credibility. Make sure the audience knows you're an expert in the area you're presenting and what your qualifications are to make the presentation. If the audience already accepts you as a credible authority, use the time you might normally spend building credibility to develop details within the message.

For Robby, a corporate pharmaceutical sales representative with experience at two large companies, understanding audience attitude toward his product and his own credentials is critical to his success. When he first started selling pharmaceuticals to doctors and medical centers 10 years ago, he relied on the presentation strategies that he learned while in training: selling the product's features. He incorporated product knowledge from training sessions into his presentations while using visual material supplied by his company. However, Robby quickly came to understand that the doctors weren't inter-

---

*Munter derives these categories from French & Raven (1959).

ested in listening to what he calls a "canned presentation"—one that didn't connect with the doctors or their individual interests. This type of presentation relied instead on the audience's goodwill to be interested in the material itself.

Therefore, Robby began to attend doctors' educational seminars and read the medical journals that his clients read. Even though he doesn't have a medical background, he started to talk with his clients about their interests to learn more about them and their profession. As a result, he focused his presentations more on the doctors' unique interests as they related to his product line than on simply pushing his products to a generic audience.

Because Robby tailors his approach and discussion to the interests of his clients, his current clients feel that he personalizes the sales transaction with them. In addition, new clients appreciate his interest in their specializations when they learn that he attends their conferences and reads the medical journals that they read. They feel he makes the time to understand their professional needs (R. P., personal communication, May 2002). In summary, Robby relies on four of Mary Munter's five credibility factors in his interactions with clients: goodwill, expertise, image, and common ground.

Without a focus on audience needs and attitude and an understanding about how an audience perceives a speaker's credibility, presenters won't be able to persuade—no matter how snazzy the graphics, how logical the argument, or how eloquent the language. An audience's skeptical or negative attitude toward a topic or presenter will influence how a presenter structures a message to establish credibility and gain agreement. Likewise, knowing an audience will be enthusiastic, presenters don't need to work as hard to build common ground and can be more direct in presenting the key message. If presenting to an audience that might be neutral on a topic, presenters can allocate presentation time to build goodwill and credibility. Learning as much as possible about audience attitude toward a topic and a presenter will help speakers organize information and present it efficiently and effectively. Chapter 3 will cover in more depth how to structure message content to support presentation goals.

Miscellaneous Factors

In addition to demographics, corporate expectations, and audience knowledge and attitude, presenters also should consider the logistical situation unique to each presentation. Ask the following questions when contacted to make a presentation.

How Many People Will Attend the Session?

This is important information to learn because the answer will help you determine how to plan for audience interaction, handle the Q&A session, manage delivery techniques, and develop handouts. As you'll read in later chapters, presenters create a message, visuals, and delivery techniques according to the number of people who'll attend the session. For example, an audience of 25 to 30 people likely won't be able to easily see material on a flip chart; a large-screen PowerPoint presentation might be more effective in this scenario. Additionally, presenters can't expect as much audience participation with a larger audience, and so they may need to build in more time for a question-and-answer session. It's difficult to generate the same quality of interaction within a large group as compared with a small group session. In another example of how audience numbers affect presentation planning, with small audiences of 3 to 5 people, presenters may feel more comfortable seated at a conference room table with the session participants than standing in the front of the room in a more formal lecture-style position.

What Type of Room Will I Be Making the Presentation In?

To plan delivery style, learn in advance as much as possible about the size and shape of the room in which you'll be presenting. If in a boardroom speaking to 10 people, you'll use a different style than if you were presenting in a larger conference room to 25 people. The smaller room will be a more intimate setting and conducive to audience participation. The larger group may expect a presenter to carry more of the speaking time. If presenting in a long, narrow room, practice projecting volume more than you might if you were speaking in a shallow, wide room to ensure your voice will carry to the back.

Knowing in advance the room setup also will be helpful. Will you have a lectern on which to rest your notes? Will you be standing at the front of the room with empty space between you and the audience? Will you be on a dais using a conventional microphone to project volume? Where does the air vent into the room? Learning the answers to these types of questions can help presenters minimize surprises. A few of the classrooms in which I teach, for example, have a particular point in the front of the room where a presenter's voice echoes off the PowerPoint projector overhead in the ceiling. Presenters who are unfamiliar with this quirk in the room acoustics often find the echo disconcerting, and presenters who are already nervous find that the unanticipated echo breaks their concentration. In another example, I often hear presenters talk about notes being blown off their podium because they didn't realize that the heating/air conditioning system vented into the room directly above where they stood. By making time to learn as much as possible about the room where they'll be presenting, presenters can tailor their delivery patterns and minimize surprises in order to shore up confidence.

What Technology Do I Need and Have Access to for the Presentation?

Before arriving at a presentation session, ask for specific technology or tools you want and then verify their availability. Some companies provide flip charts, markers, PowerPoint-enabled computers and large screens, overhead projectors, Web access, and so forth. Others may have some of these items, but you may need to provide the ones you need.

Be prepared, however, for mishaps. I once requested a liquid crystal display (LCD) projector for a PowerPoint presentation and discovered when I arrived that the organization hadn't ordered the appropriate equipment. Because much of my presentation relied on statistical information that required showing graphics, I could have run into a difficult presentation situation without PowerPoint. Fortunately, I always travel to presentations with both a disk *and* color transparencies, so I simply made my presentation using an overhead projector, and no one in the audience knew that I'd not planned on making an overhead projector presentation. Learning as much as possible about what you can expect from the technology situation of your presentation can help you prepare your message, anticipate the situation for your delivery, and give you confidence that you've prepared adequately for the presentation.

And do accept the fact that even the most prepared presenters can be surprised. Karen Moss, a vice president and controller of a small regional medical staffing company, thought she'd carefully set up every detail for an upcoming year-end board meeting with investors at a local country club. Because a key board member was out of town, Karen had arranged for him to participate via speakerphone during her presentation regarding the company performance. The country club had confirmed that they would provide a speakerphone, but at the last minute she discovered that one wasn't available. Because Karen had arrived early, she had ample time to ask someone from her office to bring a speakerphone. When it arrived, however, she found that her telephone's speaker system wasn't compatible with that of the country club. The absent board member had to participate in the meeting via a wall phone in the room, with someone telling him what was transpiring (K. Moss, personal communication, May 2002).

What if you are unable to gather as much information from an audience analysis as you might like (due to time constraints or lack of access)? You can still learn necessary details about an audience in the brief period before a presentation begins. Dennis Beaver (1998), an attorney and presentation expert, recommends that presenters arrive early to "interview" audience members as they arrive. The time before a presentation starts typically is informal with individuals greeting each other or getting refreshments before the meeting comes to order. Beaver encourages presenters to talk with individuals to learn their names and attitudes and level of knowledge about the topic. Incorporating this information into a presentation demonstrates to the audience that a speaker is connected with audience members and their concerns.

Exhibit 2.6 offers a presentation preparation worksheet. Ideally, you would ask all of the questions on this worksheet when you're called on to make a presentation. After all, the more that you know about an audience and the situation in which you'll be presenting, the more effectively you can customize the presentation. Realistically, however, you often won't have

EXHIBIT 2.6   Presentation preparation worksheet.

1. How many people will be at the presentation session? What are their positions within the organizational hierarchy?

2. Who are the key decision makers or influential people within the audience?

3. What role does the audience expect me to take in the presentation?

4. What type of presentation does the audience expect?

5. What are the various reasons these people are attending my presentation?

6. What are the demographic and cultural specifics of the audience makeup?

7. What does my audience already know about the intended topic?

8. What does the audience need to know about my topic?

9. What is my audience's attitude toward the topic I'll discuss? Why?

10. What is the audience's attitude toward me?

11. What's been happening within the company lately that's related to my topic? What's been happening within the company as a whole?

12. What is the physical room situation, and what technology will I have available?

the time to do so, and the person setting up the presentation might not have the patience to answer all these questions. So instead of trying to check off every question on the list, select a few of the key questions.

A comprehensive audience analysis offers the following presenter benefits:

- Establishes presenter credibility—understanding who audience members are, what they know, and what they value exhibits a presenter's attention to detail and attunement to each audience's unique needs.
- Determines how presenter structures message content—knowing how the audience feels about the topic and how the organization expects presentation sessions to run helps presenters decide how to organize information. Should the recommendation come early in the message? Should it be after the presenter has discussed benefits of acting on the recommendation? Or, should it be placed toward the end of a presentation after the presenter explores all other possible recommendations and then demonstrates why this particular one is the optimal solution?
- Soothes presenter anxiety—having a clear sense of what an audience expects helps presenters positively visualize the session.

Essentially, a comprehensive audience analysis demonstrates the fact that presenters have "done their homework" and are as prepared as possible.

EXERCISES   Getting Started

EXERCISE 1   Identification of Presentation Purpose and Goal

Review three presentations you've made and identify the purpose and the goal for each:

- Presentation 1

    Purpose:

    Goal:

- Presentation 2

    Purpose:

    Goal:

- Presentation 3

    Purpose:

    Goal:

EXERCISE 2   Savers Community Bank and the Softball Team

Take the role of community outreach coordinator for your local parks and recreation organization. As the coordinator, you're responsible for increasing the number of participants and teams in the adult summer softball league. You've been asked to make presentations to local corporations about encouraging employees to participate on company-sponsored teams. You heard in a recent chamber of commerce meeting that Savers Community Bank, a local bank with about 75 employees, is considering fielding a team; late last week the director of human resources from that bank left a message on your voice mail asking you to make a presentation to employees during an upcoming meeting. You pick up the telephone to call the director of human resources to settle the date and time of your presentation. What are some of the questions you should ask the director of human resources about the audience you'll be speaking with? What are some questions you should ask about the bank's interest in the softball league?

EXERCISE 3   Who's Watching What and When?

Select five television programs that air at different times of the day or different days of the week. Keep a log of what products are advertised during each show. Be sure to make a note of the following details:

- What is the theme of the show? (e.g., family-oriented, action, romantic movie, Western, comedy, sports, etc.)
- What time is the show aired?
- What day of the week is the show aired?
- What is the theme of each commercial aired during the show?
- What are the common factors that each commercial has with others aired during the same program?

Using what you've learned about audience analysis, write up a summary of the target audience you believe the advertisers are appealing to. For example, what age group are they targeting? What economic level? What educational level? What fantasy?

EXERCISE 4   Audience Analysis

Complete the Presentation Preparation Worksheet in Exhibit 2.6 for an upcoming presentation. Fill out the responses to as many questions on the worksheet as possible. Then, answer the following questions:

1. How did learning this information change the way you decided to organize the message?

Market Segment	Benefits of Joining	Potential Objections	Ways to Overcome the Objections
Married students			
Married students with children			
Skilled student athletes			
"Armchair" student athletes (those who don't participate in sports often but who enjoy watching sports)			
Students with physical disabilities			

2. What did you learn about who you'll be presenting to and what their attitude is toward you and your topic?

3. What have you decided to change, as a result of this analysis, about how you'll deliver the presentation?

4. How will you restructure your visuals to most effectively connect with this particular audience?

5. If delivering the presentation to a group outside your company, what did you learn about the group's corporate expectations and what's happening in that particular industry? How will this knowledge change your approach to developing and delivering the presentation?

EXERCISE 5   Recreational League Plan

Assume that you're in charge of setting up a recreational league for college students. Answer the following questions:

1. What would be the benefits for students in general to participate?

2. What would be the typical reasons they might give as objections to joining the league?

Once you've answered these questions, answer the same questions for the following market segments:

You'll see from this exercise that your answers will be much more specific and targeted to each audience than your responses to the questions about marketing the league to the general student population.

References

Beamer, L., & Varner, I. (2001). *Intercultural communication in the global workplace* (2nd ed.). Boston: McGraw-Hill.

Beaver, D. (1998). Your speech begins before you hit the podium [electronic version]. *ABA Banking Journal, 90*(11), 68.

Conger, Jay A. (2000). Winning them over. [Electronic version]. *Executive Excellence, 17* (5), 13.

French, J., and Raven, B. (1959). The bases of social power. *Studies in social power.* D. Cartwright, ed. Ann Arbor: University of Michigan Press.

Guffey, M. E. (2003). *Business communication: Process & product* (4th ed.). Mason, OH: Thomson South-Western.

Kotler, P. (2003). *Marketing management* (11th ed.). Upper Saddle River, NJ: Prentice Hall.

Locker, K. (2000). *Business and administrative communication* (5th ed.). Burr Ridge, IL: Irwin/McGraw-Hill.

Locker, K., & Kaczmarek, S. K. (2001). *Business communication: Building critical skills.* Boston: McGraw-Hill.

Munter, M. (2000). *Guide to managerial communication: Effective business writing and speaking.* (5th ed.). Upper Saddle River, NJ: Prentice Hall.

Thill, J. V., & Bovée, C. L. (2002). *Excellence in business communication* (5th ed.). Upper Saddle River, NJ: Prentice Hall.

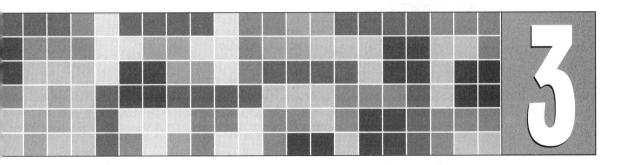

Developing an Effective Message

PERFORMANCE GOALS

After completing this chapter, readers will be able to:

- structure message using framework of audience connection, wrapping up, and transitions
- create presentations using a general presentation pattern
- create presentations using a problem-solving presentation pattern

No standard formula exists for organizing a message that will work for all presentations. Each presentation situation is unique, and each message will vary depending on purpose, audience factors, time constraints, room environment, and technology options. Incorporating these considerations into the presentation planning stage will prepare speakers to deliver a message customized for each situation. However, presenters also need to structure the organizational pattern of a message itself to support their desired goal.

Chapter 2 discussed the need to clarify the purpose and goal of a message. Do you wish to inform your service group about a procedure change? A new product line? Are you trying to persuade a potential client to hire your firm or convince a territory to adopt your department's cost-savings measures? The purpose of Chapter 3 is to map out for presenters how they can best structure a message's content to accomplish a presentation goal.

Effective presenters organize material intentionally and systematically to achieve specific outcomes; this chapter offers organizational patterns to help convey information to an audience in a logical, practical fashion. We'll discuss these patterns in the following presentation message strategies:

- Presentation frame
- General presentation pattern
- Problem-solving presentation pattern

As we examine these patterns, you'll learn what situations might call for each strategy and some benefits and drawbacks to using each.

PRESENTATION FRAME

This section of the chapter details how to develop the following presentation framework to engage an audience from start to finish:

- Audience connection
- Wrapping up
- Message transitions

These strategies support presenters in generating a customized opening, a specific closing, and logical connections between key points within a presentation.

Whatever type of presentation you might make, the beginning and the ending are crucial. Research shows that audiences consistently remember the openings and closings of most presentations (Kiechel, 1987). Audience attention is at its highest when anticipating the start of a presentation and then, while varying during a session, will spike up again when a presenter says, "In conclusion . . . " Ideally, presenters could develop a message so enthralling that the audience would hang on every word throughout a presentation. In these days of multitasking and media sound bites, however, it's virtually impossible to keep an audience's attention throughout a presentation. Realistically, presenters can capture and recapture audience attention by developing solid content and using dynamic delivery skills. A well-crafted presentation opening that connects a topic with an audience will entice the audience to follow the presenter along into the key parts of the message. And a strong call to action at the end of a presentation will direct the audience toward the goal that the presenter wants to achieve.

Two notes of caution before discussing different presentation openings:

1. Consider carefully if you want to ask the audience, "How's everyone doing today?" Ideally, presenters should network with audience members before a session begins and make the requisite pleasantries before starting a presentation. If presenting on a panel after another speaker, asking how the audience members are is a rhetorical question that the audience knows is simply that. Worse, when presenters ask the rhetorical "How are you?" question, often they don't even wait for the audience to respond!

2. Be careful about using humor as an opening. While humor might be an interesting way to open an after-dinner speech or a public speaking engagement, it might be less effective in a business presentation. Presenters who use humor run the risk of their jokes falling flat or may inadvertently use material that might be inappropriate to the audience, the company, or the industry.

Audience Connection

Probably the most basic presentation opening is *asking a rhetorical question*. Presenters who use this method to start generally intend to get an audience involved by asking them to agree with a statement or a concept. For example, in a presentation to a group of corporate communications specialists, a presenter might ask, "How many of you know about the federal government's 'Plain Language Initiative'?" From an audience analysis, the presenter would have learned that these corporate communication specialists likely completed extensive training on using plain language after the Securities and Exchange Commission's 1998 requirement that companies begin producing annual prospectuses in plain language. Thus, audience members in this example probably would nod, smile, or raise their hands to indicate that they do know about the initiative. The presenter's intent in using a rhetorical question would be to focus attention on the theme—plain language, in this example—and use the common ground of knowledge about the initiative as an audience connection.

As the first idea an audience hears in a presentation session, an audience connection links a speaker and a topic with participants attending the session. It also sets the context for what an audience can expect from the session and the presenter. An interesting opening that entices an audience to hear what will follow is a valuable tool for presenters. Simply put, audience connections ought to engage session participants and entice them to care about a topic—thus, audience members become more invested in learning about the session's topic.

A *direct statement of a presentation's goal* is another common opening. A presenter might begin by saying, "Good afternoon. I'm Jesse Carter. Thanks for giving me twenty minutes of your time to talk with your group about the cost-savings benefits we'll realize by reorganizing the Midwest division." In the first sentence, the presenter told the group he would address the reorganization of a division—and mentioned the monetary benefits of the change. This type of audience connection is particularly effective for a couple of reasons. First, some audiences prefer to hear at the beginning of a session what a speaker recommends. They'll have little patience with audience connections that try to set a context or build up to a suggested solution. Presenters should uncover this preference in an audience analysis and organize their message accordingly. Demanding audiences won't hesitate to interrupt if they believe a presenter isn't getting to the point quickly.

Second, a direct opening works well for presenters who have high credibility with an audience prior to a presentation. If audience members already trust a presenter through reputation or prior relationship, they will feel more confident in the presenter's skills, expertise, and recommendations. As a result, the presenter doesn't need to spend time at the beginning of a presentation developing a connection as a way to build credibility. The presenter already has a connection with the audience through his or her established credibility.

Customized Audience Connections

If a speaker doesn't have an established credibility with the audience or if the audience has a skeptical or negative attitude about the topic, a presenter must work harder to effectively connect with those in an audience. And according to R. Hoff (1988), the first 90 seconds of a presentation is crucial for a speaker who needs to build credibility. To gain credibility or find some measure of common ground with a skeptical or hostile audience, dynamic presenters will customize a presentation by developing a strong connection between the message they wish to convey and what they know about the audience from their audience analysis. To this end, presenters make use of startling information or concretize abstract information that they know will surprise or captivate an audience.

Following are examples of three possible ways that I considered opening a recent presentation that I gave to a civic group. The topic was the need in North Carolina for people to inform family members about their decision to sign a donor card to indicate their desire to be organ donors.

1. Hello. I'm Judy Jones Tisdale, and I'm here to talk with you for the next twenty minutes about the need to let your family members know about your decision if you've signed an organ donor card. (*direct opening about the reason for the presentation*)

2. Over 80,000 people in the United States today are waiting on a life-saving organ transplant. And, more than 2,800 in North Carolina are on that same list. (*opening provides startling numbers to catch audience attention about how many people are waiting on the national transplant list*) (Numbers as of July 2002. Source: Carolina Doner Services, n.d.)

3. How many of you already have indicated on your driver's license that you want to be an organ and tissue donor? (*could be considered a rhetorical question, depending on the audience's knowledge of the state's driver's license policy*)

The audience I spoke with was a group of community-minded people at their monthly meeting; clearly, they wanted to learn about organ donation issues. In addition, the person introducing me told the audience about my work as the project director of an annual community service event to raise awareness about organ donation issues at my university. I had credibility on the issue, and the audience members were attending the session to learn more about the topic. Essentially, they were a receptive audience. I could have opened by telling the audience why I was there, by citing a startling statistic, or by asking a rhetorical question. And if the audience consisted of a group of people who already were strong supporters of organ donation, all three openings likely would have worked fine.

However, none of these choices really are customized or bring alive the topic for a group of people who wished to learn more about a complex issue. In fact, I could have used any one of these openings for a presentation to any audience across the country, simply by changing the state statistics. Instead, I wanted to develop a stronger connection between the topic and the audience by building a bridge between information I'd gathered from my audience analysis and what I knew about the topic. I wanted to stir audience interest in the issue by illustrating for them why the topic was so urgent—thus tailoring the audience connection for this particular group of people. A strong connection may take extra time to craft, but audiences will respond more favorably to the remainder of a presentation if a speaker makes the audience connection memorable and specific to them.

By researching an audience using the methods in Chapter 2, you can learn what a group generally thinks and feels about a topic. As well, you'll learn about general audience facts that can help you customize presentation openings. In my civic group presentation example, I knew that my audience was composed of North Carolina professionals who were interested in community responsibility. I also knew, from my conversation with the contact who set up the presentation, that the majority of them were sports fans. My task was to develop an audience connection that would unite these individuals and help them conceptualize the importance of making an informed decision about being an organ donor. I ultimately decided to develop an opening that relied on two landmarks familiar to any North Carolinian interested in sports. Using the concrete example below, I helped the audience visualize exactly how many people were waiting on the national organ transplant list at that time.

> If every person on the national organ transplant list came to Chapel Hill, North Carolina, and filed into the Kenan Football Stadium (seating capacity 60,000), the ones who wouldn't be able to find a seat could walk a short distance to the Dean Smith Center (seating capacity 21,572) and fill up the seats in this arena as well. Even then, everyone wouldn't be able to get a seat. Over 80,000 people in our country are waiting for a life-saving organ transplant right now.

This opening created a mental image for people who have seen in person or on television the large football and basketball complexes at the University of North Carolina at Chapel Hill. It localized the mind-numbing number of people who need an organ transplant so that the audience could concretize the startling number I provided and begin to understand just how many people are on this transplant waiting list.

An audience connection is a bridge between what a presenter knows about a topic and what a presenter knows about the audience. What are some common factors? What areas of the topic might an audience find fascinating or startling? How can a presenter help an audience visualize key ideas of the presentation? Speakers who focus on audience interest, needs, and benefits will capture audience attention at the outset of a presentation.

Creativity in presentation openings can enliven the audience connection and make the content more visual. In one of my academic service-learning courses, for example, a student team had completed a communication consulting project for a local not-for-profit organization. The agency, a volunteer referral service, needed a database to manage the referral process and the assessment of the volunteers' experiences. In developing a presentation about the project for classmates and local not-for-profit executive directors, this team decided on an audience connection that would clearly explain how the database they created would benefit the executive director of their agency. One of the team members started the presentation by mentioning the executive director's status as the sole paid agency employee. She then mentioned two of the more weighty administrative duties the executive director was responsible for and tossed two oranges to another team member who began to juggle them at the front of the room. As the presenter continued listing key agency duties, she continued to add oranges to the juggler's total until it was impossible for him to continue juggling all the oranges that he had. The team effectively connected with an audience of very busy people—students and professionals alike—who understood the concept of attempting to juggle too many tasks. The point, of course, was that the database the student team created merged many of these duties for the executive director in order to make her job much easier to manage (Basnight, et al., 2001).

Audience involvement in the opening of a presentation can be a useful technique because it asks audience members to participate (to various degrees) in the presentation. Let me give you two examples of openings that use audience participation in very different ways. Both of the teams in these examples completed a communication consulting project for local not-for-profit organizations and then developed a presentation about the project itself for the organizations' executive directors. The presentation in Exhibit 3.1 shows the pattern they worked out to customize the audience connection. These two examples, neither of which lasted longer than 60 seconds, asked for limited participation from the audience and concretized some idea in the presentation material to set up the key points more vividly than a simple direct statement of purpose to open.

EXHIBIT 3.1   Presentation pattern for customizing audience connection.

Mental Hospital Project Team

Presentation Purpose

To explain the work that the team did to publicize the need for the community to support a special shop, open only during the December holiday season, where hospital patients may purchase gifts for family and friends.

Audience Connection

Three of the team members randomly passed out candy canes to the audience as the first speaker opened the presentation by saying the team wanted the audience to enjoy a candy cane to celebrate the season during their discussion. Next, he asked if everyone had received a candy cane; however, the team intentionally hadn't passed out enough of the goodies. Of course, those in the audience who didn't receive the candy raised their hands. The speaker then said (very sincerely), "I'm sorry that you didn't receive a candy cane to enjoy like everyone else. This disappointment and frustration must be similar in a small degree to what institutionalized patients feel if they're unable to enjoy the holiday tradition of gift-giving. The hospital's special gift store ensures that each patient can participate in the season as fully as possible by giving each one the opportunity to shop for gifts for family and friends." (Baxter, et al., 2000)

Strategy

The team was concerned that the audience might feel that it had nothing in common with hospitalized mental health patients. So, team members used the example of candy canes and holiday traditions to remind audience members of the concepts of basic tasks that they might take for granted during the season. This illustrated the idea that the hospital patients didn't have the same opportunities as the audience members. The audience connection set the context for the team's later explanation about a promotional flyer and support solicitation letters. (Aggarwal, et al., 2001)

Human Resources Department Project Team

Presentation Purpose

To explain the work that the team did to compile a summary of numerous benefits that new employees must select from when they join the organization.

Audience Connection

The first speaker singled out one audience member who was close to the front of the room and easily visible to all other members of the audience. The speaker then began the presentation by saying to this individual, "We'd like you to act as a representative of all new employees in this organization during the initial orientation session that they go through when they first come to work." The audience member

EXHIBIT 3.1   Continued

agreed, and the speaker said, "Welcome to Company X. Here is a packet on your medical benefit options. And, here is one for your pre-tax reimbursement benefit plan options. And one for your insurance options. One for your dental choices. One for your retirement plan choices. . . ." The speaker continued, giving the "new employee" a brochure, or sometimes two or three booklets, for each of the possible benefits that she mentioned. She then concluded by reminding the employee of the upcoming deadlines to make these choices and return the signed forms to the benefits office. By the time the speaker finished, the "new employee" had a stack of brochures and booklets close to four inches high in her hands and a look of panic on her face.

Strategy

The team wanted to give the audience a sense of the overwhelming amount of information that new employees receive during an orientation session about the many important decisions they would need to make in a relatively short period of time. This opening illustration helped the team emphasize the benefits of the 12-page reference guide that it had created to summarize key points, eligibility guidelines, and purposes of each of the many benefits that Company X offers its employees.

Of course, in many cases, time constraints prohibit audience involvement. If you invite an audience to participate in a less structured way than in the examples that I've provided, you run the risk of the audience becoming so involved that the session goes off task and over the time limit. Unless the point of a presentation is to involve the audience in brainstorming or problem solving, presenters need to carefully plan and control how much participation they ask for from the audience so that they can accomplish the purpose intended within the time allowed.

Here's one more example of an opening asking for limited participation that one of my students (Tse, 2001) used in a presentation to set common ground with an audience. Her goal was to persuade her classmates to attend an Asian cultural project, an annual event at the university. The student had a very limited amount of time for the presentation and realized that she wouldn't be able to open by inviting the audience to participate to any large extent. She also knew that she was speaking to college students, who were familiar with Americanized Chinese restaurants. To start her presentation, this student connected with audience members by commenting that they likely were familiar with the Asian food in American Chinese restaurants and listing a few of the more common dishes—fried rice, egg rolls, cashew chicken. Then, she told the group, "But you likely haven't come across 'Char Siu Bou,' 'Har Gou,' and 'Shu Mai' in these restaurants. I encourage you to attend the Journey into Asia program to learn about the rich cultures—food, fashion, and people—of Asia." To impress on the audience that the Chinese foods they were used to didn't begin to introduce the Asian foods that the speaker knew about, the presenter surprised the audience. She reminded them of food that was familiar to them and used the familiar to introduce them to the unfamiliar in order to encourage them to attend a cultural diversity program.

As you can see in these examples, strong audience connections can interest audience members in a presentation before getting into the details of a message. Consider the audience connection a bridge between the work you did to analyze an audience and what you want that audience to know about the presentation content. Develop audience connections for presentations in one or more of the following ways: cite startling facts, make an observation about a commonality that an audience shares with persons associated with the topic, explain to an audience the key benefit(s) they'll experience by listening to the presentation, or illustrate for audience members how they might use the information from the message.

Wrapping Up

As we discussed earlier in this chapter, audience attention tends to be highest at the beginning and ending of presentations (Bovée & Thill, 2000). To develop a presentation closing, you've got several options: summarize key points, remind the audience about benefits of acting on your recommendation, and make a call to action. Depending on the message and the presentation situation, an effective wrap-up may combine any or all of these options. Whatever the combination, however, business communication expert Mary Munter (2000) suggests the wrap-up should always let the audience know "what's in it for them" (p. 17). As with the audience connection, presenters should take time in the wrap-up to closely relate the presentation content to audience interests. Following are several strategies to develop a wrap-up.

Summarize Key Points

Summarizing key points is a basic and straightforward way of closing a presentation. This approach reminds audience members what the main topics are so that when they leave the meeting, these points are fresh and vivid; it reinforces the message. The summary wrap-up is most effective if the presentation purpose is simply to give information to a group of people who are receptive to the topic. If a team, for example, needs to inform a group of associates about an additional health care option their company will begin offering, the final presenter can simply restate the presentation's agenda to close. Audience analysis would have shown the presenters that the new health care option adds to the choices employees already have, and they'll likely either be pleased with the addition or neutral about it. As a result, the presentation goal is solely to share information about how the new option works so employees can make their own decision about signing up for it. In this case, the presenter could close with the agenda slide showing the two to three main points about the new program and give the key dates and contact information that audience members would need to know for the enrollment period.

Remind Audience About Benefits

A particularly effective presentation closing reminds audience members about the benefits of a message. This type of wrap-up helps them synthesize information they learned during a session and understand the impact it will have on them or the jobs that they do. In our new health care option scenario, if the company plans to phase out some of the current options and wants a specific percentage of employees to enroll in the new plan, the closing presenter needs to encourage audience members to investigate the details of the new plan option to make an informed decision before enrolling. The presenter could wrap up the presentation by emphasizing several ways that the new plan would benefit employees and their families in comparison to the current options. Or, in another example, a presenter wrapping up a presentation to her sales division about a new product that the company will begin offering in the next quarter could close by reminding the audience members about the rewards they'll receive from promoting the new product. The presentation closing will be even stronger in this example if she makes a case in the wrap-up about the benefits of the new product to the company's clients, the company itself, and the sales division. The presenter is emphasizing that the fact that promotion of the new product is a "win-win-win" situation for everyone involved.

Call for Action

A third option to conclude a presentation is to make a call for action. This type of closing combines a message's key points and benefits with a direct statement of the presentation goal. What does the presenter want audience members to know or to do after they leave the session? Begin handling business in a new way? If so, a strong wrap-up would urge audience members to act. Here's an example, "To conclude, I encourage you to begin using this new on-line personnel evaluation system because it will save you time, paperwork, and money." The presenter is specific about what the audience should do ("begin using the new on-line personnel evaluation system") and how the action will benefit the listeners ("because it will save you time, paperwork, and money"). To elaborate, the presenter could then remind the audience how efficient the system actually is over the current paper system and how it should streamline unnecessary paperwork for the company's human resources area. This option combines the benefits wrap-up with a direct call for action.

A good wrap-up signals to an audience that the presenter is pulling together the message with a directive about what to do with the material. An even more effective wrap-up incorporates a reminder about benefits to the audience if they act on the information provided in the presentation. And if a presentation has a persuasive bent to it, the presenter should make a clear call to action at the end; leave no doubt about what the audience should do.

Message Transitions

Just as readers need transitional words or phrases in a letter or memo to signal when and how a writer shifts from one idea to another, so audiences need verbal cues from a speaker to know when the speaker switches points or ideas. Business communication experts call such transitional phrases "oral signposts," "cues," or "idea transitions." These verbal connections are important to help an audience know where a presenter is at any time within the presentation. Remember, speakers have notes and have practiced what they want to say, so they know how the presentation should run. Conversely, audiences know the key points of a presentation only as presenters list them in agendas. Transitional words or phrases help audiences recognize that presenters have concluded one section before moving on to the next.

Don't assume that PowerPoint slide titles are enough to cue the audience that you're transitioning between major ideas. I've seen presenters simply click to the next slide, read the slide title, and then begin discussing the material. However, audience members can read the slide titles for themselves; instead, develop a clear connection between the material you've just finished and the information you're getting ready to begin.

Let's now consider how to transition effectively in a general presentation pattern to support the message structure.

Transition from Opening to Agenda

After the audience connection, introduce the agenda by stating in one sentence the two or three main presentation points:

> "The three key points that I'll address today are how to work with audience, message, and delivery in developing an effective presentation."

The first part of the sentence "The three points that I'll address today are . . ." signals to audience members that the presenter is summarizing the main ideas of the presentation. This gives the audience a verbal image of the presentation structure.

Transition from Agenda to Background

After listing the key material in the agenda, offer the audience a context to the presentation topic before beginning the first main point. In our example on developing presentations, a presenter could say,

> "Before I begin with my first point, I want to take a step back and explain a few differences between public speaking and business presentations."

The part of this sentence "Before I begin with my first point, ... " tells the audience that the speaker will comment on something before getting into the heart of the presentation. It also lets them know that this information will help them better understand the main part of the presentation.

Transition from Background to Key Point One

After completing the brief background, or context, then make the transition to the first main point. In the extended example we're using, the presenter could say,

> "Now, let's begin with my first key point about developing effective presentations: Audience."

Using the word "Now" and the phrase "let's begin" signals to the audience that he's completed the introductory part of the presentation and that he's moving into the main information. And he specifically states the title of the first point ("Audience") to remind them what that particular point is.

Transition Between Points

Just as you need to let the audience know that you've wrapped up the introductory part to the presentation, it's important to let them know that you've finished one major idea and are moving on to the next one. Do this by using phrases such as the following:

- "My next key point is ... "
- "Now that I've finished talking about _____ , let's move on to _____."
- "You've just seen _____, so we'll now turn our attention to my second point: _____."
- "Third, ... "
- "In addition to the elements we discussed in point two, I want to add _____ to it as we move on to point three."

These words and phrases cue an audience that the message is broken into organized units. Because audience members usually won't have a presentation outline to scan, transitional words and phrases help them to stay on track with the presenter throughout a presentation. If they know, for example, that a presenter will be discussing three sales regions' performance, they will clearly understand from verbal signals when the presenter has finished explaining the economic reasons for excellent performance in the north region, and they'll be prepared when the presenter begins highlighting the star performers in the west region as the keys for its stellar performance.

Transition to Wrap-Up

After finishing the final main point, it's time to wrap up the presentation. Develop a sentence to tell the audience that you're ready to conclude. Here are three possible ways to begin the wrap-up:

1. Simply pause after the last sentence in the final main point and then say, "In conclusion, . . . "
2. Start the transition by saying, "To conclude . . . " or "To summarize . . . "
3. State that you're getting ready to pull together the key information that you've just addressed, "You've seen from my presentation today how researching your audience, crafting a clear message, and practicing effective delivery techniques will result in a polished and professional presentation."

The audience will recognize any one of these transitions as the start to a conclusion.

It all seems fairly simple, doesn't it? Essentially, you tell people that you've finished a section and that you're moving on to the next part of the presentation. Audiences need this organization because of the oral nature of presentations; transitions help define boundaries between each section. You'll find that audiences like—and need—the structure of transitions between ideas.

GENERAL PRESENTATION PATTERN

A general presentation strategy can be used for virtually all presentation purposes. It's a basic model structured to convey information efficiently in a highly organized and easy-to-recall fashion. In reading written business messages, people can re-read sentences or paragraphs if they are distracted or need clarification. Audience members in a presentation, however, aren't able to go back and "re-hear" the presentation if their attention wanders. As interesting as a topic may be, people's attention will come and go throughout a presentation session. Presenters need a simple framework to offer an audience a way of visualizing the message layout. While some situations will call for presenters to modify this structure to meet a specific goal, the general presentation pattern gives presenters a solid model with which they can organize information.

This pattern consists of five steps:

1. Audience connection
2. Presentation agenda
3. Background (if necessary)
4. Discussion of agenda points
5. Wrap-up

Earlier in this chapter, we identified methods of connecting with the audience and wrapping up, so we'll now address the heart of a general presentation pattern—the agenda. Exhibit 3.2 is a template for a general presentation worksheet.

Presentation Agenda

Once a presenter establishes common ground with an audience, the next step is to reveal the presentation agenda—the presentation's bottom line. An outline of the key points that will be addressed, the agenda acts as a preview of the message.

In written business communication (memos, letters, proposals, reports, etc.), readers usually will find the bottom line of a message summarized in the subject line or concisely described in the first paragraph. Busy readers can efficiently and quickly identify the message's most important information early because it actually begins the message. Further, readers can skim written material when it's most convenient for them. They can read the initial paragraph to understand the message's purpose quickly. And if the message in that initial paragraph is somewhat unclear, readers can re-read the paragraph. If they skim the entire document quickly, they could set it aside and later go back to review the key points at a more leisurely pace.

Additionally, from simply glancing at the page layout, readers can see the following:

- How much time they must invest in reading it (from the amount of text on the pages)
- What the key elements of the message are (from headings, bold font, bullet points, etc.)

Conversely, in business presentations, audience members may only know the general topic and, typically, about how long the presentation is scheduled. They aren't able to review presenters' notes or go back hours later to hear presenters elaborate on a particular point. Thus, for audience members,

EXHIBIT 3.2   General presentation worksheet.

Presentation Purpose

I'm giving this presentation because _____.

Presentation Goal

At the end of the presentation, I want my audience to

_____.

Audience Analysis

Here's what I know about my audience:

Presentation Structure

Audience Connection

Agenda (List your two or three key points in phrases here)

Background

Key Point 1

Key Point 2

Key Point 3

Wrap-up

an agenda becomes a valuable tool to promote the message's bottom line and to remind them of the presentation's most important concepts.

As you develop an agenda, identify the elements that are important to a particular message. You should be able to deliver a thorough 20- to 75-minute presentation by fully supporting two or three main ideas. What are the most crucial two to three points that an audience needs to know (Kiechel, 1987)? Generate a two- to seven-word summary "title" for these points to establish each as a separate category and then create subpoints, using illustrations and supporting details to flesh out the sections. The summary "titles" for the categories then become the agenda that drives the presentation content. Presenters who try to address more than three main points will find that they're not able to give sufficient information to more than three ideas in the available time. Likewise, audiences probably won't be able to recall more than two or three main ideas from the session.

Of course, the more time you have available, the more in depth you'll be able to discuss each of the key points. The following example shows how I plan my agenda topics, depending on the amount of time that I'm given, for a presentation about presentation skills. When I talk with groups about effective presentations, ideally, I'd like to cover *seven* aspects of presentations: audience analysis, message organization, delivery techniques, visuals, anxieties, the question-and-answer session, and self-assessment. However, audiences can only handle so much information in any given amount of time. If I have 20 minutes for the presentation, I can discuss the general presentation pattern and touch on delivery techniques, while offering a few tips about managing presentation anxieties. Limiting my presentation to three basic points means I allot my time this way:

Connection with audience	1 minute
Agenda	15–30 seconds
Key point 1 (general presentation pattern)	5 minutes
Key point 2 (three delivery techniques)	5 minutes
Key point 3 (anxieties)	5 minutes
Wrap-up	1 minute
Q&A	2–3 minutes
Total	**20 minutes**

Clearly, 20 minutes doesn't leave time for giving information about problem-solving organizational patterns, effective visuals, or in-depth delivery discussion. And, 5 minutes for each of the three key points severely limits how much detail I can provide. On the other hand, I can offer audience members information that they can immediately apply about a few presentation components within the 20-minute time frame.

If I have 45 minutes, I might discuss in more detail a general presentation pattern, delivery techniques, and tips on managing presentation anxieties. Here's how I would structure the presentation with this expanded time limit:

Connection with audience	1 minute
Agenda	15–30 seconds
Key point 1 (general presentation pattern)	12.5 minutes
Key point 2 (three delivery techniques)	12.5 minutes
Key point 3 (anxieties)	12.5 minutes
Wrap-up	1 minute
Q&A	<u>5 minutes</u>
Total	**45 minutes**

You can see that the topics are identical to those that I may have used in a presentation 25 minutes shorter. However, I prefer to use the extra time to give the audience more in-depth information, examples, and perhaps even practice rather than expand the number of topics that I address. More time to develop supporting illustrations and examples for each of the key topics helps the audience better understand each one. Audience members can only absorb so much information in a limited time period, and I'd prefer to give them specific details about a few key presentation guidelines instead of general, overly broad tips about a number of elements. The example below shows a presentation planning chart I use to determine key points based on what I know about a presentation's purpose, audience, and time limit:

Purpose

What is the purpose of my presentation?

Why was I asked to present?

Audience

What does the audience already know about my topic?

How does the audience feel about my topic?

What does the audience need to know about my topic?

Time Limit

How much time do I have?

If this sounds like the planning and audience analysis work covered in Chapter 2, that's exactly what it is! Based on what I know about why I was asked to present and the audience I'll be presenting to, I customize my presentation content to fit each audience's need for a specific amount of information within a given time period.

Obviously, presenters can't address, even in longer presentations, as many main ideas as they might wish to. At the end of a presentation, to ensure an audience knows that there's more to be learned, speakers could give a handout about a few tips on the parts of their topic that they didn't have time to discuss and offer to speak again with the group about these ideas at a later date. You can read more about supporting handouts in Chapter 6.

So how to decide what to include and what to leave for another session? If you're not sure what might be the most important elements of a topic, scratch out an outline. The old-fashioned outline format using the capital Roman numerals (I, II, III, etc.) for headings, the capital letters (A, B, C, etc.) as subheadings, or the numbers (1, 2, 3, etc.) and lower-cased letters (a, b, c, etc.) will be helpful in deciding how to prioritize and organize information. Use the main headings (I, II, III, etc.) for the main category "titles" (the agenda).

If a presentation appears overly complex and might beg for more than three key points, look closer for commonalities among key headings to see where and how to consolidate ideas. If you could only cover only two to three key points, what would those be? The answer will be your agenda. Resist the temptation to use more than three main ideas in a 20- to 75-minute presentation—even though you might believe the extra information is critical. Doing so will keep a presentation detailed, memorable, and within the time limit. It will be difficult to do all of these if you have more than a few key points to discuss. Further, as you'll learn in Chapter 8, the long points that you can't fit into a particular presentation because of time limitations may become the basis for the Q & A for that presentation.

Background

Once you've decided what the main points in an agenda should be, next consider a brief background, or context, for the presentation. Think about the background section as a way to share (briefly) information about a topic that will enhance how an audience understands a message. For example, when I speak with a group about presentations, I explain in the background section that the material I'll address focuses exclusively on business presentations. Too often, audience members come to a session on presentations thinking they'll learn about public speaking. But, in the background section, I briefly explain the major differences between business presentations and public speaking engagements. Doing this helps the audience understand the approach that I take in the remainder of the presentation.

Another way to think about the background is as a section to share information about a topic that is important but doesn't really fit within one of the main agenda points. For example, a presenter speaking to potential clients about their company's human resource services might mention in the background section what she knows about how their human resources area currently operates. This cues the audience to recognize that the presenter has done her homework on the company; it also sets the context that the presenter knows how their system works in comparison to what she'll recommend. The background then paves the way for the presenter to explain in the main part of the presentation how her human resource services plan could be more efficient.

Here's one final example of material useful for the background section. If you're making a presentation to an audience that might not be familiar with the topic, the background is an appropriate place to offer explanations or definitions and ensure everyone in the audience has the same basic understanding of terms or concepts. For example, if presenters for a not-for-profit organization are soliciting funds from potential corporate donors, the presenters may need to provide a brief history of the not-for-profit agency and its mission as the background section. The heart of the presentation then can be dedicated to explaining how the organization plans to spend funds and what benefits donors will receive for providing financial support. Likewise, if a presenter speaks with an audience that has mixed levels of expertise or familiarity with a topic, the presenter may need to define some terms. Giving a brief background allows everyone in the audience to have the same grounding about the presentation material.

Key Points and Support

Once presenters outline the agenda and explain any background information, they then begin the main section of a presentation. Here presenters flesh out details about each of the two to three key points outlined in the agenda, using either a topical or a chronological model to develop the ideas. In the former, the two or three agenda points are grouped by topic. Speakers identify the points they'll discuss and then elaborate on each. In the latter, presenters base their message structure on events within a time progression and address the events in sequential order.

To compare, let me show you how I would organize a 20-minute presentation on speaking anxieties differently depending on whether I used the topical or the chronological model. First, the topical:

Connection with audience	1 minute
Agenda	15–30 seconds
Topic 1 (why presentations make us nervous)	7 minutes
Topic 2 (how to reduce presentation anxieties)	8 minutes
Wrap-up	1 minute
Q&A	2–3 minutes
Total	**20 minutes**

You can see from the description of the main ideas in this example that I could switch Topics 1 and 2 and discuss how to reduce presentation anxieties before explaining why presentations make us nervous. There's no reason to order them sequentially.

In a chronological presentation pattern, on the other hand, I instead might explain how presenters could manage their presentation anxieties by focusing on stages within the presentation process. Here's how I would order my material in chronological order:

Connection with audience	1 minute
Agenda	15–30 seconds
Stage 1 (minimizing pre-presentation nerves)	5 minutes
Stage 2 (handling nerves during the presentation)	5 minutes
Stage 3 (managing nerves after the presentation)	5 minutes
Wrap-up	1 minute
Q&A	2–3 minutes
Total	**20 minutes**

In this example, each stage builds on the one before, and I focus on how presenters can use their time during each stage to minimize and manage anxieties about speaking in front of a group of people. Instead of organizing by general categories with each one being approximately equal in importance to the others, however, the chronological pattern organizes information by time progression. It wouldn't make much sense for me to *start* a presentation about anxiety by discussing how presenters can manage their nerves *after* a presentation in order to prepare for the next one. Nor would it be logical to position the section on minimizing pre-presentation nerves as the last main point in the presentation. As you can see, a chronological presentation pattern follows a narrowly defined path—time progression.

Sample Presentation Model

Using a topical pattern, Exhibit 3.3 shows an outline for a 20-minute presentation on an organ donation information session. Of course, the presentation outline is just that—an outline. It doesn't include all that a presenter will address. For example, in the presentation on organ donation issues, I usually take time to elaborate on the facts and myths of organ donation and give more details in each area. The outline can be as comprehensive as necessary, and it's fine to have a list of subpoints under each key topic to help presenters determine that they've included all the material they need.

In presentation outlines, avoid using complete sentences. If you plan on using this outline as presentation notes, it's too tempting to read the sentences while delivering a presentation. Most presenters who read to an audience come across sounding stilted or overly formal. Additionally, presenters who use paragraph form for notes (not outline form) run the risk of

EXHIBIT 3.3 Organ donation information presentation.

"Think You're an Organ and Tissue Donor? Not If You Don't Tell Your Family!"

Audience Connection

If every person on the national organ transplant list came to Chapel Hill and filed into the Kenan Football Stadium, the ones who wouldn't have a seat could walk a short distance to the Dean Smith Basketball Center and fill up the seats in this arena as well. Yet, even then, everyone wouldn't have a seat. Over 80,000 people in our country are waiting on a life-saving organ transplant right now. *(Note: this opening would only be effective for an audience familiar with the size of these sporting arenas.)*

Agenda

   I.   Learning a Few Facts and Myths About Organ Donation
  II.   Becoming a Donor in North Carolina
III.   Informing Your Family About Your Decision

Background

Organ donation has only been around for a few decades, but already thousands of people have experienced a better quality of life and a longer life span as a result of having an organ transplant. Most people in North Carolina believe that the little heart on their driver's license indicates their legal decision to be an organ donor.

EXHIBIT 3.3 Continued.

Key Points

Presentation goal: to inform audience members about organ donation facts so that they can make an informed decision for themselves—and share that decision with their family members.

I. Learning the Facts and Myths About Donation Issues
 A. Facts
  1. One organ donor can save up to 8 lives and improve the quality of life for up to 50 others through tissue donation (Carolina Donor Services, n. d.).
  2. The majority of the world's religions either support organ and tissue donation or believe that it's a choice left up to each individual.
 B. Myths
  1. Doctors won't try to save you if they know you've signed an organ donor card.
  2. Your body won't be suitable for an open casket funeral after organ and tissue donation.
  3. Rich people or celebrities receive special consideration for higher priority on the transplant lists.
II. Becoming a Donor in North Carolina
 A. Driver's license
  1. Your driver's license is an indication that you want to be an organ donor, but it's not a legal document.
 B. Organ donor card
  1. As of December 2001, a signed, witnessed organ donor card is a legal document.
III. Informing Your Family
  1. Donor cards often aren't found with individuals who have been in accidents.
  2. Telling your family guarantees your decision to be an organ donor will be honored.

not being able to find the point they might need during a presentation. It's more difficult to find a specific point, for example, two-thirds through a text paragraph than to glance at subpoint 3 under key idea 2.

Wrap-Up

Below is an example of a combination summary and call to action wrap-up that I use in my organ donor awareness presentations.

"Today, you've learned a few facts about organ transplantation issues. You've learned about some of the most common myths and misconceptions about transplants. And, you've learned that just having the little heart on your driver's license isn't enough to guarantee that your wishes about organ donation will be carried out. Make time to talk with family members about your decision so that they won't have to add yet another decision to an already difficult time in the event of your death. And, while you're having the discussion, you may find that it's a good time to learn about the donation wishes of your family members."

In the first three sentences, I summarize my key points. Then, I develop in this example a call to action (make time to talk with family members about your decision) and provide an indirect benefit (save your family members a decision during a difficult time).

PROBLEM-SOLVING PRESENTATION PATTERN

When presenters need to offer a group a recommendation to resolve a problem—or gain consensus about a decision a company needs to make—the most effective organizational model will be the problem-solving pattern. Following is an example of a situation that calls for this type of presentation.

The supervisor of a department asked an assistant manager to examine the viability of the company offering a credit card payment option for its customers. (The company's payment policy up to that point had been cash or check only.) The assistant manager spent a significant amount of time learning about how the automated system would work and talking with associates inside and outside his department to understand how each department would need to incorporate the new procedure. He discovered that a number of departments would be involved in the new payment system: billing, the customer service center, the programming areas, the collections area, and the marketing department, just to name the primary ones. Additionally, he talked with several credit card vendors to learn their basic pricing structures and service support capabilities. After extensive research and a thorough cost-benefits analysis, the assistant manager concluded that an automated credit card payment option would offer the following benefits:

- Establish another payment option for customers
- Provide convenience to customers by allowing them to use a Touch-Tone telephone system on their own time to pay their bill
- Require the credit card company processing the payments to collect late or defaulted payments
- Impact the company's bottom line positively because the system is automated

- Increase on-time payments from customers
- Streamline paper handling and costs

However, he learned that several of the departments or areas that would be involved didn't see the value in the automated credit card payment system because they didn't understand how the change would affect the company; they were used to working in their own "silo" (or department) and didn't grasp how substantial the change could be. One department manager even told him, "Why do we need to change a system that's working just fine?" Once he had finished his research and the cost-benefit analysis, the assistant manager sent his supervisor a brief report on the findings. The supervisor then asked him to develop a 15- to 20-minute presentation to deliver to a group of department and area heads outlining his findings and recommendation.

In this scenario, the assistant manager learned about how an automated credit card payment system would work; how it would benefit the customers, the departments, and the company; and how individuals in the various departments felt about it. He identified the value in the system and discovered that anyone presenting the new payment system as a company initiative would need to persuade department managers to support the system because they didn't yet understand it. A problem-solving organizational pattern would be the most effective way for the assistant manager to explain his research and demonstrate that his recommendation is beneficial for the company and all parties involved.

The same preliminary planning questions that we examined earlier in the general presentation pattern would be a good place for the assistant manager to start developing his presentation:

Purpose

What is the purpose of my presentation?

—to inform department managers about new customer payment system

Why was I asked to present?

—because I did the research on the system

Audience

What does the audience already know about my topic?

—most know only how the system would impact their respective departments

How does the audience feel about my topic?

—most aren't pleased because they believe it will create more work for their departments or will result in loss of job responsibilities

What does the audience need to know about my topic?

—how the new system works and would affect the individual departments, what alternatives I've considered, and how it will benefit the company

Time

How much time do I have?

—15 to 20 minutes

By answering these questions, the assistant manager can then begin to decide what information he needs to include in the presentation to meet his goal. Because his research revealed the audience attitude toward the topic isn't positive, he needs to address the audience's potential objections and emphasize the benefits of the system to the department heads, their departments, and the company. A problem-solving presentation pattern would give him the structure to explain his recommendation by demonstrating why the automated credit card payment system is a sound decision for the company.

In a problem-solving presentation format, presenters outline challenges and benefits of potential solutions to a need or a problem. After covering the necessary material, presenters then demonstrate why one recommendation is the best solution, or they open the floor for the audience to select the most optimal one based on the choices presenters offer. Because there usually are several ways to resolve issues, acknowledging and explaining advantages and challenges to each option preemptively addresses possible objections to any one recommendation and answers potential questions. Additionally, this strategy evidences a speaker's knowledge of and credibility with the issue. Problem-solving presentations require research and presenter credibility in order to convince individuals that the recommended option is the best one or that the several choices offered are the strongest solutions from all possibilities.

Here's what a problem-solving presentation might look like in outline form:

I. Audience connection

II. Explanation of the shared problem/issue/goal

    a. What the problem/issue/goal is

    b. Why it's a problem/issue/goal for the company/division/employees/etc.

III. Key recommendations (discussion of strongest possible solutions to shared problem/issue/goal)

    a. Benefits of each solution

    b. Drawbacks to each solution

IV. Highlight of the recommended solution
    a. Drawbacks of this solution
    b. Benefits of this solution
    c. Explanation of why it's the best solution
V. Wrap-up and call to action

Of course, if a presenter's goal is to give a group the information they need to make the decision themselves from several options, simply collapse point V into point IV and eliminate the highlighting of any one option as the optimal solution.

Let's walk through the stages of a problem-solving presentation pattern using the example of an HR (human relations) specialist who wants to convince senior management to develop and fund a corporate citizenship outreach program. Exhibit 3.4 offers a template for a problem-solving presentation pattern.

In this example, assume that senior managers have given the HR specialist 30 minutes to present options for the company to consider. The following time schedule could be used to develop a problem-solving presentation:

Connection with audience	1 minute
Explanation of shared goal	5 minutes
Option 1	4 minutes
(donate experts and money to support defined causes)	
Option 2	4 minutes
(establish challenge grants for community projects)	
Option 3 (recommended solution)	9 minutes
(partner with school for tutoring/mentoring purposes)	
Wrap-up and call to action	1 minute
Q&A	4–5 minutes
Total	**30 minutes**

Although the HR specialist likely discovered numerous ways for the company to be involved in the community, you can see in this time schedule that he identified three options for management to consider. Limiting the number of choices allows the presenter to thoroughly explain the benefits and drawbacks to these three before pointing out the desirable one or asking session participants to decide which one they prefer. If presenters offer more than three options, they won't have enough time to share details about

EXHIBIT 3.4   Problem-solving presentation strategy worksheet.

Presentation Purpose

I'm giving this presentation because _____.

Presentation Goal

At the end of the presentation, I want my audience to

_____.

Audience Analysis

Here's what I know about my audience:

Presentation Structure

    <u>Audience Connection</u> (common ground or shared goals)

    <u>Context</u> (explain the current situation and why it's an issue or challenge)

    <u>Possible Solutions</u> (including strengths and challenges)
        A. Possible Solution 1
          a. Strengths
          b. Challenges
        B. Possible Solution 2
          a. Strengths
          b. Challenges
        C. Possible Solution 3
          a. Strengths
          b. Challenges

    <u>The Solution</u> (if you're charged with making a recommendation)

    <u>Reminder of Benefits and Call to Action</u>

any of the possibilities. Of course, at times presenters need to disclose more than two or three options (perhaps the executives attending the session are notorious for wanting to know what ideas presenters *discarded* to understand how they came to select the ones being presented); if so, presenters could simply mention them in the explanation of the shared goal and—without going into detail—mention why they weren't selected as the top viable choices. If the audience wants to revisit these other options, they can do so during the Q&A session.

Audience Connection

A strong audience connection in a problem-solving presentation is crucial to establishing credibility. The presenter should connect with the audience immediately—establish common ground by identifying shared goals or interests. Why should an audience be interested in the topic? How will it benefit them to listen to—and then act on—a presentation? If a presentation purpose is to give people details they need to know to do their jobs more efficiently (an informative presentation), an appropriate audience connection might be an explanation about how much money, effort, or time can be saved by a new process the presenter will introduce. In a problem-solving presentation, couch the connection in terms of a shared problem or goal. A process change, for example, might be a controversial one, so a presenter could open by discussing shared difficulties that departments might have with the current process. Or, if the current process works fine for one department but not for another, open with the shared benefits that the entire company will experience as a result of the change.

In our example about the recommendation for a more comprehensive corporate citizenship program, audience analysis might indicate that management and employees are satisfied with the current corporate matching funds donation program. Thus, an effective audience connection might be to talk about the shared goal—the positive impact the corporation has on the community with its current program. The executives attending the presentation will agree that the program has been successful in making an impact on the community and in raising awareness about the company's efforts. This common-ground connection kicks off the presentation by celebrating past results and gaining agreement about the importance of being involved with the community.

Explanation of Shared Goal

A detailed explanation of a shared goal or problem should follow an audience connection and set the context of the recommendation(s). Why does the audience need to spend time resolving a particular issue? What's the importance of solving the problem for the company or the department? Why does this issue matter? Explaining the answers to questions like these helps the audience understand the importance of proactively resolving the issue. In our corporate citizenship example, if the company's current program is a success, why does it need to expand or change the program? Why should the company need to create an outreach program for associates if the current program of matching donations is working well?

Key Recommendations

Once a presenter sets the context for why an issue needs to be resolved, the next step in a problem-solving presentation pattern should be to identify and explain to an audience the strongest possible options to resolve the issue—including solutions and challenges of each. Doing this emphasizes the presenter's credibility by demonstrating an expertise in the topic. It also sets the stage for the audience to understand the benefits and drawbacks of all reasonable options. Exhibit 3.5 shows what a problem-solving presentation outline might look like in the corporate citizenship example. Simply an outline, this gives the presenter the framework of a problem-solving presentation to walk an audience through the benefits and challenges of each option in order to select the most feasible one.

Wrap-up

A problem-solving presentation wrap-up should reemphasize the call to action. Close by leaving the audience considering both the benefits of the alternative that you recommend and an encouragement to act on the recommendation. Or, if the presentation goal is to have the audience decide the most feasible option, end the presentation by encouraging the participants to select a solution; urge them to act and remind them of the benefits of choosing one of the recommendations. Be clear about what you want the audience to do.

In our corporate citizenship program example, the HR specialist might use the example below as a wrap-up.

CLOSING

"I encourage you to create and fund the adopt-a-school corporate citizenship program that I've recommended because it will raise our profile in the community, motivate our employees, and help to develop our community's children." (*goal: to persuade audience to adopt the recommended solution*)

or

"I encourage you to create and fund one of these corporate citizenship programs that I've recommended because doing so will raise our profile in the community, motivate our employees, and help to develop our community's children. We now have some time to discuss the options and select one." (*goal: to convince the audience to select one from the options presented*)

Remember, the audience needs to hear—again—why the company should establish a citizenship program above and beyond its current donation matching program; establish the need for change and then explain how it will produce results.

EXHIBIT 3.5   **A problem-solving presentation.**

"Let's Get Involved"

Audience Connection

In the past three years, our employees have donated over $800,000 to 65 different not-for-profit agencies in our community. Through our 50 percent matching donations program, our company donated $400,000 more to these agencies. XYZ corporation has made a difference in our community to the tune of $1.2 million.

Explanation of Shared Goal

We donate considerable funds to the community. Can we do any more? Should we do more? Research shows that corporate citizenship can impact a company's bottom line in several ways.

Corporate citizenship contributes to:

I.   Better public relations
II. Better trained and more motivated employees
III. Development of future market and customers

(continued)

EXHIBIT 3.5 Continued.

Key Recommendations

Presentation goal: to convince management to create and fund a corporate citizenship outreach program.

I. Donate "experts" and equipment to support selected causes (literacy, homelessness, health care, etc.)
   A. Benefits
      1. Gives organizations people resources and materials they need but can't afford
      2. Sends selected associates out in the community
   B. Challenges
      1. Limits the number of associates involved
      2. Need to select which not-for-profits to assist
      3. Need to determine budget for donated equipment
      4. Determine how to adjust work schedules and duties to accommodate employees who go out into the community
II. Set up grant funding program to encourage initiatives in the community
   A. Benefits
      1. Focuses our donation efforts on needs in community
      2. Encourages associates and people in the community alike to partner with our corporation
   B. Challenges
      1. Doesn't get associates out in community on any regular basis
      2. Need to set funding guidelines for grants
      3. Need to establish follow-up structure
III. Partner with school for mentoring or tutoring programs
   A. Benefits
      1. Sends associates out in community on regular basis
      2. Focuses company involvement in one specific area
      3. Involves limited direct expenses
   B. Challenges
      1. Need to select one school
      2. Determine how to adjust work schedules and duties to accommodate employees who go to the school during work hours
IV. Recommendation and call to action
V. Discussion of recommendations and Q&A

EXERCISES   Developing an Effective Message

EXERCISE 1   Starting My Message: Audience Connection and Agendas

For each of the following two mini-cases, write an audience connection that will link the topic with an audience's interests and list the two or three main agenda points that you would discuss if you were going to develop a presentation on these topics.

A. CPAs and ABCs

You've been asked to make a presentation to a professional accounting organization about the importance of clear and concise written communication skills. Each year at its annual conference, the organization holds a professional development seminar series, and this year, communication competency is the focus. On the agenda with you will be speakers who will address business presentation techniques, interpersonal communication skills, voice messaging tips, and electronic mail guidelines. You know that most of the conference attendees are interested in polishing up their communication skills, but few have had any formal training in how to write business messages. What they've learned has been on the job. You also know that the accounting organization recently completed a field study that indicates that most practitioners are concerned about the quality of writing skills among entry-level accountants. These employees, working under tight deadlines and budget constraints, must send numerous letters, memos, analysis reports, and audit reports with little support from office staff or mentors. As a result, some accounting firms worry about the possible lack of professionalism or increased risk of liability if new associates aren't trained how to write effective business messages.

Your task: Develop an audience connection on effective written communication skills. Think about what you already know about your audience and create a link between the importance of clear, concise writing skills and what you know that your audience values.

B. College Recruiting for XYZ Corporation

Your manager invited you to go on a recruiting trip to several local colleges and universities. Each of these academic institutions has one day a year designated as "Career Day," when businesses can come to the campus and talk with juniors and seniors about career options. Each campus also sets an agenda for participating organizations so that no one organization will have a competitive advantage over another. For the campuses you'll be visiting, speakers will make one 15-minute presentation about their business and will then be available to the students at booths set up in the school cafeterias.

Your task: Drawing on your knowledge of a business organization, think about what qualities might attract recent college graduates to work for this firm. Develop an opening that will create a bridge between your firm and the students. Then, list the two or three key ideas that you'd like to discuss about this firm during the presentation.

EXERCISE 2   Creating My Presentation

Select one of the following scenarios and develop a presentation agenda and outline (including key points and subpoints) directed to an audience of your peers.

A. Your favorite vacation spot

B. The importance that your department has to the company as a whole

C. One side of a controversial issue in your professional field

D. How to select plants to decorate your landscape

E. How to pick a puppy or kitten

F. An important trade journal article that you've read recently

G. The most difficult sale you've ever been satisfied with

H. One of your favorite products/services that your company makes/offers

I. Time management issues

J. How to decide which computer to purchase

K. Business interview etiquette

L. Writing performance evaluations

M. Deciding which nonprofit to volunteer with

N. Stress management issues

O. The importance of networking

P. Deciding on or switching careers

EXERCISE 3   Wrapping Up My Message

Using the information you have in the mini-cases in Exercise 1, develop an effective wrap-up for each of the two presentations.

EXERCISE 4   Making a Presentation to the Shareholders

Select a company that interests you and print or copy the CEO's letter to the shareholders from the annual report. Read the letter and create a presentation using the chronological presentation pattern highlighting two to three key ideas in the letter. Consider the audience to be a group of shareholders and title the presentation, "Our Year." Alternatively, develop a presentation using the topical presentation pattern titled, "What We Anticipate for the Upcoming Year."

EXERCISE 5   Offering a Problem-Solving Recommendation to the Shareholders

Using one of the two examples in Exercise 4, select an issue the company listed as a challenge that it experienced during the current year or expects to face in coming years. Develop a problem-solving presentation, addressed to the company's executive management team, to recommend a solution to the challenge.

References

Aggarwal, G., Brannon, B., Celiesius, K., Chau, C., Mayer, K., & Reynolds, T. (Spring 2001). UNC-Chapel Hill Benefits Department team presentation for BUSI 100.

Basnight, A., Edwards, B., McConnell, I., Poplin, L., & Stading, M. (December 2001). Volunteer Orange team presentation for BUSI 100.

Baxter, B., Beaudin, J., Bucklew, S., Evans, A., & Larson, M. (December 2000). John Umstead Hospital team presentation for BUSI 100.

Bovée, C. L., & Thill, J. V. (2000). *Business Communication Today* (6th ed.). Upper Saddle River, NJ: Prentice Hall.

Carolina Donor Services. (n.d.). Retrieved May 22, 2003, from www.carolinadonorservices.org. Numbers as of June 2002.

Hoff, R. (1988). "I can see you naked," *A fearless guide to making great presentations.* Kansas City, MO: Andrews and McMeel.

Kiechel, W., III. (1987, June 8). How to give a speech. *Fortune, 115*(12), 179–182.

Munter, M. (2000). *Guide to managerial communication: Effective business writing and speaking* (5th ed.). Upper Saddle River, NJ: Prentice Hall, p. 17.

Munter, M., & Russell, L. (2002). *Guide to Presentations.* Upper Saddle River, NJ: Prentice Hall.

Tse, K. (Summer 2001). Presentation for BUSI 100.

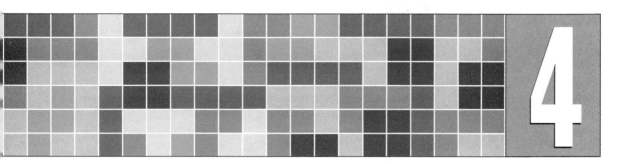

Delivering
with Impact

PERFORMANCE GOALS

After completing this chapter, readers will be able to:

■ hone volume, rate and articulation, and conversational tone to enhance speaking voice

■ identify and refine non-verbal communication cues to convey professionalism and support the message itself

■ develop presentation notes to manage anxiety

We've spent considerable time in Chapters 2 and 3 discussing the importance of analyzing an audience and developing a well-organized message. Presenters must thoroughly analyze audiences to tailor a message for a specific purpose. Similarly, presenters need to craft a well-organized message to convey information efficiently. These presentation components are critical building blocks to inform and/or persuade an audience. However, knowing an audience and generating content material alone don't equate to an exceptional presentation. Dynamic delivery techniques can support message content, enhance an audience's impressions of a speaker and topic, and play a significant role in elevating a good presentation to an extraordinary one.

Even though some people may appear to have a natural talent for speaking in front of groups, most effective presenters have worked hard to polish their delivery skills. They know how to use specific techniques to connect with an audience and to support message content. Chapter 4 addresses these three delivery considerations:

■ Speaking voice
■ Nonverbal cues
■ Presentation notes

Additionally, you'll find at the end of this chapter a section called "Habits to Avoid," a brief discussion about how to correct ineffective delivery habits.

The exercises at the end of this chapter are particularly important in helping presenters polish delivery skills. To develop a strong professional presentation presence, it's critical for presenters to objectively analyze their own delivery methods. Effective use of body language, vocal intonations, movements around the room, and eye contact establish the presenter as a confident expert and signal the message is comprehensive and credible.

SPEAKING VOICE

In written business communication (letters, memos, reports, proposals, etc.), writers have many techniques available to highlight key ideas. For example, in a memo about policy changes, a manager can draw readers' attention to information about an upcoming meeting by using bold font to highlight the date, time, and place of the meeting. When readers skim the memo, the bold font stands out from the rest of the document. Or, if an executive wants to stress several key points in a letter explaining an organizational process to a potential client, the writer can indent the information and use a bulleted or numbered list. Either of these emphasis techniques encourages readers to notice specifics different from the general document layout. The white space surrounding indented text creates an inviting look. And readers expect that material in bold font or bulleted format will be a quick summary of important information.

In business presentations, speakers also need to be able to draw an audience's attention to key elements of their message, and their voice is one of the strongest tools they have available to do so. Beyond simply highlighting key points, however, the sound of a presenter's voice conveys a significant amount of information to an audience about the presenter. In communication theory, Carl Leathers found that from the sound of and variations in a speaker's voice, listeners infer confidence, credibility, and personality, as well as a speaker's likeability (1992). This section examines the following ways that presenters can use their voice to underscore information in a presentation and create a favorable impression on the audience:

- Volume
- Rate and articulation
- Conversational tone

Because each presentation situation will be unique, however, there are few "hard and fast rules." Sometimes presentation situations require that a presenter speak more loudly than in others. A rapid pace might be necessary in some situations, but not appropriate in others, because a presenter may need to closely match an audience's typical rate of speech. A more formal tone might work best in some sessions and a much more informal tone in others, depending on the speaker's relationship with individuals in the audience and the presentation purpose. With that said, there are some basic strategies you can use to hone vocal patterns for a successful presentation.

Volume

On the most basic level, of course, speakers need to project loudly enough so that everyone in the room can easily hear them. But a sudden shift to a louder or softer level from regular volume calls attention to specific words or phrases. Volume is a tool presenters can use to emphasize essential elements in a message.

Planning appropriate volume levels at various points in a presentation also is critical because audience members use volume cues to assess a speaker's confidence and likability. In the U. S. business environment, for example, audiences expect that assertive presenters will use a louder, more forceful volume than submissive or anxious presenters. On the other hand, overly loud presenters will be seen as excessively dominant or unlikable (Leathers, 1992). This section focuses on how to vary volume to project clearly and emphasize key points in order to create a confident, professional speaking style.

Project Clearly

Let's start with how loudly or softly you speak in general conversation to determine how to modulate volume and projection in a presentation. The following tips show how to diagnose conversational speaking volume and then modify it for presentation situations.

SOFT-SPOKEN VOICES

Are you a quiet person who tends to speak in a soft voice? Do people often ask you to repeat what you've said because they had difficulty hearing you?

Strong volume sends a signal to audiences that a presenter has solid self-esteem and is enthusiastic about discussing the presentation material and interacting with the audience. Overly soft volume, on the other hand, suggests a nervous speaker or one who may be uncomfortable with the information being presented. Volume is one of the primary indicators of dominance in interpersonal communication theory.

If you naturally speak softly or quietly in general conversation, practice speaking in rooms of various sizes and ask a colleague to sit in on these rehearsals to let you know how well your voice projects to the back of each room. As you begin to increase volume, you may feel that you're almost shouting when you speak to the back row of seats. You may even feel a bit rude and too loud. However, audiences need to be able to hear you easily—and a strong volume will establish you as a confident speaker. Therefore, while you'll feel uncomfortable at first speaking louder than you might normally, push yourself out of that comfort zone during presentations. With practice, you'll begin to naturally adjust volume and projection in various rooms without feeling a sense of discomfort. In other words, you'll more easily draw on practice and experience to adapt volume to each presentation situation.

BOOMING VOICES

Do you have a voice that's naturally loud? Do you find that people often tell you to "tone it down" or they lean slightly back as you're talking because your volume might be a bit loud?

Audiences may view excessively loud presenters as overly dominant and less interested in audience interaction. While a strong volume gives the impression of a presenter who is confident, credible, and in control of the material, too much volume could undercut the message by alienating an audience.

If your voice naturally carries well in general conversation, work on moderating how loudly you project it for presentations. Such vocal energy is an asset because presenters who project well convey enthusiasm and competence. On the other hand, excessively loud speakers may convey anger and aggressiveness. Practice delivering presentations in rooms of various shapes and depths with a colleague sitting near the front of each room to offer feedback on volume level. As you're practicing using a restrained volume level, you may feel uncomfortable that you're not talking loudly enough. But give your test audience the opportunity to let you know how well you're coming across. As you become more comfortable speaking at a more moderate volume level, you'll find it easier to adapt that volume to the room situation and number of participants in each audience.

Check Room Acoustics

Some rooms are more conducive than others for presentations, and voices will project differently in various sizes or types of rooms. If speaking in a small room with just a few people, you may not need to increase volume much at all; everyone in the room should be able to hear a strong conversational volume. If you're in a room with tall ceilings or if audience members are seated considerably back from where you'll be speaking, project your volume level so that those in the back of the room will easily be able to hear the presentation.

Additionally, presenters need to adjust volume and projection for any background noise. You may find yourself having to speak over the whirring sound of an overhead projector fan, construction noise, ringing telephones, traffic, or any number of other sounds. Take a moment to identify the acoustical situation and the potential competing sounds in the room where you'll be presenting. Doing this will help you compensate and adjust how much you need to moderate or project your volume.

Emphasize Key Points

Now that you've identified some strategies to diagnose your typical volume level and moderate it to adjust for various situations, let's examine how to vary the levels of volume to make details "come alive" for the audience. If presenters normally speak in an assured conversational manner, they can grab an audience's attention when they increase or decrease volume suddenly to emphasize a particular element of a message.

Audiences certainly don't want to be shouted at, but using a volume that's slightly louder than a normal presentation voice for a few words or a phrase will prompt them to take notice of the change. A sudden volume variation signals a presenter may be excited, happy, or concerned about something, and a shift to a louder voice cues an audience to focus more closely on what a presenter is saying. Alternatively, presenters can generate the same attention from an audience if they suddenly drop their volume and speak as softly as possible—yet still be audible for those in the back row—for a few phrases. The change from a normal volume to a much louder or softer one will motivate an audience to concentrate on what a presenter is saying because the change will surprise them. It's a shift from the volume levels they've been listening to and expect from the presenter.

Of course, speakers need to carefully decide when to use the loud/soft volume techniques for emphasis because too much of either could annoy an audience. As is the case with written business communication, the key is to use emphasis sparingly to underscore the most important elements in a message. The example below shows a paragraph from a memo that over-uses bold font to make key points.

> "I'm **impressed** with the amount and quality of work that each department has devoted to **our** community service project, and I'm **proud** to be working on a team with **you.** Please make sure that you **set aside** time for our **next project team meeting on Tuesday from 6:00 to 8:00 P.M. in Room 2050. Thank you** for all that you're doing!"

Read this paragraph out loud, raising your volume for each word in bold font and then returning to a normal (general conversational) volume for each word that isn't in bold font. Hear what sounds like false enthusiasm? Now try the opposite technique; read the same paragraph out loud, lowering your voice to almost a stage whisper for each word in bold font. You'll hear that the technique quickly wears thin either way; an audience will have a difficult time distinguishing what's important because so much seems to be emphasized. Use volume to highlight significant ideas—but use it sparingly.

This next example shows the same paragraph that you just read out loud, but this time the words in bold font emphasize only the most essential points. Read this paragraph out loud, emphasizing the words in bold font with a raised or lowered volume to hear how much more effective volume shifts can be if used less frequently.

> "I'm impressed with the amount and quality of work that each department has devoted to our community service project, and I'm **proud** to be working on a team with you. Please make sure that you set aside time for our next project team meeting on **Tuesday** from 6:00 to 8:00 P.M. in Room 2050. **Thank you** for all that you're doing!"

EXHIBIT 4.1   Notes emphasis (Tisdale, 2001).

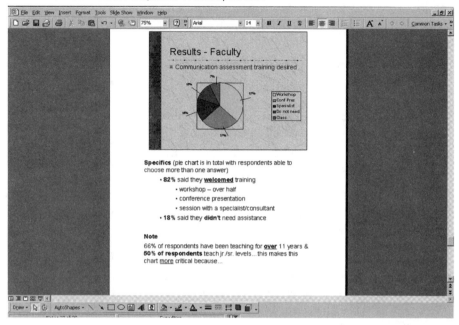

If the speaker wants to emphasize, in this example, when the next project team meeting will be, naming the day either in a louder or softer volume will attract the audience's attention because the volume varies from what the speaker says in the remainder of that particular point.

As you practice delivering presentations, highlight in your notes those areas where you want to raise or lower volume as an attention-getter. Exhibit 4.1 illustrates a notes page that emphasizes particular information for a specific part of a presentation. In this example, the bold font and underlining in the two major points (**Specifics** and **Note**) on this slide remind the presenter where she wants to raise her volume or slow her pace in order to accentuate information from the survey she was discussing.

Rate and Articulation

Let's now address rate and articulation in presentations. A moderate rate of speaking combined with clear articulation sends a message to an audience that a presenter is prepared and comfortable with the material. Speaking too rapidly could signal that a presenter is overly anxious. Additionally, audiences may not be able to easily follow the thought process of someone who talks too rapidly; research shows that understanding is impeded if a speaker uses more than 275 to 300 words per minute (Leathers, 1992).

How quickly or slowly do you typically speak in general conversations? The most obvious way that you know you talk too quickly, of course, is recognizing that colleagues or friends may, at times, have difficulty comprehending what you say:

- Do people often stop you to repeat a phrase or word that they didn't understand?

- Do you feel that you stumble over sentences because you're thinking several points ahead of what you're saying?

- Have you noticed people looking at you with a blank or puzzled expression when you're excitedly talking . . . because they have to take a few seconds to process what you just said?

If you answered "yes" to any one of these questions, you likely have a habit of talking a bit too quickly for normal conversation—and this means you need to make a concerted effort to slow down in presentations.

Your usual speech pace may not have created problems for you in general conversations because you live and work in an environment where friends, family, or colleagues are used to your speech patterns—after all, they interact with you every day. In presentations, however, you may speak to people who aren't as familiar with the way you talk. When reading written material, individuals can go back and review information in earlier paragraphs if they don't understand something that they've read. Conversely, in a presentation listeners can only grasp what they've heard. If a presenter speeds through material, audience members might still be absorbing and processing something the presenter said a sentence or two prior to a key point—and thus possibly miss or misunderstand the key point itself.

The typical speaker uses 125 to 150 words per minute, and this is a comfortable, measured pace for presenters (Bovée & Thill, 2000). Of course, it's difficult to keep up with how many words you use within a time frame while presenting. Instead of trying to count words, experience instead what the recommended pace sounds and feels like so that you can strive to match that pace in a presentation session. The paragraph prior to this one contains 128 words. Test your speech rate by timing yourself when reading it aloud at the rate that you normally use in general conversation. If you read the paragraph in about a minute, you're using a consistently moderate rate.

To slow down your speech rate, start by carefully articulating each word—not by pausing slightly between sentences or phrases. Read the sentence in the example below out loud and listen for yourself how an audience might hear someone who speaks quickly and doesn't enunciate clearly.

"WhadI wanyou to realize about the salesfigures I've jushown you is that they're froma yearnwhich theconomy was booming."

Audience members who aren't familiar with a presenter's rate of speech might have a difficult time distinguishing between many of these words. A rapid pace doesn't allow for clear articulation. As a result, an audience might assume that a presenter has difficulty pronouncing words when, instead, the presenter might simply run words together because of a rapid speech pattern. Try saying the same sentence example out loud, paying particular attention to speaking each word clearly and pausing slightly between each word, as shown in the example below.

"What • I • want • you • to • realize • about • the • sales • figures • that • I've • just • shown • you • is • that • they're • from • a • year • in • which • the • economy • was • booming."

Now, of course, if you were to make presentations using such an exaggerated pause between each word, you'd sound halting, stilted, or overly formal. Try it again without the slight pause, but take time to completely pronounce each word. Articulating each word in the sentence ensures that a presenter will maintain a moderate pace.

"What I want you to realize about the sales figures that I've just shown you is that they're from a year in which the economy was booming."

Presenters who have always had a fairly rapid rate of speech will find this pattern to be a difficult habit to change. In fact, they may feel as if they're talking in "slow motion" when they enunciate each word. They may even worry that audiences think that they're talking too slowly! But audiences need speakers to use a slow pace. As people listen to someone speak, they must be able to process the spoken words. Presenters will appear more competent and assured when articulating clearly and using a measured rate of speech.

Before leaving this section on rate and pronunciation, I want to address a common concern that a pronounced accent or dialect might lessen the effectiveness of a presentation. If presenters have a strong regional accent, they don't necessarily have to minimize their accent. Instead, first determine how strong the accent is. Would a presenter's dialect from one geographic region impede how audiences from another region understand the message? Would an audience pay more attention to how a presenter pronounces particular words than to the ideas conveyed in any given sentence? For most presenters, regional dialect would not be an issue. Speakers might have a "New York accent," a "Texan twang," or "a Southern drawl," but chances are good that people from other regions of the United States can easily understand what they say. If, however, presenters do have unusually thick accents or challenges with pronunciation, they may want to work on these issues with a professional speech therapist or coach—if the particular speech pattern will be prohibitive for an audience to understand what the presenter is saying. It won't matter how brilliant the material is or how snazzy the graphics are—if audience members can't understand a presenter, they won't understand the message.

These same general guidelines about accent and dialect hold true for international presenters in the United States who speak English as a second language. Many are overly anxious about how native English speakers understand their pronunciation. In my work with international graduate students, however, I've found that their pronunciation generally is not what impedes audiences in understanding their message—instead, pace is more of an issue. One international student I worked with recently, for example, was surprised to learn that he needed to slow down his speaking rate. He felt that he would blend more easily into the U. S. culture by talking as rapidly as native English speakers did. However he was running words together within his sentences, and it was difficult to distinguish what he was saying. But once he took time to articulate each word—even though he still had a strong accent from his native language—he pronounced his words much more distinctly and was significantly easier to understand. If presenters who speak too rapidly (non-native and native English speakers) will slow their pace in order to articulate words, audiences will have a much easier time understanding the message.

Conversational Tone

One of the most difficult—and yet the most simple—keys to delivering a dynamic business presentation is approaching it as a *conversation with your audience*. We typically understand speeches as a rhetorical mode of addressing large crowds; the speaker, usually standing behind a podium, speaks mostly from scripted material, and uses oratorical devices to emphasize points. Personal interaction during a speech with individuals in an audience will be limited because of the number of people in the audience. Addresses at political rallies, after-dinner speeches for professional organizations, or CEO messages at large annual shareholder meetings are common examples of public speaking engagements.

But because most business presentations address audiences of 5 to 25 people (Bailey, 2002), this type of presentation is very different from a speech. In a business presentation, a presenter has an opportunity to talk **with**—not **to**—an audience. Presenters interact significantly more with an audience in this smaller setting, and the situation lends itself to a more informal approach, even if presenters aren't literally generating discussion with an audience during the presentation. Nick Morgan (2001), a communications consultant and editor of *Harvard Management Communication Letter*, believes that audiences attending presentation sessions prefer a personal approach. In fact, Morgan theorizes that people now *expect* a more intimate speaking style (closer space and a warm, disclosing style) than they do from typical public speeches as a result of the development of broadcast communication, specifically television. According to Morgan, television offers the "illusion of physical closeness . . . [and creates] in audiences an expectation of intimacy, both spatial and emotional, from a speaker" (p. 115).

It might appear to be natural for presenters to talk conversationally. Nonetheless, here are a few reasons that some speakers might not have as natural a tone as possible:

1. *Hesitation to stray from notes.* Presenters may feel the need to stick strictly to the message that they've written. They likely have spent substantial time crafting sentences they wish to say, and they believe they need to use as much of the language that they've carefully written as possible.

2. *Anxiety.* Many presenters might use an overly formal tone because they're anxious about their material or the presentation situation itself. As a result, they may memorize the message in order to shore up confidence. These presenters believe that memorizing content will help them feel less nervous and look more professional.

3. *Professionalism.* Some presenters believe that they write much better than they speak in a presentation, and they want to make sure that they stick to a "script" so that they can say exactly what they want to.

Any of these reasons for wanting to communicate exactly what's written in a message are valid. However, even though written business communication today uses plain English with common words, contractions, and pronouns, we still just don't speak exactly the way that we write. Orally, we don't use complete sentences, we leave out articles, we shorten complete thoughts to numerous simple sentences or phrases, and we use an animated tone to convey emotion.

The most effective technique presenters can use to develop a conversational tone is pitch variance, or a range of vocal tones. These pitch ranges convey feelings and attitudes to audiences—enthusiasm, tiredness, happiness, anxiety, delight, frustration. Studies by H. B. Fisher (1975, as cited in Leathers, 1992) have shown that factual information is typically communicated in a more narrow pitch range than more emotional communication. Further, an apathetic speaker will use an extremely limited range, significantly more monotone than someone who simply provides information.

Effective presenters use a wide variety of pitch because they're genuinely interested in the opportunity to be in front of an audience talking about a message that they believe has value for that particular audience. The enthusiasm and energy that they show through varying vocal pitch, supported by complementing nonverbal communication, can convey more to an audience than the words themselves (Mehrabian & Wiener, 1967). In fact, one study even contends that audiences receive 38 percent of a message's meaning through a speaker's tone of voice (Mehrabian, 1971).

You don't need to exhibit a bouncy, cheery attitude, if that's not your normal personality, but you *do* need to be enthused about your topic and energetic about its implications for the audience. If the topic is a serious one, the audience needs to hear the energy and emotion in your voice through a wide variety of pitch as you discuss the issue. Stated simply, if you sound upbeat and enthusiastic during a presentation, chances are the audience will view you and your material as more interesting. If you don't sound excited about a topic, an audience won't see any reason to be enthused either (Hoff, 1988). As one of my students so aptly put it during a discussion about why pitch variance is important in delivery techniques, "We need to prove to our audience that we care about what we're saying."

Presentation content and visuals by themselves won't carry a dynamic presentation. Demonstrate your confidence in yourself and in your material by using a wide range of vocal pitch to appear energetic and enthusiastic about the topic. Show the audience that you're delighted to be there and sincerely pleased to share information or make a recommendation.

NONVERBAL CUES

One of the key benefits of communicating information to an audience via a presentation versus a written memo, letter, or report is the chance to interact with the message's recipients. And, probably the most effective tool that presenters have in their chest of presentation techniques is nonverbal communication (facial expressions, posture, body movements, eye contact, use of space, clothing).

What presenters express nonverbally can support and enhance a message, as well as signal a presenter's confidence and professionalism. Audiences interpret nonverbal communication in the same way they do a presenter's speaking voice: to form an impression of a speaker's likability and assertiveness (Leathers, 1992). Further, nonverbal cues signal to an audience the presenter's status and credibility (Gabbott & Hogg, 2000; Leigh & Summers, 2002). Understanding how audiences might interpret nonverbal communication gives presenters the opportunity to manage their behavior to create the most positive impression possible.

As you learned in the prior section on conversational tone, much of the meaning presenters convey to an audience is not what they know or say—but *how* they convey the information. In terms of nonverbal presentation communication, studies show that 65 to 90 percent of what a speaker communicates to an audience is nonverbal (McKay & Rosa, 2000)!

Another study suggests that audience reliance on the spoken word may be even less than 10 percent. According to A. Mehrabian (1971), a speaker's facial expressions and tone of voice actually account for 93 percent of meaning communicated, leaving only 7 percent for the spoken word. Mehrabian's data suggest that facial expressions alone account for just over half of meaning conveyed in a message.

So, if nonverbal communication has such a strong impact on audience perceptions of a speaker, why worry about the spoken message itself? The answer is that presenters need to be aware of and manage audience perception of nonverbal signals in order to consistently support message content. Communication research finds that audiences will accept a message as more credible if the nonverbal communication cues are uniform with the verbal cues (Burgoon, 1994; Mehrabian & Wiener, 1967). In other words, audiences are more likely to believe presenters whose nonverbal messages illustrate their confidence in the quality and substance of the spoken message. Additionally, audiences will rely more heavily on nonverbal signals to interpret meaning from a message if the nonverbal communication isn't consistent with the verbal message (Burgoon, 1994; Mehrabian & Wiener, 1967).

This section addresses how you can polish the following nonverbal communication cues to support the message you want to convey and to present yourself as professionally as possible:

- Eye contact
- Body language
- Use of space

Pay close attention to a presenter who effectively exhibits these signals—who seems expressive, uses a good bit of space in the room, maintains eye contact with individuals in the audience, and gestures with purpose. You'll note that audience members respond more positively to this presenter because he or she promotes a highly interactive speaking situation.

Eye Contact

Eye contact is an important nonverbal communication sign to demonstrate a presenter's confidence and credibility. Further, it helps a presenter assess an audience's interest. A study by Janik, Wellens, Goldberg, and DeLosse, (1978) found that listener attention is focused on the speaker's eye region for 43.4 percent of the interaction. Clearly, effective eye contact is one of the most critical nonverbal cues presenters can employ to promote themselves positively *and* to gauge an audience's reaction.

Direct eye contact with audience members offers presenters opportunities to see how the audience responds to verbal messages, and presenters can adjust accordingly. If noticing puzzled or resistant expressions on individuals' faces, for example, a presenter could respond by adding a few more examples to support that particular point—audience members would be indicating that they need to hear more details before they'll buy into the message. Alternatively, supportive expressions and friendly responses from an audience will reinforce a presenter's comfort level and suggest that session participants agree with or are interested in the topic and presenter.

Equally important, eye contact lends presenters an aura of credibility and confidence. In the United States, listeners tend to perceive speakers who look at them directly as more believable because direct eye contact in the U.S. culture signals knowledge and honesty (Locker, 2000, p. 318). Research has also proven that presenters who look at an audience during at least 63 percent of their presentations are judged by the audience to be more sincere than presenters who don't look as much at the audience (study cited in Locker, 2000, p. 494).

In U.S. business presentations, audience members may interpret minimal eye contact as a sign that a presenter lacks self-confidence, feels uncomfortable with the message, or has little to no interest in the audience or the presentation itself (Dovidio & Ellyson, 1985; Hoff, 1988). However, not all cultures rely on eye contact to assess a presenter's credibility and interest. Some Asian and Muslim cultures, for example, interpret indirect or limited eye contact as a way of showing respect; in these cultures, direct eye contact is considered rude and overly assertive (Beamer & Varner, 2001; Locker & Kaczmarek, 2001; Munter, 2000). Presenters speaking to groups that include individuals from these cultures should be aware of the differing perceptions of eye contact across cultures and not assume that the style they're used to is acceptable in all cultures (Beamer & Varner, 2001).

Of course, many presenters don't make eye contact simply because they're nervous. They may feel extreme anxiety knowing that everyone in the presentation session is looking at them. Other presenters avoid eye contact because they've heard the adage that to reduce presentation nervousness they should look just above the heads of individuals in an audience. This advice works in a larger public speaking situation (a speech) because the people in the front of the room think that the presenter is looking at those in the back of the room, and those in the back can't really see where the presenter is looking. However, audience members attending a speech don't really expect to be singled out; they're there as members of a group. In business presentations the dynamics of the small size of most audiences demand that presenters interact with them in a more intimate manner—eye contact. If a presenter looks directly at individuals in a business presentation setting, audience members feel more engaged and involved in the presentation than if the presenter didn't use eye contact effectively.

So, what's the best way to know how much eye contact is just enough or not enough? You want to be able to truly look at and see the face and eyes of most (if not all) of the audience members at various points in a presentation. Practice looking at your audience in a "scan pattern." The sketch in Exhibit 4.2 demonstrates what a scan pattern might look like. A presenter starts by looking at an individual in one corner of the room and follows a straight line across the audience as if drawing one line of an "X" until reaching the other

EXHIBIT 4.2   Eye contact scan pattern.

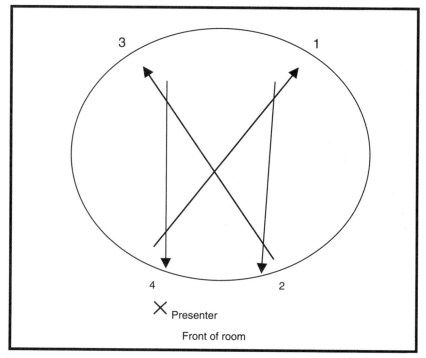

end of the room. At that point, the presenter starts at a different point and follows another straight line, drawing the corresponding line to form the "X" until reaching the end of the room again. Thus, the presenter's gaze moves from the front left of the room to the back right of the room. Then, it moves up to the front right before going to the back left of the room and then returning to the front left. The "X" pattern allows presenters to "eyeball" each audience member on a consistent basis throughout a presentation. If you use this pattern, however, take care that you don't "scan" the room too quickly—looking at audience members so fleetingly that you don't really see them. Instead, make eye contact for at least one to two seconds with each person in the room.

Keep your eye contact balanced and consistent among all members of an audience and avoid focusing only on one side of the room or on one individual. It's easy to maintain eye contact longer with individuals you already know or who appear to be responding positively to the message (for example, those who are nodding or smiling at appropriate times during a presentation). Instead, include as many audience members as possible when looking around the room because you need to know how everyone is responding to the message. Engage those who don't appear interested or who appear skeptical of your topic just as much as those who appear to accept your ideas.

Special Note About Presenter Eye Contact During PowerPoint Presentations

One of the most common mistakes that experienced and inexperienced presenters alike make when they're using PowerPoint slides is to look more often at the on-screen image than at an audience. Probably the main reason speakers do so is because they're using the PowerPoint slides as presentation notes. Admittedly, it's tempting to want to make the slides double as notes. However, when presenters look back at the slide screen too often (and particularly when presenters talk to the screen instead of to the audience), audience members may interpret the lack of eye contact as a sign the presenter is insecure with the message and uncomfortable being in front of a group. Additionally, a presenter who looks back too often at the screen loses valuable opportunities to connect with an audience during the message and observe how the message is being received.

Should a presenter ever look back at the slide screen? Certainly! It's fine to check that slides are transitioning properly or that information is ap-

pearing on a timely basis. However, presenters should simply glance back and quickly return to the audience. Here's the key: If you need to look at the slide screen to ensure a slide or bullet point appears properly, pause whatever you're saying until you turn back to the audience. A second or two of silence is fine, it is better for a speaker to pause for a brief instant while checking a slide than to talk to the screen and appear to be an insecure—or worse, unprepared—speaker.

Body Language

Nonverbal expressions and body movements support and enhance a presenter's message if the presenter uses them consistently with the verbal message (Burgoon, 1994; Mehrabian & Wiener, 1967). Close attention to nonverbal body language signals can help a speaker eliminate habits that may reveal anxiety or send mixed messages to an audience. This section addresses the following key nonverbal body language cues:

- Facial expressions
- Gestures
- Use of space

Keep in mind that these signals are cultural, and this section focuses on body language in the U. S. culture. What may appear as assertiveness and confidence in one ethnic group could come across as aggression, rudeness, or even the opposite of the intended meaning in another culture. While the following sections offer examples showing how cultures view these nonverbal cues differently, it's important to consult resources specializing in international communication in order to research effective nonverbal communication if presenting to audiences globally (see Beamer & Varner, 2001).

Facial Expressions

When presenting, speakers should exhibit an alert, animated expression to signal interest in the topic and in the audience. In the U. S. business culture for example, smiling at appropriate times helps an audience find a presenter to be more likable and attractive (Burgoon, 1994; Hoff, 1988; Leathers, 1992). Audiences want a presenter to convey interest in them and in the message, and an alert expression combined with a smile demonstrates a presenter's engagement.

In general conversation with individuals, we're rarely expressionless. We use facial gestures—raised eyebrows, an intent gaze, a smile—to show surprise, intensity, or agreement. Listeners use these expressions, in part, to interpret verbal messages. For example, a verbal scoff accompanied by a pleasant smile could be accepted as a simple form of teasing or supportive collegial concern if a speaker already has a trusting relationship with a listener. On the other hand, the same remark without a smile could be viewed as a criticism.

Facial expressions should be natural and consistent with a message's verbal content. A presenter should never smile, for example, during a section in a presentation that addresses a particularly sensitive matter; doing so could suggest that the presenter takes the idea lightly. A presenter's quizzical or amazed expression may be appropriate during a section of a presentation when discussing the many possible ways to resolve a problem. The same expression may signal bewilderment or an inability to deal with all the options during a section of a presentation when the presenter needs to make a strong recommendation or call to action in order to resolve the problem. Additionally, excessive smiling or smiling at inappropriate times during a presentation could suggest that a presenter is overly anxious, acting submissive to individuals in the audience, or unsure about message content (Leathers, 1992).

If you're presenting to an international group, an understanding of the cultural expectations about smiling can be critical. Intercultural communication experts L. Beamer and I. Varner (2001) note that smiles aren't necessarily interpreted the same way universally. For example, the Japanese and Koreans believe in keeping emotions private, so they rarely smile in public. North Americans smile often to show openness, while many East Asian cultures believe a smile indicates embarrassment or discomfort. People in Arab and Latin cultures frequently smile and laugh, but those in the German culture are more reserved and don't smile as often (Beamer & Varner, 2001).

Gestures

One of the most common nonverbal delivery concerns presenters have is what to do with their hands: They wonder how much—or even if—they should gesture. Gesturing can be an effective way to emphasize points; it's another benefit of delivering a presentation versus sending a written message—you can emphasize key ideas to reinforce visually the spoken word.

Speakers who naturally use gestures during general conversations should feel free to do the same during a presentation. But gestures shouldn't be aimless; they ought to support the verbal message content. Effective gestures illustrate specific points. A presenter could, for example, hold up three fingers while saying, "The third way that we can better serve our customers through this reorganization is . . . . " By using this gesture, the presenter shows the audience the numerical concept (and thus emphasizes it) while talking about that particular point. Similarly, a presenter talking about increasing levels of sales performance can help an audience visualize the concept by holding out a hand at waist level, then moving it upward to elbow level, and then up just above shoulder level progressively. This gesture demonstrates the per-

EXHIBIT 4.3 Ineffective delivery habits.

Gesture	Why to Avoid Overusing It
Arms folded and crossed in front	Protective gesture—may appear as if speaker is setting a shield between the speaker and the audience.
Holding the podium/console/lectern	Protective gesture—may appear as if speaker is either nervous or using the prop as a security blanket.
Hand(s) in pocket(s)	Casual gesture—overly informal. Speaker also runs the risk of nervously jingling change or keys in pockets during the presentation, thus distracting an audience.
Leaning on podium/console/lectern	Casual gesture—overly informal. Speaker may appear to be tired or overly anxious and needs support.
Twisting notes	Nervous gesture—crinkling paper sound and repetitive gesture will distract audience.
Repeated up-down hand movement (chopping or waving motion)	Nervous gesture—distracts audience with repetitive nature; also difficult for audience to know what's really important if everything is emphasized.
Arms rigid and straight at sides	Nervous gesture—audience will perceive speaker as too stiff and formal.

formance level's upward progression—the hand movement is consistent with the verbal message.

Similarly, gestures point an audience's attention toward something a presenter wants to stress. For example, a presenter can show a graphic on a slide and talk about the graphic in general. To redirect the audience's attention to a specific point in the graphic, the presenter can step back toward the slide screen and point toward the graphic. This gesture literally aims the audience's eyes toward the information on the screen.

To learn your gesture habits, videotape yourself delivering a presentation and note how (and when) you move your arms or hands. In particular, focus on how often you might use repetitive or distracting gestures. If, for example, you frequently pump your right hand clinched in a fist up and down in a quick gesture to emphasize what you're saying, work on limiting how often you use that gesture. Otherwise, an audience won't get a sense of what's really important; such a repetitive gesture appears to highlight everything. Or, if you frequently wave one hand up slightly in the air as you're elaborating on points, audiences may not be sure what's being emphasized.

Exhibit 4.3 lists some of the more common gestures to avoid using excessively and a brief description about why they're not effective in presentations.

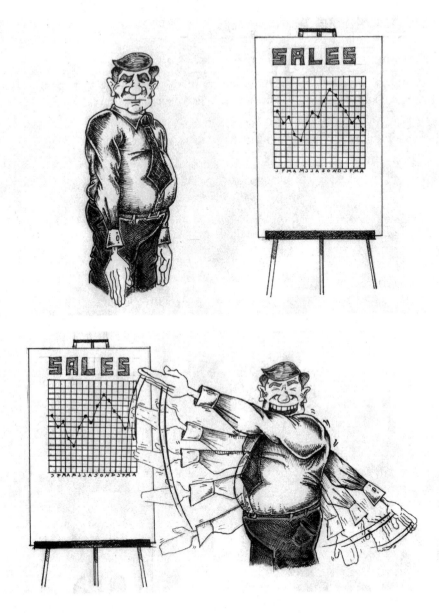

The problem with overusing these gestures is that they can distract an audience from what a presenter is saying in the message. Twisting notes once or perhaps twice, for example, won't detract from the spoken message. However, incessantly massaging notes will; audience members likely will begin to focus more on how and why a presenter keeps rolling those papers than on what's being said.

Can you ever use the gestures in Exhibit 4.3? Certainly! Limited use of gestures is fine. If a presenter is comfortable speaking with arms crossed for a moment or so, that particular gesture won't distract an audience. It's simply important to avoid overusing gestures so that they don't become a distraction or signal anxiety. To limit excessive or aimless gestures, plan when you want to use gestures to stress specific points and then practice them. When not gesturing, hold your arms loosely by your side to indicate you're relaxed and confident. If you're not comfortable holding your arms by your side for long, cross your arms in front of your body for a few moments, then drop them down by your side. Vary arm movements from time to time, as you feel comfortable, so that your position won't appear stiff or overly formal.

Use of Space

As is the case with gesturing, some presenters feel that they just have to move. Others believe that they should stand perfectly still. Either technique or combination of the two can work fine for most presenters, depending on their comfort level. One of the most polished, professional speakers I've seen (an internationally recognized expert on customer satisfaction) gave a presentation standing perfectly still with her arms down by her side. She looked relaxed and used eye contact, voice inflections, and animated facial expressions to engage her audience. This speaker didn't need to move around the front of the conference room to interact with individuals in the session.

On the other hand, speakers can give just as polished, professional presentations by moving to different parts of the room during a discussion. Movement can dramatically change the dynamics of presentations, as speakers more directly engage audience members by moving closer to them. Both approaches (the still approach and the movement approach), however, can backfire if used in the extreme. If you prefer to stand still, practice this technique so that you look and feel relaxed. Avoid standing stiffly and make a special effort to vary pitch, use eye contact, and show facial expression. Conversely, if you prefer moving during a presentation, harness your energy and move purposefully.

To plan movements during a presentation, try the technique illustrated in Exhibit 4.4. Stand toward one side of the front of the room and take one or two steps to the front center. Wait for a moment or so and then take a few steps toward the back left of the center part of the room. A short time later, move to the front again and then return to the side of the room where you started. If you'd rather limit movements to a smaller space (perhaps you're presenting in a fairly small area), try a two-step pattern. Take two steps forward or slightly forward. Hold steady in that spot for a moment or so, and then take two steps backward to the position where you started. This pattern allows presenters flexibility to move within a small space.

Whatever movement pattern you select, practice using it so that you're comfortable with the pattern. Use of movement as a visual aid demonstrates confidence, emphasizes points, and engages the audience.

EXHIBIT 4.4   Movement pattern.

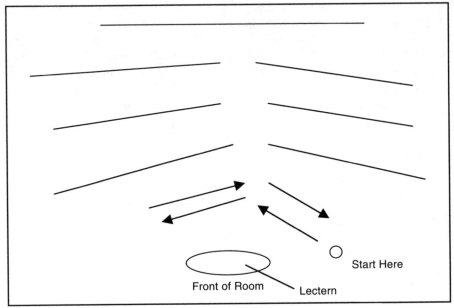

Understanding the space issue distinctions is important when giving presentations because presenters must carefully consider where they stand in relation to an audience. Hall (1968) categorized acceptable communication distances in the U.S. culture (see Exhibit 4.5). Even in the U. S. culture, however, Hall (1968) cautions that acceptable distances may vary depending on gender, age, status, and so forth (as cited in Leathers, 1992). Comfort with spatial distances also varies dramatically from culture to culture. People from Latin American and Middle Eastern cultures, for example, are comfortable with less space between individuals than those from Japanese and German cultures, who prefer an even greater distance between people (Beamer & Varner, 2001).

EXHIBIT 4.5   Communication discourses and distances.

Communication Discourse	Acceptable Distance
Intimate space	0–18 inches
Personal distance	1½ feet–4 feet
Social distance	4–12 feet
Public distance	12 feet or more

In addition to being sensitive to varying comfort levels with space, presenters must also keep in mind audience expectations for where presenters should stand during a session. For example, in a public-speaking situation, an audience typically expects a speaker to stand in front of the audience, usually behind a podium of some sort. But in a business presentation, speakers often will be talking to an audience seated around a table or at numerous tables in a conference room. Decide where you will stand based on the speaking situation (the number of people who will attend and the space you'll have available) and your goals for each presentation. To promote a more formal atmosphere in which you'll give information and the audience will listen until you invite questions, use a podium or lectern during the presentation to reinforce the environment you want to foster. Audiences will recognize this convention and respond to it accordingly. However, to encourage *more* participation and interaction with individuals in an audience, step out from behind the podium/lectern and move closer to the audience. This way, you'll eliminate a barrier between you and the audience.

Nonverbal First Impressions

Ron Hoff (1988) writes that the impression a presenter makes in the first 90 seconds of a presentation will color an audience's opinion of the speaker and the message. However, audiences don't wait until a presenter starts speaking before they begin assessing credibility. Presenters are actually "onstage" *before* they stand up in front of the audience and begin speaking. What audience members might see prior to a presenter clicking on the PowerPoint title slide can shape their first impressions of the speaker and the message. Judee Burgoon (1994) found that research shows first impressions "may serve as a template through which all subsequent information is filtered and assimilated" (p. 251). This means that the nonverbal cues that signal confidence, likability, and credibility can positively affect how an audience will understand the spoken message. Alternatively, ineffective nonverbal signals may also indicate a presenter is overly anxious or dominant, and these signals could negatively affect the audience's opinion about what a speaker has to say.

Speaker assessment begins before a presenter even steps to the front of the room. Audience members often will know who the speaker will be when they walk into a room, and they form a quick impression about the speaker from that first glance. Frequently, in fact, audience members have an opportunity to introduce themselves to a presenter during the informal time before a presentation or meeting begins. Audiences, consciously or unconsciously, assess a presenter's posture, attire, attentiveness to what's happening in the room, and general appearance. If, for example, a presenter sits at the corner of a boardroom table avoiding any interpersonal interaction and hurriedly flipping through notes, those in the meeting will wonder how prepared the speaker is. If a presenter isn't involved in what's happening in the room—paying attention to earlier presenters or seeming attuned to opening remarks—an audience may assume the presenter is detached and not interested in the surrounding events and people. However, if a presenter sits confidently (listening carefully to what's going on and making eye contact with those around the conference room table), audiences will feel more engaged with the speaker before the presentation begins.

It's important to remember that speakers are always "on stage," and audiences will judge credibility, likability, and professionalism before a presentation starts. Presenters should use appropriate body language and facial expressions to communicate an unspoken impression that they're delighted to be in front of that audience and that they have something valuable to share with each person in the room.

PRESENTATION NOTES

Notes are probably one of the most misunderstood tools of an effective presentation. Many presenters feel that they look more professional if they don't appear to need notes. Some presenters may worry that they'll lose spontaneity if they have to stick with a "script." Others believe that they need everything they're going to say on their notes so that they can give the best presentation possible and not overlook an important point.

Actually, the most optimal use of notes lies somewhere in-between all of these ideas. Many accomplished presenters use notes, and I encourage presenters to have notes available so that they can refer to them if necessary.

Think about notes as your personal outline for a presentation. If you're worried about inadvertently leaving out some important points, by all means, list them on an outline. But resist the urge to write out the notes in paragraph or even sentence form. Too much text on notes increases the risk of overreliance on them. If presenters are slightly uncomfortable in front of an audience, for example, it's tempting for them to look down toward the notes instead of toward the audience. As a result, presenters may *read to* the audience the written sentences instead of *talking about* the ideas in the presentation. Remember that most people speak even more informally than they write, and if a presenter reads complete sentences from notes, it probably will sound scripted and overly formal.

Additionally, presenters can experience difficulty attempting to locate a particular point within a paragraph of text. Thus, if presenters scan sentences or paragraphs to find the information they need, they run the risk of losing eye contact and connection with the audience . . . as well as possibly feeling the general discomfort of "losing their place" in the notes.

To develop effective presentation notes, reduce text to an outline format, much like an outline for a written report. Use Roman numerals (I, II, III, etc.) for main headings, capital letters to indicate subheadings (A, B, C, etc.), and regular numbers for sub-subheadings (1, 2, 3, etc.). And for points under the sub-subheadings, use lower-case letters (a, b, c, etc). Consider an outline to be a table of contents for a presentation.

Look at the example below, an outline for the first key point (Learning the Facts and Myths About Donation Issues) from the presentation on organ donation in Chapter 3.

LEARNING THE FACTS AND MYTHS ABOUT DONATION ISSUES

I. How many affected?
   A. 1. One organ donor = estimated potential 8 lives saved
      2. Types of organs donated
   B. 1. One tissue donor = estimated potential 50 persons receive improved quality of life
      2. Types of tissue donated
II. Viability
   A. Kidney
   B. Liver
   C. Heart

Clearly, a presenter using these notes would have a lot more to say than what is listed here. However, the notes text in this example is limited to show only the key information. In Point I, the speaker will elaborate on how one organ or tissue donor can affect the numbers of people listed, giving specifics about each organ. In Point II, she'll discuss the limited window of time that doctors have between when a decision is made to donate and when an organ needs to be transplanted.

Boil down the points on a notes outline to words or phrases (rarely more than 5 to 10 words per point). Exhibit 4.6 is a sample notes page for a presentation I recently made on a survey I'd completed. Notice that a couple of the bullet points have more than 10 words. These same bullet points are in phrase form, however, and the other bullet points number 7 or fewer words each. Eliminate all unnecessary words and, if necessary, create a new subpoint. By outlining a written message, presenters can focus on what's most relevant in the presentation and filter out nonessential information to simplify the amount of text on the page. Additionally, refining text or rough notes into a manageable outline for presentation notes helps presenters review content and become more comfortable with presentation material.

Once you've developed a notes outline, decide what format the actual presentation notes should take. There are many theories about the "best" notes format: 3-by-5-inch or 5-by-7-inch note cards, 8½-by-11-inch paper, and so forth. Following are some of the advantages and disadvantages of two of the most popular types of notes:

EXHIBIT 4.6   PowerPoint notes view (Tisdale, 2001).

Slide 4

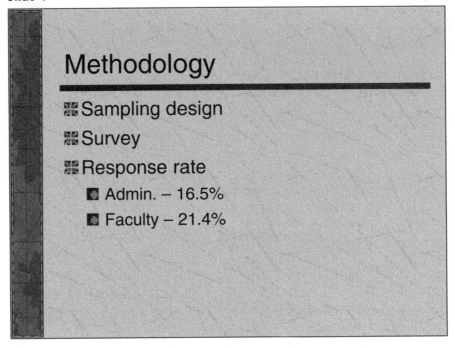

Sampling Design
- Respondents selected randomly from 188 colleges/universities from over 950 offering grad/undergrad accounting degrees
- Included programs in all 50 states
- Selected schools ranged from small enrollments to universities with 40,000 to 50,000 students

Survey
- Email request
- Website response
- "Cold" mailing

Response Rate
- Typical rates for "cold" surveys are 10 to 20%

■ *PowerPoint notes.* The PowerPoint program offers presenters a method to generate notes while developing a presentation—and they print out in a clean professional format (see Exhibit 4.6 for an example of a PowerPoint note page). This option gives you the advantage of seeing each slide on the top part of the page and the notes below it on the same page. The drawback is that these notes are printed on $8^1/_2$-by-11-inch paper, and some presenters feel that these pages are too large to hold during a presentation. If you should decide to use PowerPoint notes, staple the pages together so that you don't have to worry about a page (or more than one) slipping out of your grasp and floating to the floor during a session.

■ *Note cards.* These are probably the most popular types of notes. The cards are small, flexible, and easy to hold. Use only one key point per note card, and add additional cards for subpoints within each key point. Be careful not to put too much information on each card, or you'll run the risk of making the text too small to read at a quick glance. Additionally, it's important to number the cards just in case they get out of order. Note cards do have two drawbacks. First, like PowerPoint notes, they could slip out of a presenter's hand and fan across the floor. Typically, these cards are too small to staple, so presenters will need to practice often with the cards to reduce the risk of dropping them. Second, most presenters write their notes on note cards, and handwritten notes simply don't look as polished as typed notes.

Whatever type of notes that you choose, they need to be crisp, clean, and easy for you to use. If a presenter has note cards that are yellowed and dog-eared, audiences may wonder just how long that speaker has been using the same material.

Finally, avoid writing on the back of the notes and highlighting too much text on the front. Notes with scribbling on the back or lots of color on the front may distract an audience; remember that notes pages should be a simple prompt for a presenter—not a source of curiosity for an audience. Additionally, avoid last-minute writing on typed notes. People sitting in the front of a room can see what's on a presenter's notes, and scribbling could appear to an audience to be the work of someone who did last-minute preparation on the way to the presentation.

Habits to Avoid

Be yourself during a presentation and use effective delivery techniques to portray yourself and your message in the most professional way possible. The audience is continually evaluating you—and a presentation reflects your (and your firm's) credibility. To this end, Exhibit 4.7 details some habits to avoid.

EXHIBIT 4.7 Correcting ineffective delivery habits.

Habit	Solution
Not being ready to present when called upon. Presenters who exhibit one or more of the following behaviors will appear unprepared: • Shuffle notes to get them back in order • Go back to seat to get a handout that should have been in hand • Sort through briefcase to find a computer disk	✓ Before leaving for a presentation session, check to be sure that you've got the necessary supporting material. ✓ When you first arrive at the room in which you'll be presenting, take a moment to organize supporting material so that all you need to do is pick it up and begin.
Not having a backup plan. Think about worst-case scenarios here. What should a presenter do if the computer disk won't open? What should a presenter do if the network server is down and Internet access isn't available? What should a presenter do if the overhead projector lightbulb burns out during a presentation? In other words, what will a presenter do when the unexpected happens?	✓ By thinking about these types of worst-case scenarios before arriving at a presentation, you're preparing yourself as much as possible. For example, consider bringing a backup disk or handouts of your PowerPoint presentation just in case the computer system or overhead projector doesn't work. ✓ You'll not be able to predict all the possibilities that might occur, so just remember that it won't really matter what unexpected event happens . . . it matters how you handle it. If a disk won't open, for example, try it a couple of times and then begin the presentation as if you'd planned to do it without the computer.
Apologizing—If you either directly or inadvertently apologize during a presentation, you lose credibility with your audience. A direct apology, of course, might be when a presenter says, "I'm sorry that you won't be able to see my presentation because I'd expected an overhead projector, and we don't seem to have one." An indirect apology might be when a presenter says, "I just learned yesterday that I'd be speaking with you, so bear with me."	✓ Don't.
Chewing gum or eating candy. It's difficult to talk clearly if you're chewing gum or eating candy while making a presentation.	✓ Don't.

EXERCISES   Delivering with Impact

EXERCISE 1   Rate—How Do I Hear My Pace?

Tape yourself reading the sample paragraphs on page 82 at the recommended paces. Then listen to the tape to hear how an audience might hear each of them. How does the third reading sound to you compared with how it felt when you read it?

EXERCISE 2   Rate—How Might Others Hear Me?

This exercise is a quick, easy, and fairly painless way for you to hear yourself as others do. Call your telephone answering machine and—at your normal rate of speaking—leave yourself the message given in the example below. Then, play back the message and listen to yourself. Play back the message several times because most people worry far too much about their dialect or accent the first few times they hear themselves on tape instead of listening to how articulately they're speaking.

> "Shane, we need to block off some time in our schedules tomorrow to meet with the strategy planners. I'm thinking that we'll need about a half hour so that we can discuss where they see our department moving over the next three to eight years. Email or call to let me know when might be good for you. Thanks. Good-bye."

EXERCISE 3   Notes—What Do I Need?

Read the scenario on pages 64 to 65 in Chapter 3 (about the HR specialist who needs to make a presentation about a new credit card payment system to a group of resistant department heads). Develop a notes outline for a problem-solving presentation you would use if you were delivering this presentation.

EXERCISE 4   Eliminating Verbal Clutter

Videotape yourself giving a three- to five-minute presentation (or three to five minutes of a part of a presentation). Watch the tape simply to count how many times you say one or more of the following words: "uhm," "aah," "like," "you know." If you said any of these verbal clutter words more than ten to fifteen times, deliver the presentation again focusing on reducing the number of times that you use these words. Videotape this second rehearsal also and watch the tape again. Do you realize that you said "uhm" in a particular sentence? Did you recognize that you were getting ready to say, "aah" and stopped before you did? Count how many times you said these verbal clutter words. Did you drop the number from your first count? Try this exercise one more time and compare your word clutter count with the first two practices.

EXERCISE 5   Delivery—How Might Others See Me?

Videotape yourself giving a five- to seven-minute presentation. Watch the presentation from beginning to end three times using the following guidelines:

1. On the first time, just watch and try not to judge or comment on your delivery style or how you sound.

2. The second time, watch the tape and put yourself in the place of an audience member. What do you notice? What stands out? Additionally, have a colleague or friend complete the presentation checklist in Exhibit 4.8.

3. The third time, watch and then complete the presentation checklist in Exhibit 4.8 on your own performance. How does your assessment compare with the assessment your colleague or friend completed?

References

Bailey, E. P. (2002). *Writing and speaking at work: A practical guide for business communication* (2nd ed.). Upper Saddle River, NJ: Prentice Hall.

Beamer, L., & Varner, I. (2001). *Intercultural communication in the global workplace* (2nd ed.). Boston: McGraw Hill.

Bovée, C. L. & Thill, J. V. (2000). *Business Communication Today* (6th ed.). Upper Saddle River, NJ: Prentice Hall.

Burgoon, J. K. (1994). "Nonverbal signals." In *Handbook of Interpersonal Communication.* (2nd ed.) Eds. Mark L. Knapp and Gerald R. Miller. Thousand Oaks: Sage Publications, 229–285.

Dovidio, J. F., & Ellyson, S. L. (1985). Patterns of visual dominance behavior in humans. In S. L. Ellyson & J. F. Dovidio (Eds.), *Power, dominance, and nonverbal behavior* (pp. 129–149). New York: Springer-Verlag.

Fisher, H. B. (1975). *Improving voice and articulation* (2nd ed.). Boston: Houghton Mifflin.

Gabbott, M., & Hogg, G. (2000). An empirical investigation of the impact of non-verbal communication on service evaluation [Electronic version]. *European Journal of Marketing, 34*(3/4), 384–398.

Guffey, M.E. (1977). *Business communication: Process and product* (2nd ed.). South-Western College Publishing, p. 45.

EXHIBIT 4.8 **Presentation checklist.**

Message Content

- How did the opening connect with the audience?

- Did the presenter give an agenda? Did the agenda have the appropriate number of key points for the time allotted?

- What was the context of the presentation?

- Did the presenter list and then provide support for each of the key points?

- How did the presenter wrap up the presentation?

Delivery Techniques

- What were the strengths of the presenter's voice (e.g., rate, tone, volume)?

- What were the weaknesses of the presenter's voice (e.g., rate, tone, volume)?

- How did the presenter move?

- How much verbal clutter did the presenter use (e.g., "ah," "uhm," "like," "you know")?

- How did the presenter's notes look?

- How enthusiastic was the presenter?

- Did the presenter stay within the time limits?

Overall

- What were the key strengths of the presentation?

- What were the major weaknesses?

Hall, E. T. (1968). Proxemics. *Current anthropology*, 9, 83. As cited in Leathers (1992).

Hoff, R. (1988). *"I can see you naked," A fearless guide to making great presentations*. Kansas City, MO: Andrews McMeel.

Janik, S. W., Wellens, A. R., Goldberg, M. L., & DeLosse, L. F. (1978). Eyes as the center of focus in the visual examination of faces. *Perceptual and motor skills*, 26, 34–35.

Leathers, D. G. (1992). *Successful nonverbal communication, principles and applications*. New York: Macmillan.

Leigh, T. W., & Summers, J. O. (2002). An initial evaluation of industrial buyers' impressions of salespersons' nonverbal cues [Electronic version]. *The Journal of Personal Selling & Sales Management*, 22(1), 41–53.

Locker, K. (2000). *Business and administrative communication* (5th ed.). Boston: Irwin McGraw-Hill.

Locker, K., & Kaczmarek, S. K. (2001). *Business communication: Building critical skills*. Boston: McGraw-Hill.

McKay, M., & Rosa, E. (2000). *The accountant's guide to professional communication: Writing and speaking the language of business*. Orlando, FL: Harcourt.

Mehrabian, A. (1971). *Silent Messages*. Belmont, CA: Wadsworth, p. 44. As cited in Guffey (1997).

Mehrabian, A., & Wiener, M. (1967). Decoding of inconsistent communications. *Journal of Personality and Social Psychology*, 6(1), 109–114.

Morgan, N. (2001, April). "The kinesthetic speaker: Putting action into words." [Electronic version]. *The Harvard Business Review*, 112–120.

Munter, M. (2000). *Guide to managerial communication: Effective business writing and speaking* (5th ed.). Upper Saddle River, NJ: Prentice Hall.

Tisdale, J. (2001). Preparing accounting students to communicate effectively in the profession. Presentation to the Association of Business Communication, annual conference.

5

Using PowerPoint Wisely

PERFORMANCE GOALS

After completing this chapter, readers will be able to:

- design slides effectively using text features, color, and white space
- organize information effectively using an agenda, slide transitions, and planned slide builds
- create visuals to illustrate message concepts with graphics, illustrations, or pictures

PowerPoint is—simultaneously—a beloved and reviled presentation tool.* It's become an expected part of meetings, sales presentations, and academic classes. Yet businesspeople and students alike have horror stories about enduring sessions wherein presenters rely too much on slides with dense text, hyperanimated pictures, snazzy graphics, and bullet points that zip in and out seemingly at random.

Although PowerPoint has become an accepted medium for presentations and offers creative approaches to designing visuals, the program is also experiencing a backlash. Recent business trade magazines carry articles with titles such as "The Case Against PowerPoint" (Bly, 2001), "When Was the Last Time PowerPoint Made You Sing?" (Simons, 2001), "Ban It Now! Friends Don't Let Friends Use PowerPoint" (Stewart, 2001), and "The Trouble with PowerPoint" (Nunberg, 1999). These articles document the business community's attraction to and frustration with the PowerPoint program.

Executives have responded to the frustration by attempting to set guidelines on how to use multimedia presentations. In 1997, Scott Mc-Nealy, chairman and chief executive of Sun Microsystems, outlawed use of PowerPoint in all company presentations (Zuckerman, 1999). (His edict wasn't enforced.) In 2000, General Hugh Shelton, the chair of the U. S. Joint Chiefs of Staff, directed military personnel using PowerPoint to minimize the number of bullet points, computer-enhanced graphics, and sound effects in presentations (Jaffe, 2000). And Rebecca Ganzel (2000) believes that many more companies attempt to limit electronic presentations but refuse to admit their efforts because conventional business wisdom demands that presenters use electronic presentations as evidence of professional expertise (p. 55).

This chapter doesn't address how to use the PowerPoint program—we'll cover *how to use it wisely.* The following page lists key points for effective PowerPoint presentation.

---

* The market offers several electronic presentation programs, such as Lotus Freelance, Sun Microsystems' StarOffice, and Corel Corporation's Presentations. However, the program that's become synonymous with electronic presentations is Microsoft's PowerPoint (Zuckerman, 1999).

- The power of PowerPoint (do we really need it?)
- Slide design
- Information structure
- Slide enhancements

This information gives you strategies to design a dynamic PowerPoint presentation to support your message content.

THE POWER OF POWERPOINT (DO WE REALLY NEED IT?)

If companies are starting to restrict the use of PowerPoint, do businesspeople really even need the program? To answer this question, researchers have begun to conduct studies on the value of electronic presentations. Focusing on audiences' responses to presentation effectiveness, researchers believe that PowerPoint indeed offers presenters several significant advantages. One recent study (*Presentations* and 3M, 2000) found that electronic presentations, specifically PowerPoint, have more impact on audience recall, comprehension, and perception of product/presenter professionalism in comparison with presentations made using overhead transparencies and text documents. Further, the study notes that electronic visuals strongly affected the audience's perceptions of the product quality and presenter professionalism more so than overhead transparencies and text documents. (Overhead presentations were rated lower than electronic presentations, even though the overheads were prepared using the same PowerPoint slides as the electronic presentation.) Conversely, however, test audiences rated an electronic presentation about the same or lower than a text document in terms of personal engagement and presentation quality. The program sets for the audience a heightened expectation that presenters should have a more polished delivery style, message, and visuals. Clearly, in the hands of presenters who know how to use it well, PowerPoint can be a powerful tool.

SLIDE DESIGN

One of the most important concepts to building professional PowerPoint presentations is effective slide design. The way that a presenter arranges material on slides should enhance slide readability and the presenter's credibility. Otherwise, a presenter risks slides becoming the presentation itself, thus obscuring the real message. For example, to provide all the necessary material, presenters may crowd slides with text, leaving little white space to emphasize key points. As a result, audience members may be intimidated by the amount of text on the slide and tune out the presenter.

This section will teach you how to design slides so that you can use PowerPoint to support—not be—your message. We'll address the following techniques of slide design:

- Text
- Fonts
- Colors

While PowerPoint offers many options in these categories, select carefully from all the possibilities and design slides to create the maximum intended impact on an audience.

Text

How much text on slides is too much? If presenters are tempted to use slides as notes, they likely will put almost everything they want to say on the slides as a prompt. And if presenters are dealing with complex issues or terms, they may want to fill each slide completely so they can minimize the number of slides. Instead, design simple slides with plenty of empty space so that each slide emphasizes its one purpose: to support or illustrate what you want to say at that particular point in the message. The slides themselves shouldn't be the presentation text, script, or notes.

One of the most basic concepts to arrange text effectively and make each slide as visually appealing as possible is the use of open (or white) space. Space around text or graphics draws the eye toward it and enhances the impact. And minimizing the amount of text on each slide opens up more space. Design each slide so that it won't have more than five or six bulleted points on it—and avoid using more than six or seven words per bullet. Many presentation experts even encourage you to use a "6 by 6 rule":

- No more than six bullets per slide
- No more than six words per bullet point

In fact, I encourage presenters to further limit the number of bulleted items on their slides. My recommendation is to have no more than four bullet points per slide.

Of course, you'll often find exceptions to this guideline. Sometimes a presenter may need to have eight words in one bulleted line but stick to the "rule" in the other three bullets. Or perhaps a presenter wants to use a brief quote in its entirety to illustrate a point. In general, however, slides need to be easy for audience members to skim at a quick glance. To accomplish this, use phrases instead of complete sentences. This gives the audience, quite literally, the key words at each point in a presentation. Audience members won't see a lot of text on the slide and can then focus on the presenter. The complementary visual on the screen simply reinforces the verbal message.

EXHIBIT 5.1 **Excessive text.**

Interview Strategies

- Create a confident first impression by introducing yourself, smiling, offering a firm handshake, and using the recruiter's name

- Be as specific as possible in your answers to questions. Include details about why you may have acted as you did in specific circumstances.

- Be comfortable with a few seconds of silence if you want a little time to think about an answer to one of the questions. You don't have to have all the answers immediately ready!

- Explain what you can do for the company and why you're interested in that specific company.

Let's look at some slide examples to see how streamlining text creates a more visually appealing slide. Exhibit 5.1 is an example of how a presenter might explain interview strategies. Notice that it's difficult to find the key words quickly because each bullet point is a complete sentence. Readers can rapidly skim complete grammatical sentences, but it slows them down to read each word—and too much text makes the slide design unnecessarily dense. An audience should pay attention to what a presenter says instead of reading sentences on a slide. For example, a presenter talking about interview strategies may wish to elaborate on how to be more specific when responding to interview questions (the second bullet point in Exhibit 5.1). However, audience members reading that same bullet point may not be listening closely because they're instead reading the 24 words in that sentence and perhaps thinking about job interviews they've had where they didn't answer the question as fully as they may have wanted to.

Exhibit 5.2 shows the same material on interview strategies in a more concise version. This slide uses key words instead of sentences for an audience to skim as the presenter discusses the material on this particular slide.

EXHIBIT 5.2   Streamlined text.

Interview Strategies

☞ Create positive first impression

☞ Give detailed answers

☞ Use pauses if necessary

☞ Show interest in the company

EXHIBIT 5.3   Side-by-side comparison.

Interview Strategies

☞ Create a confident first impression by introducing yourself, smiling, offering a firm handshake, and using the recruiter's name.

☞ Be as specific as possible in your answers to questions. Include details about why you may have acted as you did in specific circumstances.

☞ Be comfortable with a few seconds of silence if you want a little time to think about an answer to one of the questions. You don't have to have all the answers immediately ready!

☞ Explain what you can do for the company and why you're interested in that specific company.

Interview Strategies

☞ Create positive first impression

☞ Give detailed answers

☞ Use pauses if necessary

☞ Show interest in the company

The points simply highlight the message instead of displaying virtually every word the presenter plans to say.

To further emphasize how sharp and clear bulleted phrases can be in comparison to complete sentences, Exhibit 5.3 shows the two example slides side by side. You clearly can see in this side-by-side comparison which of the two slides audiences would prefer. The one on the right, the more concise

EXHIBIT 5.4   Slide sorter view (Tisdale, 2001).

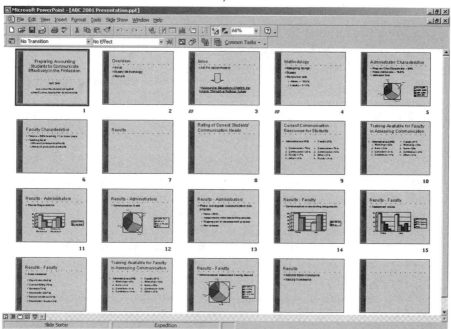

one, quickly and easily shows audience members key points the presenter will cover. This slide acts as a cue, and the audience can focus on what the presenter has to say about those key points.

As you're designing PowerPoint slides, run one or more of the following three checks to determine if you have too much text on your slides.

1. *Phrase check.* Carefully examine the text on each slide. Do you have any complete sentences? If so, reduce the amount of text and open up more white space by changing those sentences into phrases. Remember the "4x6" guideline!

2. *Slide sorter view check.* On your PowerPoint toolbar, pull a drop-down box from "View." Click on "Slide Sorter," and you'll see a miniature version of each slide in a layout that puts the slides in the order you'll show them. Exhibit 5.4 gives an example of what a slide sorter view might look like. In this version, you have a bird's-eye view of the presentation and can see that a few of these slides look more dense than others. If you notice that some slides appear too heavy on text, you'll know these are the ones that need to be more concise.

3. *The "big screen" check.* Practice your presentation on a screen size similar to the one that you'll use for your presentation. In fact, make a habit of doing do. Stand in the back of the room and look at the

slides as an audience member in the back row will. How cluttered or clear does each slide appear?

If you're unsure about how much text might be too much on any given slide, be conservative. Either pare down the material on the "heavy" slides or create another slide to finish those particular points. Audiences would rather see an extra slide than be faced with a screen full of bulleted text.

Fonts

Size

A 12-point font is the norm for written business correspondence and documents, but considerably larger text is necessary for presentation slides. The PowerPoint program has templates with preprogrammed font sizes for each slide title and bulleted point. Most of these templates use 44-point font size for slide titles and 32-point font size for body text. You don't have to stick with these sizes, but they're effective guides if you've not used the program often. Experienced presenters will manipulate the font size to customize slides for a presentation. However, the minimum font sizes for PowerPoint slides should be 32-point font for slide titles and 18-point font for the body of each slide. Although 12- or 14-point font text looks large enough to read comfortably on a personal computer or laptop, the smaller font sizes are difficult to read from the vantage point of someone sitting in the back of a conference room.

Type

The type of font that presenters select also contributes to attractive, easy-to-read slides. Sans serif font projects a clean, sharp image on-screen. Sans serif font is font without the "feet" that serif font has. Times New Roman is a serif font; its design style connects one letter to another to help the reader's eye move more smoothly across lines of text on a page. Below is an example of a sans serif font. The sans serif font (literally "without feet") projects better on a large screen than the serif font.

    KEEP YOUR SLIDES SIMPLE

The example below gives the two font types side by side, both in 14-point size.

Keep Your Slides Simple   Keep Your Slides Simple

If you hold this page at arm's length, the sans serif font phrase (right) will appear larger and slightly darker than the serif font phrase (left)—even though both text fonts are the same size.

EXHIBIT 5.5   Font comparison.

SANS SERIF

28-point size Arial font
22-point size Arial font
18-point size Arial font
12-point size Arial font

SERIF

28-point size Times font
22-point size Times font
18-point size Times font
12-point size Times font

To further illustrate how important font size and type are, look next at Exhibit 5.5. The sans serif font simply is easier to see when viewed from a distance. And the last line (the 12-point size) in both examples appears reasonably large on the printed page, but it would be almost unreadable to someone sitting in the back of a room during a presentation.*

Exhibit 5.6 gives one final example to illustrate how much more clearly an audience can view slides with sans serif font, showing two slides about interview strategies. The text on the left slide is serif font (Times New Roman). The text on the right slide is sans serif font (Arial). Glancing at these two slides side by side, you'll notice that the text on the right appears

---

* Thanks for this example of font type comparison to Catherine Gihlstorf, Program Director, Center for Innovation in Learning, the UNC Kenan-Flagler Business School.

EXHIBIT 5.6 Font side-by-side comparison.

Interview Strategies

- Create a confident first impression by introducing yourself, smiling, offering a firm handshake, and using the recruiter's name.
- Be as specific as possible in your answers to questions. Include details about why you may have acted as you did in specific circumstances.

Interview Strategies

- Create positive first impression
- Give detailed answers

sharper and even a bit larger than the information in the slide on the left—even though the font sizes are the same!

Experiment with various font types as you're developing presentations, but the two most common types for PowerPoint presentations are Arial and Tahoma. Keep a close eye, however, on the default font type in the Power-Point templates. Many of the templates do have a sans serif font–type default, but some default to Times New Roman font.

Colors

The PowerPoint program offers many templates to choose from, and each template already has a color design default. Presenters certainly can create their own color combination design by selecting a blank presentation when they begin, but it's important to consider contrast when venturing beyond the program's templates.

Effective slides need a sharp contrast between the slide background and the text or illustration. Black text, for example, is a nice contrast on a white background. Or, white text on a dark blue background. Exhibit 5.7 shows an example of a dark background-light text contrast. Even though the exhibit isn't shown in color, you can see that Exhibit 5.7 looks sharper than Exhibit 5.8. The first slide was designed with a dark blue background and bright yellow text. The second slide was created using the same background but with light-blue text. You might think that light blue text against a dark blue background would contrast nicely, but unless you're using a very high quality projector, the two blues will blend together slightly and won't provide the clear contrast needed. Additionally, some bright colors won't create a sharp contrast. For example, most shades of red and green text on a dark background won't show well; a light background would be more appropriate for either of these colors. The PowerPoint templates offer effective text/background color

EXHIBIT 5.7 Dark slide background with light text.

Dark Blue Background

- New product features
- Customer benefits from new product
- New sales goals

EXHIBIT 5.8 Dark slide background with dark text.

Dark Blue Background

- New product features
- Customer benefits from new product
- New sales goals

EXHIBIT 5.9 Contrast comparisons.

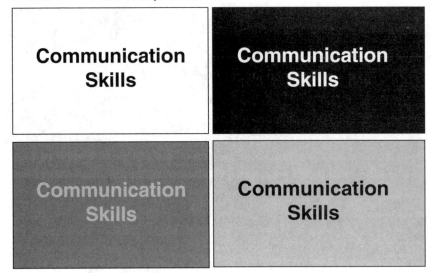

contrasts, and you can rely on them for sharp, clear slides. Exhibit 5.9 shows other examples of effective and less effective uses of contrast. Use the same principles when creating visuals or placing graphics on slides. To illustrate, a light company logo might not show well on a light background, and a picture with dark colors will be difficult to see on a dark slide background.*

Use a similar contrast concept in creating a watermark for a PowerPoint presentation. This is a slide background (imported images from the Internet, scanned pictures, or special illustrations) that enhances and customizes a presentation's slide design. The watermark function lightens these images so that they appear in the background of each slide, thereby helping to vary the standard mono-color slide backgrounds of many templates. Essentially, these backgrounds create a fresh, unique impression on each slide. To create a watermark, follow these steps:

1. Select an object (clip art, illustration, picture) and paste it onto a slide.
2. On the picture toolbar, click the "color" icon.
3. Click on "washout."

To create the same watermark on each page, paste the image onto the master slide. To design a watermark for one slide only, paste the image on that particular slide. Make the watermark a background object by right-clicking on the object, clicking on "order," and then clicking on "send to back."

But take care that a watermark isn't too busy for any text or graphic on the slides. Exhibit 5.10 is an example of a watermark that distracts from the

---

* Special thanks for this excellent example of slide color contrast to Catherine Gihlstorf, Program Director, Center for Innovation in Learning, the UNC Kenan-Flagler Business School.

EXHIBIT 5.10 Distracting watermark.

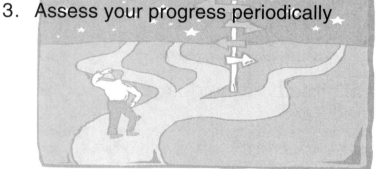

text. Not only is the text difficult to read over the watermark, but the busy watermark picture itself clutters up the slide. Exhibit 5.11 shows a good example of how a watermark can enhance a slide. In this example, a slide for a presenter to discuss email conventions, the ubiquitous email symbol underscores the electronic theme of the presenter's discussion.

INFORMATION STRUCTURE

How can presenters build information on slides to keep an audience alert and interested? This section addresses using slides as a framework for a presentation—slides can prompt an audience to recognize transitions between key ideas during a presentation. We'll discuss the following techniques that cue an audience about the different stages of a presentation message:

- Using specific slide titles and an agenda
- Using consistent slide transitions
- Using planned slide builds
- Preparing to take questions

Presenters use verbal transitions to let an audience know when they're shifting from one point to another in their presentation. The transition and build functions that PowerPoint offers can complement and support the verbal transition.

EXHIBIT 5.11 **Effective watermark.**

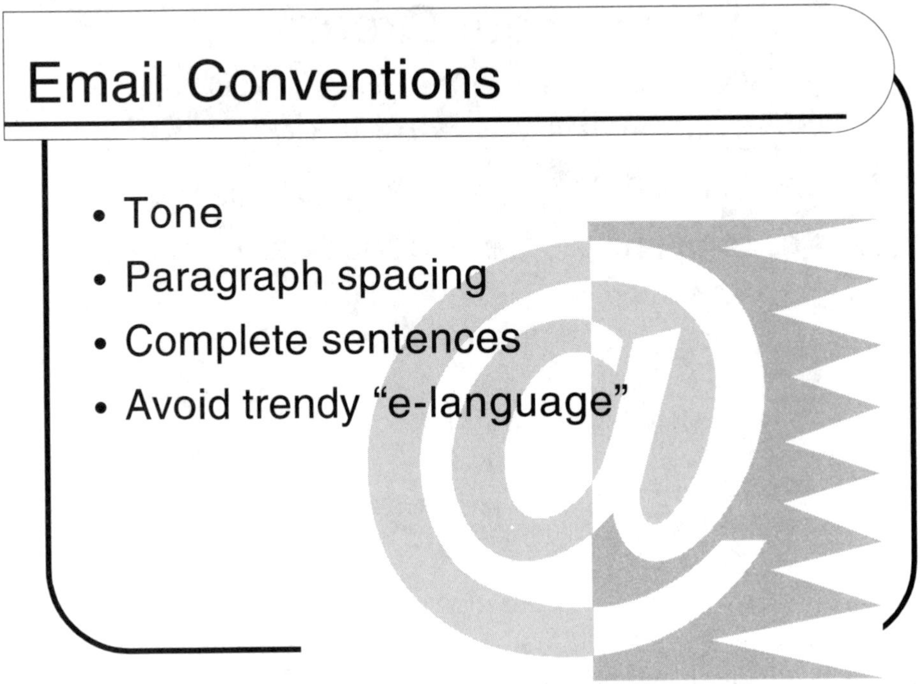

Email Conventions

- Tone
- Paragraph spacing
- Complete sentences
- Avoid trendy "e-language"

Using Specific Slide Titles and an Agenda

One of the devices that presenters use to let audiences know the "thesis" of each slide—and thus what will be discussed at that point in the presentation—is the slide title. Serving the same function for PowerPoint slides as headings in written business communication, a slide title should be a three- to five-word summary of what follows. For example, an audience can anticipate from the slide title in Exhibit 5.12 that the presenter will talk about each group's performance as a percentage of annual goals. As the presenter shifts to the next key point, the audience can expect to see the slide title change to reflect the new idea.

Another method to keep an audience in touch with a presentation's structure is to create an agenda slide or graphic that updates an audience each time a presenter shifts from one key idea to the next one. Edward Bailey (2002) calls this technique a "moving blueprint" (p. 163). Presenters indicate which point they want to emphasize by dimming the point(s) they've already covered and those they've not yet discussed. This technique creates a contrast by leaving the idea the speaker wants to address in regular-font type on the slide. Exhibit 5.13 shows an example of an agenda slide that tells the audi-

EXHIBIT 5.12   Specific slide title.

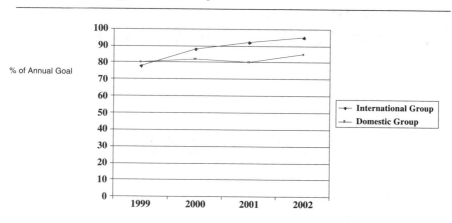

Tracking Group Performance

EXHIBIT 5.13   Agenda with emphasis—"moving blueprint."

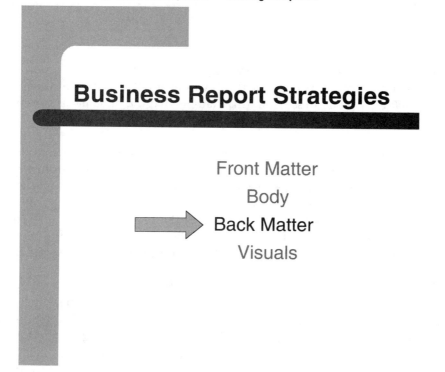

EXHIBIT 5.14   Agenda at bottom of slide—"moving blueprint."

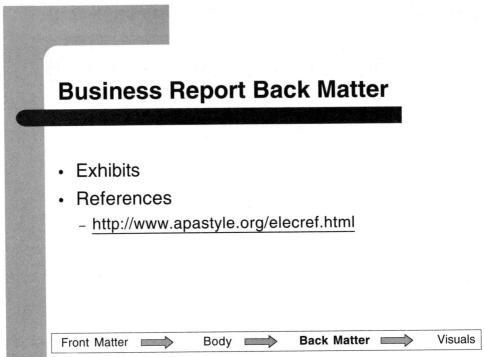

ence that the presenter just wrapped up point two of the presentation (the body structure of a business report) and will next talk about point three (the back matter). It's easy to see from this example that the presenter is switching into the third point because both the arrow and the regular font type emphasize it.

Alternatively, presenters can create a small graphic on each slide to show the audience at all times which section of the presentation they're discussing. Exhibit 5.14 is an example of a slide with this type of agenda prompt. The agenda is at the bottom of each slide, and you can see from the arrows and the bold font what stage of the presentation the presenter is covering. In this example, the presenter has finished discussing the sections dealing with Front Matter and Body and next will address the Back Matter.

Because presenters spend considerable time researching, developing, and practicing their presentations, they know at all times where they are within the presentation organization and how they plan to talk about the material. But, audiences will better be able to follow along if they clearly understand a presentation's structure. Think about the "moving blueprint" as a way to provide an audience with a basic outline to review as you explain the transitions between main ideas.

Using Consistent Slide Transitions

"Slide transition" is the term that business communication experts apply to the way that speakers change from one slide to another. Ideally, presenters should move smoothly and consistently between the different slides in a presentation so that the transition itself doesn't become a distraction for an audience.

The PowerPoint program offers numerous transition choices: Checkboard Across, Blinds Vertical, Dissolve, Split Vertical In, and so forth. Experiment with these transitions to find the ones that you like. Then, choose *one* for your primary transitions throughout each presentation. Many inexperienced presenters enjoy the possibilities that PowerPoint's variety of transitions offers, and they happily zip new slides in and out from different directions. After the first few transitions, however, an audience likely will begin to pay more attention to where slides are coming from and going to than to what the presenter has to say.

Of course, to emphasize a particular point by using a different type of transition, it would be appropriate to do so when you change to the slide you wish to stress. For example, you may have all of your slides simply appear—except for one slide with the recommendation that you've been building up to. For that slide, consider transitioning to it by using a "cover up" transition. Infrequently switching up slide transitions will subtly startle your audience because the change differs from the transitions you've been using; it will catch their attention as a novel movement. Whatever you choose, however, be consistent throughout each presentation so that audiences focus on you and your message and not on the slide transitions.

Using Planned Slide Builds

Presenters reveal information on each slide through a method called a "slide build." Inexperienced presenters often take one of two approaches: either show all information on any given slide or reveal every bullet point separately on all slides. However, presenters who take control of their presentations use a combination of these two methods. To this end, presenters should consider how to reveal the slide content so that it corresponds with the material that they want to discuss at each point in a presentation.

If you have three bullet points on a slide and won't be talking about one or more of them for any length of time, there's no need to bring up bullet points separately. Let's say a presenter is just going to mention, for example, three keys for marketing strategy: product, pricing, and placement. The presenter doesn't need to show each of these points separately. To do so would mean that the speaker would have to glance at the screen four separate times—once to make sure the slide had transitioned from the prior slide and three times to make sure that each of these points appeared properly. And why bring up each point separately if the main idea of this particular slide is that the three points—together—are keys for marketing strategy?

EXHIBIT 5.15 Dimming bullet point for emphasis.

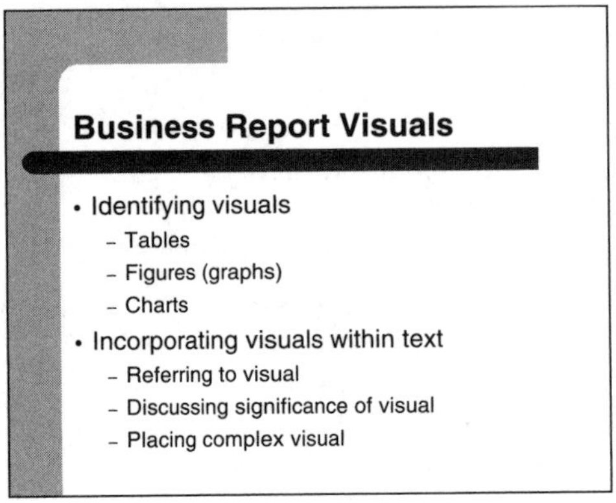
Business Report Visuals
• Identifying visuals
- Tables
- Figures (graphs)
- Charts
• Incorporating visuals within text
- Referring to visual
- Discussing significance of visual
- Placing complex visual

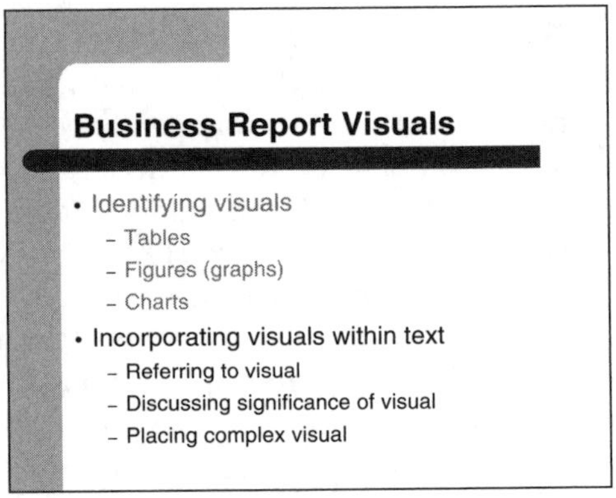
Business Report Visuals
• Identifying visuals
- Tables
- Figures (graphs)
- Charts
• Incorporating visuals within text
- Referring to visual
- Discussing significance of visual
- Placing complex visual

If, however, the presenter planned on *discussing in detail* how "product" fits into a marketing strategy and then how "placement" fits, he might consider revealing the bullets separately. To do so puts the presenter in control of the presentation. If all of the bullet points are on the screen at the same time, an audience may "read ahead" in the presentation and might miss something important about one or more of the earlier bullet points. Presenters should reveal only the information that thay want an audience to see so that they can take their time discussing the point they wish to address.

To further accent the build on each slide, use the PowerPoint "dim" feature to focus an audience's attention on any particular point in the presentation. This feature literally dims the text in one bullet point when the presenter has clicked to the next bullet and reinforces the verbal transition to the next idea. Notice the difference in Exhibit 5.15: these two slide examples have two key points with subpoints. The slide on the left has all the text visible to the audience, while the slide on the right has the first set of points dimmed so that the audience will focus on the idea (the second set of points) that the speaker wants to discuss.

Finally, as with transitioning from one slide to another, be consistent in building points throughout a presentation. The PowerPoint program has as many ways to build a slide as it does to transition between them. Some of the build options include "Unfold," "Compress," "Spin," "Zoom," and "Ascend." Inexperienced presenters can become overwhelmed with these options and vary the text directions frequently in an attempt to keep an audience alert. Like slide transitions, however, an inconsistent build technique may grab an audience's attention at first, but audience members can quickly become more entertained by where the text might be going to or coming from than they are with the message itself. Be consistent in building information on most slides so that the build effect doesn't detract from the message.

Preparing to Take Questions

After conducting a PowerPoint presentation, you want the audience's attention focused on you to begin the Q&A.* The audience already will recognize that the presentation is closing from transitional phrases such as "In conclusion," "To wrap up," or "As you've seen in today's presentation." To emphasize the fact that the presentation has ended, close out the presentation with a black slide. Doing so draws an audience's eyes from the slide screen to focus on the presenter.

Here are the two easy steps for setting this option

1. Go to "Tools" on the toolbar and click on "Options."
2. On the "View" tab, make sure the box for "End with black slide" is checked.

As you click to the black slide, turn the lights in the room back up and invite questions. You've verbally prepared the audience to move into the Q&A portion of the presentation and visually readied them by drawing attention to you as the Q&A session begins. Of course, you can also have an ending slide that is a blank slide of the template that you've used in the presentation, but the audience may wonder if you'll be bringing up information on it as you've done throughout the presentation.

Once the Q&A session ends, "blank out" the projector before closing the PowerPoint presentation and program. You don't want an audience to see the "work view" of the presentation and watch you log off the computer system. You've finished the Q&A with the impression you want the audience to have of your professionalism and credibility; don't leave an audience with an impression of a visual that you didn't intend to show. Exhibit 5.16 shows an example of the "work view" of the final key point in a presentation draft that I use whenever addressing career interview strategies. This, however, is not what I wish individuals in the audience to see. I don't want them to see the cluttered notes on the left side of the slide screen. Nor do I want to deliver my wrap-up as the audience continues to consider the post-interview reflection points on the slide. Therefore, I encourage presenters to show the audience only the prepared slides and blank out the projector while closing out a presentation.

SLIDE ENHANCEMENTS

We've spent considerable time in this chapter addressing how to effectively use text on PowerPoint slides. More important than text, however, are graphics and visuals. Audience members will better understand presentation

---

* Special thanks for the details on this method to begin the Q&A session to Catherine Gihlstorf, Program Director, Center for Innovation in Learning, the UNC Kenan-Flagler Business School.

EXHIBIT 5.16 PowerPoint "work view."

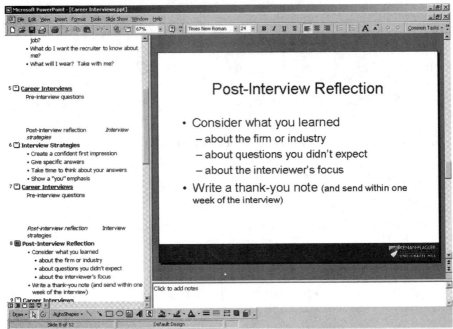

content if the verbal message is reinforced visually (Clayton, 2002). Graphics and illustrations help audiences quickly and efficiently visualize difficult concepts or numerical data.

With the many options available on the Internet and in the PowerPoint program, presenters have no excuse for developing plain slides loaded with bulleted text. But how to select from the limitless numbers and types of graphics and visuals available? Following are the types of slide enhancements we'll cover in this section:

- Graphics
- Pictures or illustrations
- Motion and sound
- Hyperlinks

You'll learn that slide enhancements drive home a point to an audience much more quickly than text—particularly if discussing statistics or abstract concepts. Let me give you a quick example. Exhibit 5.17 shows a slide that presenters wanted to use to discuss how low North Carolina ranked in one study in three specific health care issues. The slide gets the point across fairly quickly using text only to convey ideas. However, the visual representation of these same ideas in Exhibit 5.18 is more memorable. As you can see in Exhibit 5.18, the text has been rearranged on the slide so that it isn't in the typical bullet line order, and the cartoon shows the image of an over-

EXHIBIT 5.17 All text slide.

North Carolina Ranks:

- 36th in the nation in controlling smoking
- 36th in the nation in adequate nutrition
- 38th in the nation in levels of physical activity

Information from Behavioral Risk Factor Surveillance System, CDC, 1998

Source: Evans, et al. (2000).

EXHIBIT 5.18 Illustration slide.

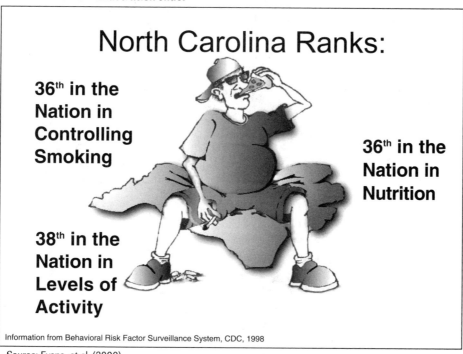

North Carolina Ranks:

36th in the Nation in Controlling Smoking

36th in the Nation in Nutrition

38th in the Nation in Levels of Activity

Information from Behavioral Risk Factor Surveillance System, CDC, 1998

Source: Evans, et al. (2000).

EXHIBIT 5.19 **Table example.**

Graphic	Description	Use
Table	Rows and columns that include either numerical or text data	Compare information side by side
Graphs	Visuals that include the following types: bar graphs, pie charts, line graphs	• Bar graphs show comparison of numerical data • Pie charts show comparison of numerical data as a percentage of a whole • Line graphs show comparison of numerical data over a period of time

weight teenager enjoying pizza and a cigarette—illustrating the concepts of physical inactivity, poor nutrition, and a smoking habit.

Graphics

PowerPoint and Excel offer presenters many types of graphics to use when quantifying ideas or illustrating points. Exhibit 5.19 shows you the two most common types. As you design slides, follow a few basic guidelines for each of these types of graphics to illustrate ideas effectively.

Visuals Guidelines

Tables

■ If you're simply displaying information, label the top row of each column so that an audience will know the content of each section. And, if you're comparing information, label both the top row of each column and the left side of each row.

■ Give each table a descriptive title (see Exhibit 5.20).

Graphs

■ *Pie charts.* Pie charts nicely show percentages of a whole. Label each piece of the pie outside the graph (black font text is often too difficult to read on the various pie chart colors) and place a legend either on the right side of the visual or at the bottom. Start the pie "slices" at noon and place them clockwise. The information that is most important should be the first slice of the pie (beginning at noon). If no one piece of the pie is more important than the whole, place the largest piece of the pie first and then add

EXHIBIT 5.20 Table example.

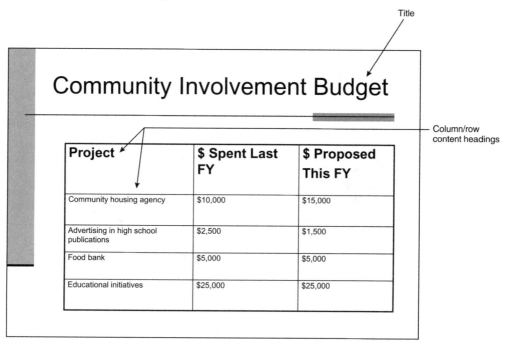

Title

Column/row content headings

Project	$ Spent Last FY	$ Proposed This FY
Community housing agency	$10,000	$15,000
Advertising in high school publications	$2,500	$1,500
Food bank	$5,000	$5,000
Educational initiatives	$25,000	$25,000

the slices in descending order. Finally, avoid having more than five to seven slices in the pie; otherwise the visual becomes too complex, and audiences will have a difficult time distinguishing the information. Be sure to title each pie chart as specifically as possible. See Exhibit 5.21 for an example.

■ *Bar graphs.* Bar graphs can be used for comparison purposes or to show trends over time. Label both the horizontal and the vertical lines so that an audience can read the visual accurately. Don't label inside the bars because you'll typically use darker colors to fill in the bars, and the text will be difficult to read. Avoid using more than four colors on a bar graph to keep the visual simple. Include a descriptive title, like the example shown in Exhibit 5.22.

■ *Line graphs.* Line graphs show comparisons of information over time. Label both the horizontal and vertical lines and avoid using lighter colors for a line because they may appear faded and difficult to read alongside darker lines. Use up to three lines per line graph; more will create difficulty for audiences to distinguish between the lines. Label the graphic with a descriptive title (see Exhibit 5.23 for an example line graph).

For all types of visuals, keep the graphics simple and fairly large. Just as you want slide text to be clear, graphics should look the same way. If you've got a complicated organizational chart or a large numerical table that may not fit on one slide unless the text is reduced below 14-point font, create a

EXHIBIT 5.21   Pie chart example.

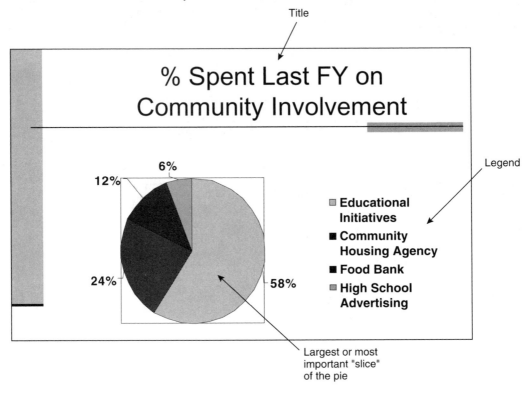

EXHIBIT 5.22   Bar graph example.

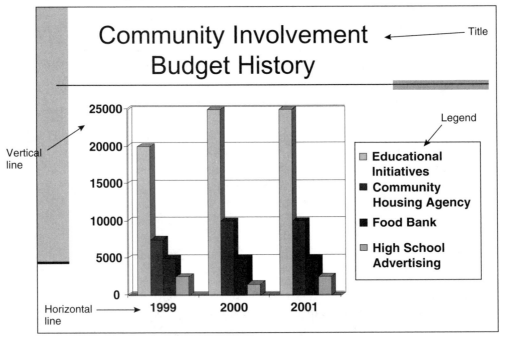

EXHIBIT 5.23   Line graph example.

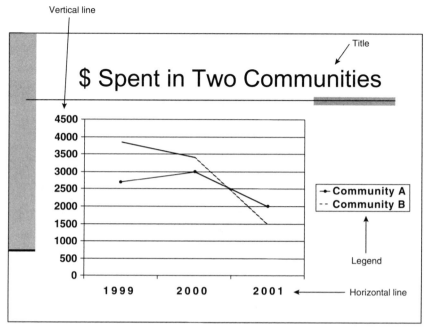

handout of this visual instead of putting it on-screen. Too often presenters show a visual that the majority of the audience either can't see or has to squint to make it out. Avoid this situation—create a handout and talk your audience through the handout instead of discussing a visual that they can't see clearly. Finally, whenever you use a graphic or visual that you've either copied or relied heavily on in creating your own visual, be sure to credit the source. Place the phrase "Source: _____" in small font (typically 10- to 12-point font) right justified under the graphic or visual. Exhibit 5.24 shows how the reference should appear.

You can see the source for this information in the lower right corner of the exhibit.

Pictures or Illustrations

Presenters have innumerable other visual images to choose from to illustrate ideas, including clip art, images imported from the Internet, line drawings, photos, and so forth. If you pull an image from the Internet, obtain permission from the owner if it's copyrighted before you use it. However, many images are free, such as Microsoft's ClipArt gallery (http://dgl.microsoft.com/), or you can create your own.

Whatever visuals you choose, test the images on a screen similar to what you'll use in a presentation. What looks sharp on a personal computer

EXHIBIT 5.24   **Citing a source.**

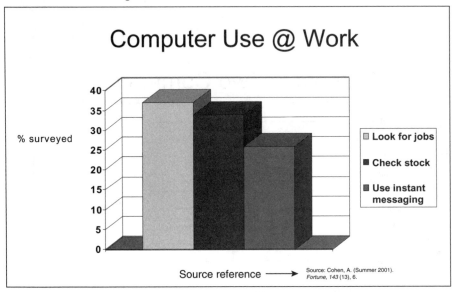

or laptop doesn't always enlarge well. Some Internet images, for example, lose clear resolution when they're projected onto a larger screen, or if the projector doesn't have high resolution. When these visuals are enlarged, they become grainy or fuzzy, and the image quality is compromised.

Additionally, be selective about the images used in a presentation. Clip art has been overused, and presenters should carefully consider the professionalism of some of the cartoon-like characters. Decide what your presentation purpose is, who your audience is, and how you want to be viewed by the audience. If you're looking for some light humor or if the presentation situation will support it, feel free to use the clip art cartoon drawings. But, you'll also find plenty of free, high-quality Internet photos that will make your visuals more refined. Or, you can scan in quality photos of your own. Compare the images in Exhibit 5.25 that a presenter could use to symbolize the quickness with which companies can adapt to change. On both slides, the greyhound represents power, agility, and grace. However, the actual picture in the slide on the right looks more polished and professional than the drawing in the slide on the left.

Motion and Sound

Catherine Gihlstorf, Program Director, Center for Innovation in Learning, the UNC Kenan-Flagler Business School, has an apt motto for using motion and sound in a PowerPoint presentation: "Just because you can, doesn't

EXHIBIT 5.25   Image choices.

Flexibility and Speed

Flexibility and Speed

How Companies Adapt to Change

Flexibility and Speed

How Companies Adapt to Change

mean you should." The PowerPoint program has many creative features that can enhance a presentation, but some features should be used sparingly. Motion and sound, in particular, are two such features. Presenters can create images or text that dance or sway during a presentation; audiences may or may not be enchanted. Audiences may also be irritated by a character that continually bounds across each slide on the screen throughout a presentation or pops up on slides unexpectedly at odd times. Additionally, audiences may become more interested in the cute character that bounces around a slide or a graphic and continually changes colors or shapes than they are in the presentation content. As a result, a presenter must work harder to regain audience attention.

To illustrate this particular point in presentations workshops, I place an animated baseball pitcher cartoon character in one corner of one slide. As I'm talking about clip art and illustrations, this little pitcher continuously winds and pitches. The image probably would work well for a specific audience of sports fans. However, the continual motion is distracting to a general audience, and I prefer the professional look of real photographs to a clip art character for most presentations.

Does this mean that animation won't do at all in a presentation? Of course not! Simply plan carefully for it to support your message. For example, an arrow that drops from the top of a slide to point to one particular area of a visual that you're getting ready to discuss can be an effective way of signaling a transition to an important point. Or, text that flashes once a different color to let an audience know that you'll next be addressing the information on that particular area of the slide will grab an audience's attention. Use this feature sparingly, however, because an audience will come to expect it—and it then loses its novel effect to attract attention.

Sound is another feature to use sparingly. PowerPoint offers presenters the opportunity to animate bullet points as they're shown with sound features such as a whoosh, a gunshot, screeching brakes, or breaking glass (among many others). If the sound is relevant to your point, it can enhance your message. Some presenters overuse this feature, however, and what might be effective if used judiciously turns into a painful experience for the audience and presenter alike. I attended one such presentation where a presenter reasonably decided to use the breaking glass sound to illustrate a particular point about auto safety. But she used the sound to bring in each bullet point. The result was a breaking glass sound every time she clicked the remote control mouse. For five minutes, the audience and the presenter cringed each time she started a new point because they knew that they were about to hear breaking glass. Had the presenter used the sound once, or maybe twice, to illustrate a key idea, it would have had the effect she intended. Instead, she put the audience through an excruciating experience every time she moved to her next point; as a result, the audience tuned out her message.

When used judiciously, sound can enhance a dynamic presentation. I recently heard a good illustration of effective sound use in a presentation about a museum. The team making the presentation wanted to use the museum's upcoming exhibition about a famous folk singer as their presentation opening. They played one of his songs very softly in the background as they developed their audience connection, and they identified the singer as the subject of the upcoming exhibit; they then played the background music again when they closed their presentation. What made this use of sound so effective was that the team accurately understood that the music should complement their message; it shouldn't be the focus (Brand, et al., 2001).

Hyperlinks

One additional visual feature that presenters can use to create dynamic presentations is hyperlink capability. This technique allows presenters to connect within a presentation to a Word or Excel document or even go directly to an Internet page. If you choose to use a hyperlink, however, have a reason for moving from the PowerPoint presentation to another program or to the Internet. In a presentation about an on-line bookseller's marketing techniques, for example, don't link to the Internet simply to show an audience the on-line seller's home page. Use the visual as you would any graphic that you've inserted into your presentation. In the on-line bookseller example, you might link to the seller's home page and talk about the marketing strategies illustrated on that specific site.

You can use either words or pictures as a hyperlink. In Exhibit 5.26, for example, a presenter could use the industry names or the clip art (the visual representation of the industry) to connect to websites of leading companies in these industries and illustrate how each of these companies designs its website. To create a hyperlink, simply select an item by clicking on the text.or the picture and then click on the hyperlink icon. A box will open for you to select a representative company's website to link. Note, however, that the link won't be active in the "work" view of the PowerPoint program. It's only active in the "slide show" view.

EXHIBIT 5.26 Hyperlink icon example.

Using PowerPoint Wisely

EXERCISE 1 **Slide Design—Take Another Look**

Print out a PowerPoint presentation that you've recently used (print the 6-to-a-page view). Examine each slide for the following elements of effective slide design:

Space

- How many bullet points do you have on each slide?
- How many words per bullet on each slide?
- How many different types of visuals (text, graphics, hyperlinks, etc.) do you use in the presentation?

Font

- What size font do you use for the body text on each slide?
- What font type do you use on each slide?

Color

- What type of color contrast do you use on each slide for the background and the text?
- Does your watermark interfere with the readability of the text or visual on each slide?

Once you've assessed your PowerPoint presentation using these questions, revise your slides to apply the techniques you've learned from this chapter.

EXERCISE 2   Information Structure—How the Audience Sees My PowerPoint Visuals

Using the same presentation slides that you revised in Exercise 1, analyze the presentation in the computer "slide show" view. Slide by slide, ask yourself the following questions:

- ❏ Do I have an agenda slide? If so, what key points do I say I'll address?
- ❏ Do my slide titles match my agenda slide?
- ❏ How do I transition between slides? Am I consistent?
- ❏ How do I build information on my slides?
    - If I show all bullet points at the same time on any slide, do I spend enough time talking about any one bullet point to warrant dimming the others?
    - Do I need to show every bullet point separately on every slide? How much time do I really talk about each bullet point?
    - How do I reveal the bullet points? Am I consistent?

EXERCISE 3   Slide Enhancements—Using Appropriate Visuals

Put one of your recent presentations on the "slide show" view and answer the following questions:

- How much text do I have compared to graphics or illustrations?
- Can I change some of my text into graphics to make a few of my points more concrete?
- If I have tables, can audience members in the back row easily see the text inside the tables?

- If I have graphs, do I have a good contrast between the color of my bars or pie pieces and the text showing the names or percentages of each?
- Do I cite my source if I've used someone else's information in creating graphics?
- If I've used images from the Internet, are they sharp? Do they support my message?
- If I've used animation or sound, is it effective for the point I want to make?
- If I've used hyperlinks, do I switch to another program or to the Internet for a specific reason? Why am I leaving PowerPoint?

EXERCISE 4   PowerPoint Effectiveness Test

Ask a colleague to assess the effectiveness of your PowerPoint slides using the following checklist:

POWERPOINT SLIDE EFFECTIVENESS CHECKLIST

	Yes	No
Does the presenter use a pleasingly aesthetic template that includes color?		
Do you see a title slide?		
Do you see an agenda slide where the presenter outlines the key presentation points?		
Does the presenter rely on slides composed mainly of text?		
Do all slides contain text large enough to read easily?		
If the presenter uses colored font, is the text easily visible against the slide background?		
Do any of the slides appear "text heavy" (too much text)?		
Do you see any text slides that the presenter could convert into slides with graphics (e.g., statistics)?		
Are the slide transitions and build effects consistent?		
Does the presenter control the presentation by revealing bulleted text only when ready to discuss it?		
Do graphics (line graphs, pie charts, etc.) have titles and clear legends?		
Do the illustrations (pictures, clip art, etc.) appear appropriate for the intended audience and presentation purpose?		
If the presenter uses pictures on any slides, are they high-quality resolution?		
Is the information in the slide graphics easy to see?		

References

Bailey, E. P. (2002). *Writing and speaking at work: A practical guide for business communication* (2nd ed.). Upper Saddle River, NJ: Prentice Hall.

Bly, R. W. (2001). The case against PowerPoint [Electronic version]. *Successful Meetings* 50(12), 5.

Brand, D., Ferraro, M., Freeman, A., Sekulic, G., & Wallance, J. (Spring 2001). Chapel Hill Museum team presentation for BUSI 100.

Clayton, J. (October 2002). How to make a picture worth a thousand words. [Electronic version]. *Harvard Management Communication Letter*, 1–5.

Evans, K., Hill, M., Sullivan, S., Watson, D., & Ziebell, J. (Fall 2000). NCPP team presentation for BUSI 100.

Ganzel, R. (2000). Power pointless [Electronic version]. *Presentations* 14(2).

Jaffe, G. (April 26, 2000). What's your point, Lieutenant? Just cut to the pie charts—the Pentagon declares war on electronic slide shows that make briefings a pain. *The Wall Street Journal*, p. A1.

Nunberg, G. (1999, December 20). The trouble with PowerPoint [Electronic version]. *Fortune*, 140(12), 330–334.

Presentations and 3M (Minnesota Mining and Manufacturing Co.) in conjunction with two independent researchers from Portland State University—Dr. Hayward Andres, Ph.D., and Dr. Candace Petersen, Ph.D. (2000). This study supports the basic results of an earlier one (1986) also completed by 3M and the University of Minnesota on the effectiveness of multimedia visuals. It showed that presenters using overhead transparencies and slides were 43 percent more persuasive than those who didn't.

Simons, T. (1999). Handouts that won't get trashed [Electronic version]. *Presentations*, 13(2), 47–50.

Simons, T. (2001). When was the last time PowerPoint made you sing? [Electronic version]. *Presentations*, 15(7).

Stewart, T. A. (2001, February 5). Ban it now! Friends don't let friends use PowerPoint [Electronic version]. *Fortune*, 143(3), 210.

Tisdale, J. (2001). Preparing accounting students to communicate effectively in the profession. Presentation to the Association of Business Communication, annual conference.

Zuckerman, L. (April 17, 1999). "Words Go Right to the Brain, But Can They Stir the Heart? Some Say Popular Software Debased Public Speaking." *The New York Times*, section B, page 9, col. 3.

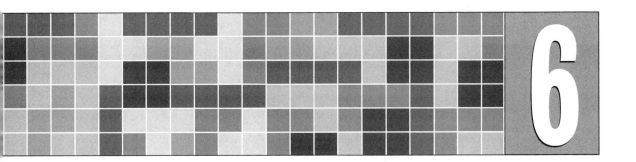

6

Using Other Visuals

PERFORMANCE GOALS

After completing this chapter, readers will be able to:

- design effective overhead transparencies using text features, information placement, and visuals

- use flip charts and white boards to organize key topics and generate audience participation

- create summary or supporting handouts to give an audience a physical "takeway" of the presentation message

Before Microsoft introduced the PowerPoint program in the late 1980s, presenters used a combination of visuals (e. g., overhead transparencies, handouts, flip charts) to support their message. Now that PowerPoint offers a dynamic, multimedia effect, most presenters rely heavily on it. However, the conventional visuals are still useful for business presentations—and some are more effective even than PowerPoint in particular situations. Presenters can use them in conjunction with PowerPoint or fall back on them if access isn't available for an electronic presentation. As is the case with the PowerPoint program, conventional visuals are tools to enhance, support, or illustrate a presenter's key points.

Although there are many types of visuals available, this chapter addresses the following:

- Overhead transparencies
- Flip charts and white boards
- Handouts

For each of these, we'll examine appropriate strategies for using them and how to maximize their effectiveness.

OVERHEAD TRANSPARENCIES

The PowerPoint program appeared to make overhead projectors obsolete. However, some businesses don't have PowerPoint available in a conference room format, and some small companies and not-for-profit organizations might not have the technology at all. If presenters don't have the appropriate equipment to take with them for use with a laptop, they can't convert their PowerPoint slides into a presentation. Further, laptop presentations to small groups (one to three people) may not be the most efficient use of time in front of an audience, depending on the presenter's goal.

Audiences are more likely to be persuaded if a message is supported with visuals, but don't despair if PowerPoint isn't available or accessible for an upcoming presentation (Bovée & Thill, 2000). Most businesses and not-for-profit agencies still have an overhead projector, and presenters can use it to show PowerPoint slides in a transparency format.

The special nature of transparencies, however, dictates a different perspective on creating and then incorporating these visuals into presentations. Overhead transparency presentations have limitations that electronic presentations don't. Speakers using transparencies, of course, don't have the benefit of seamless transitions between slides or crafted build techniques to reveal information separately on each slide. Additionally, there's no capability to connect with the Internet or any other program during this type of presentation. On the other hand, overhead transparency presentations allow for the opportunity to use well-designed visuals to help an audience conceptualize ideas or digest numerical data. They promote audience understanding almost as effectively as electronic presentations. In fact, a recent study funded by *Presentations* and 3M (2000) found that audiences rated informational multimedia presentations and overhead projector presentations almost equally in terms of effectiveness and professionalism.

In this section, we'll cover the following two principles of developing overhead transparencies:

- Transparency design
- Information structure

As you'll likely use the PowerPoint program to generate transparencies, note that I'll use the word "slide" instead of "transparency" in discussing the process of designing an overhead transparency presentation.

Transparency Design

To design overhead transparency slides, focus on the following design principles:

- Space
- Layout
- Font
- Color

Many of the issues we'll address for each of these principles are similar to those in Chapter 5 on creating PowerPoint slides, and I encourage you to read that chapter for more in-depth discussion on slide design strategies after you finish this section.

Space

Many presenters crowd slides with text because they want to rely on the slides for notes and because they believe they'll look more prepared if they

EXHIBIT 6.1   **Side-by-side slide text comparison.**

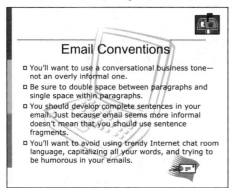

don't appear to have notes. However, the result is that these presenters put everything they plan to say on the slides, and audiences may walk out of these presentation sessions wondering about the necessity of attending the sessions; the presenter could have simply sent the presentation visuals instead so that audience members could have read them for themselves. After all, why set aside time for someone to read material to you that you could read yourself? Additionally, these presenters inevitably use the slides as a crutch, looking back at them on the screen too long and possibly even reading from them instead of talking about the points they want to convey.

An overhead transparency presentation should simply illustrate or support the ideas you want to discuss with an audience; it shouldn't be the message itself. Therefore, instead of using slides as notes, develop them as two separate documents because they have different purposes: *slides should enhance and support a presentation, while notes act as a prompt or support for a presenter.* Once notes are eliminated from the slides, presenters can then focus on generating appealing slides that will showcase ideas in an organized and professional fashion.

Limit the amount of text on each slide; use the "4 by 6" guideline that we discussed in Chapter 5: no more than four bullet points per slide and no more than six words per bullet point. Exhibit 6.1 shows a side-by-side comparison of a slide that's too busy and one that uses space effectively. The slide on the left contains too much text in the bullet points and unnecessary clip art. It's difficult to know what might be important—or even where to begin looking on that slide. Conversely, the slide on the right uses space to give audience members the key points in a few bulleted phrases and carefully selected clip art illustrations. Exhibit 6.2 is another side-by-side example of an ineffective slide and an effective one. In this example, the first slide

EXHIBIT 6.2 Ineffective versus effective slide design comparison.

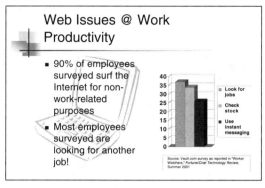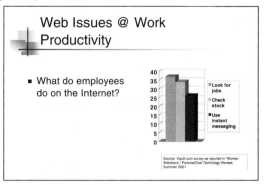

has more text than it needs, and it uses unnecessary clip art that clutters up the design. The second slide shows minimal text, eliminates the clip art, and lets the graphic illustrate the concept the presenter wants to emphasize. This slide encourages an audience to focus on the data included in the graphic placed on the right of the slide; the bulleted text on the left is simply an outline used in discussing the material that the slide supports. When transparencies are placed on an overhead projector, audience members should be able to quickly skim the material on the slides and then turn their attention to the presenter who will talk about the information, using the slides simply as support or evidence.

Minimize the amount of text in each point and maximize each slide's white space by using graphics or developing bulleted phrases instead of sentences. As with PowerPoint slides, transparencies don't need complete sentences for bullet points. The text and graphics on slides exist only to give the audience a tangible reference to key ideas. Further, be creative in designing slides and eliminate bulleted text when possible. Exhibit 6.3 shows how a presenter can eliminate the dry text-only slides and spice up discussion of a particular point simply by using a graphic instead of bulleted text (Evans, et al., 2000). You'll see in the slide on the left that the three key ideas for this point in the presentation are listed. Alternatively, the slide on the right illustrates the concepts of these points using an image combining those ideas.

Layout

For overhead transparency presentations, the "portrait" view is the most appropriate way to build a slide because it approximates the shape of the projector screens. A PowerPoint presentation, in contrast, uses the "landscape" view. When designing a transparency presentation on PowerPoint, however, avoid adding more points just because the layout is taller. Even though a

EXHIBIT 6.3   Enhancing text-only slides.

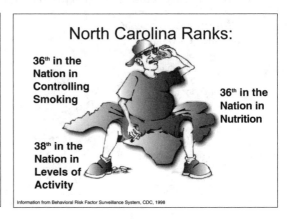

NC Prevention Partners

North Carolina Ranks:

- 36th in the nation in controlling smoking
- 36th in the nation in adequate nutrition
- 38th in the nation in levels of physical activity

Information from Behavioral Risk Factor Surveillance System, CDC, 1998

North Carolina Ranks:

36th in the Nation in Controlling Smoking

36th in the Nation in Nutrition

38th in the Nation in Levels of Activity

Information from Behavioral Risk Factor Surveillance System, CDC, 1998

slide may appear as if it has more space available, you can't have as many words on each line because the page isn't as wide as in the "landscape" view. Exhibit 6.4 gives an example of each slide view with the same text. You can see that the "landscape" view allows you to have each bullet point on one line if your points are fairly brief. Though the "portrait" view might not allow you to keep your points to one line each, you will have more open space above and below your text.

Fonts

Use the same principles for font size and typeface when building slide transparencies as you do for PowerPoint slides. Even though the slides will be on 8.5-by-11-sized transparencies, the images will still project on a larger screen, and the principles about making the text and graphics easy to read apply similarly for transparency and PowerPoint presentations.

Design information on slides to appear sharp, clear, and easy for an audience member anywhere in the room to read. This means the font size should be much larger than you normally would use for a conventional typed message on an 8.5-by-11-size page. Of course, as you customize presentations to meet each unique situation, you may need to vary font sizes. Avoid, however, using less than 32-point font for titles and 18-point font for the body text of each transparency. If you're fairly new to creating presentations, the PowerPoint program has many templates available with default-sized font, and you can rely on these templates to ensure the font size is large enough for an audience to read easily.

As is the case in designing PowerPoint slides, select a sans serif font for transparencies because it displays a sharper image when the font projects

EXHIBIT 6.4 Landscape versus portrait slide layout.

Anticipated Expansion Possibilities
- Europe
  - Consumer division by Q3
- South America
  - Commercial division by Q3
  - Consumer division next year
- Asia
  - Commercial division next year

Anticipated Expansion Possibilities
- Europe
  - Consumer division by Q3
- South America
  - Commercial division by Q3
  - Consumer division next year
- Asia
  - Commercial division next year

on a screen. Any sans serif font will be fine for transparency presentations; the most common types are Arial and Tahoma. Just remember that the PowerPoint program has numerous templates that default to the Times New Roman (or serif), and this type of font doesn't translate well on the screen. The sans serif font shows up as much more clear and sharp than serif font. Chapter 5 goes into more detail about font size and type in PowerPoint presentations and provides useful information in designing slides.

Colors

One of the more significant differences between designing slides for PowerPoint and overhead transparency presentations involves the use of color. Because LCD projectors are more powerful and clear than overhead projectors, a PowerPoint slide with a dark background contrasts nicely with light text. However, the color contrast on a transparency with a dark background and light text won't show up as well with an overhead projector. The background will appear too dark, while the lighter text or graphics won't have enough strong light showing through in order to project a clean image on the screen. Therefore, work primarily with light background–dark foreground templates when designing transparency slides. Additionally, test each slide on an overhead projector to determine the effectiveness of the contrast selected.

Printing needs also will be different if using overhead transparencies. It's important to have access to a color laser printer to print out clean, professional transparencies. On many basic ink-jet printers, colors may not adhere well to a transparency page. A high-end ink-jet printer may print clear transparencies if there isn't too much of any one color on the page.

Information Structure

As you do with PowerPoint presentations, structure information on each transparency slide with a careful eye to helping audiences know where they are at any given time in the message. Conversely, transparency presentations have two unique features that require prior consideration by presenters:

- The moving blueprint
- Transitions between slides

Because overhead transparency presentations have limited technology benefits, presenters simply cannot substitute a PowerPoint presentation for a transparency presentation without careful planning for transitions.

The Moving Blueprint

Transparency slides must be manually changed each time a new slide is required. Because of the awkward nature of physically switching one transparency to the projector while taking another off the screen, I advise against using separate transparencies for a "moving blueprint" (Bailey, 2002). This concept involves a separate slide showing only the presentation agenda each time a presenter shifts into a new point within a presentation. For example, Exhibit 6.5 shows a "moving blueprint" slide. Notice the first and last bullet points are in a lighter font than the second bullet point. In a typical PowerPoint presentation, presenters can quickly click to this slide between main ideas to visually reinforce the transition from point 1 (in this example, "pre-presentation") before beginning the discussion of point 2.

EXHIBIT 6.5 **A "moving blueprint" slide.**

EXHIBIT 6.6 A slide showing the moving blueprint at the bottom.

In an overhead transparency presentation, however, a presenter would have to remove the last slide used for the first key point discussion, place the agenda slide on the projector, remove it after just a transitional sentence or two, and then put up the slide starting the section on the second key point. That means handling the slides more than necessary, and presenters run the risk of losing connection with an audience because the focus would necessarily be on adjusting the transparencies on the projector. Instead, a more efficient way of using a "moving blueprint" might be to develop it on each slide. Exhibit 6.6 shows an example with the agenda at the bottom highlighting the second key point within the presentation. The slide itself begins the information for the second section, and the moving blueprint at the bottom signals the shift to another topic. A moving blueprint at the bottom of each slide keeps an audience aware of presentation structure and minimizes the number of times a presenter has to change transparencies.

Transitions Between Slides

When planning a transparency presentation, decide—and practice—how to reveal (or build) information on each slide. For a basic approach, presenters can place a transparency slide on an overhead projector and discuss the points shown. This technique is effective if the presenter is briefly touching on each of the points—it equates to the presenter revealing all points at the same time on a slide in a PowerPoint presentation.

If, however, a speaker needs to elaborate on a point and would like the audience to focus on a particular idea, it's more effective to reveal points separately. In a PowerPoint presentation, presenters can click a mouse to reveal material on a slide or change from one slide to another. Of course, in overhead transparency presentations, this build effect has to be done manually. To show only specific information on each slide in a particular order means that presenters need to place a large index card on the transparency, thus covering the material yet to be discussed. When ready, presenters can then move the card to go on to the next point.

To transition from one slide to the next, presenters also need either to change the transparencies themselves or ask someone to do it for them. These strategies can be either effective or distracting, depending on how well the presenters plan ahead. The advantage to having someone else change the transparencies is that a presenter can focus on the audience's reaction and interest in the message; there's no diversion from the audience in switching out the transparencies on the projector. The disadvantage, of course, is that an assistant may not know the presentation as well as the presenter, and the presenter will have to prompt the assistant each time a slide needs changing.

If using an assistant to change slides, practice in advance so that the assistant knows when to build information by moving the index card on each transparency and when to transition to the next key point by switching to the next transparency. If it's not possible to practice this in advance, take a few moments prior to the presentation to give the assistant cues for the changes. For example, you might suggest that you'll look over at the assistant and nod when you're ready to move to the next slide.

The following practical tips will help you build points on each slide and transition smoothly from one idea to another in an overhead transparency presentation:

1. Purchase a cardboard transparency frame for each slide and carefully tape the transparency to it; this provides stability for the transparency sheet and blocks glare from the overhead projector light.

2. Number the slides on the frame and arrange them in the order they should be shown. You might also write the title of each slide alongside the number on the frame. In the unlikely event that frames get out of order, you can look for the proper slide either by the number or the title on the frame.

3. Practice changing slides on the overhead projector. It might appear to be easy to pick up a slide that's already being shown and replace it with a new one. But, you'll find it to be more awkward than you might imagine if you've not practiced. First, decide where you'll place the slide that you're removing: on the podium? On the bottom of the stack that you're holding? On a side table? Second, place the

new slide straight on the overhead projector screen; moving it about to get it straight can make an audience dizzy. And, finally, make time to practice delivering the message while changing transparencies.

4. Keep transparencies in a clean folder with a hard copy of the slide on top of each transparency. This enables you to know what slide you're getting ready to place on the overhead projector at any given point in a presentation.

These tips will help you think about how to build information on each slide and transition smoothly between transparencies in a presentation. Additionally, they will make the presentation—message, delivery, and visuals—more cohesive.

FLIP CHARTS AND WHITEBOARDS

Flip charts and whiteboards (or dry erase boards) are ideal visuals to use when you wish to involve an audience in a participatory presentation. They give individuals the opportunity to conceptualize ideas in a concrete format in front of an audience. In addition, they can illustrate the process by which a group of people reach a consensus or come to an understanding of differing ideas in a presentation session.

Following are some of the most common reasons to use flip charts or whiteboards in presentations:

- *Brainstorming.* To generate as many ideas as possible in a short time period
- *Audience participation.* To invite an audience to be more active in the issue being presented
- *Problem solving.* To stimulate audience ideas in a problem-solving format (helps audience identify a problem, come up with as many potential ways to solve the problem as possible, and then decide on the most efficient method to resolve it)
- *Simplicity.* To help an audience talk its way through a complex training exercise or a process

Additionally, as David Dehaas (1999) notes, flip charts (and, by extension, whiteboards) are excellent organizational tools for presenters. Each heading on a page signals a separate topic to an audience. As presenters complete one page and turn to the next (or erase the board to begin filling it up again), audiences recognize a clear end to one section of a discussion and the beginning of the next.

Essentially in a flip chart or whiteboard presentation, individuals in the session act both as audience members and as presenters with these visuals. In fact, the physical presence of these tools sets the context for this type of presentation. When people walk into a boardroom and see a flip chart or whiteboard positioned near the front of the room, they recognize that they'll be expected to participate actively in a discussion—instead of being interested, but passive, listeners.

This section addresses the following tips on effective use of flip charts and whiteboards for presentations:

- Record audience ideas
- Invite active audience participation
- Generate ideas from material on the visuals

One note of caution, however, about using flip charts or whiteboards: Avoid asking audiences to use these visuals to answer rhetorical questions or enact trivial exercises. Use them only if the presentation purpose truly calls for collaborative participation. Audiences have little patience with a presenter or a participatory type of presentation if they don't think that they're contributing to the ideas—that is, if they think a presenter has a specific idea in mind (the "right" answer) and simply wants them to verbalize or confirm it.

Record Audience Ideas

Flip charts and whiteboards are tools to help presenters to structure a participatory presentation because audiences can visualize key headings and

EXHIBIT 6.7 Team presentation feedback.

Group Feedback

What Presenter Did Well   What Presenter Needs to Work On

Presenter Goals

Strength Goal   Challenge Goal

---

then contribute to fleshing out the information for each heading (Dehaas, 1999). When a presenter solicits participation on a particular topic and turns to write the responses on the flip chart or the whiteboard, this action signals to the audience that these visuals are a specific component of a presentation—much like the "moving blueprint" slide in a PowerPoint presentation.

I often use this flip chart technique, for example, in smaller presentation workshops to help presenters learn from others in the group. After a presenter has finished delivering a presentation, I ask participants in the session to give the presenter positive and constructive feedback. As individuals begin commenting, one group member records the feedback on a flip chart page. Once the feedback portion of the session is complete, the person recording the comments tears off the completed flip chart page and gives it to the presenter; then we move to the next presenter. Exhibit 6.7 shows this response page outline.

The two main headings on this exhibit indicate the key points of the workshop: Group Feedback and Presenter Goals. The subheadings and open space under the headings invite audience members and presenters to reflect on strengths and challenges of each presentation. This format (headings, subheadings, and open space) keeps the group focused on the goals for the session. And at the end of the session, presenters take their flip chart pages with them as "notes" about the feedback the group offered, as well as a tangible reminder about the goals that they set for themselves.

Ideally, presenters should ask someone from the audience to record group ideas so that they can more effectively moderate the session and stay connected with the audience and the discussion flow. Whether a presenter or a volunteer acts as recorder, however, it's important that the recorder clarify ideas as they're being written down. The most efficient way to do this is by restating key ideas. Another method is to ask a question to double-check what's been said; this ensures that all members of the audience have the same understanding of the idea as it's recorded. Finally, try as much as possible to use abbreviated versions of exactly what a speaker says instead of trying to "massage" it into fitting the theme of the presentation. This is one reason that an audience member often will work better as a recorder than will a presenter—audience members who act as recorders will be more likely to write what fellow audience members say. The close attention to each contribution to a discussion validates audience members' ideas and opinions. They'll be more likely to believe their views are truly heard and not feel that they're going through an exercise simply to give rote answers that a presenter wishes to hear.

Invite Active Audience Participation

If using just one flip chart or whiteboard with a small audience (typically 5 to 15 people), place it near the front of the room. It can then be moved forward when the presenter needs it. If an audience consists of more than 20 people, a flip chart or whiteboard may not be the most effective visual because audience members in the back of the room probably won't be able to see the visual and, thus, can't or won't participate.

There is, however, an exception to the guideline of using flip charts as a visual only with a small audience. If a presenter's goals include the use of breakout group exercises, several flip charts or whiteboards positioned in various places around the room create an ideal environment to generate ideas from several small groups broken down from the larger group. Exhibit 6.8 shows a diagram illustrating easy access to flip charts when the presenter breaks the larger group into smaller ones for exercises.

Generate Ideas from Material on the Visuals

If you want an audience to split into breakout groups to generate ideas, Exhibit 6.8 shows how to position flip charts or whiteboards around the room so that each team will have its own work space. Then, when the exercise is complete, ask each team to explain to the larger group (using the visual that they created) the ideas they worked on and the conclusions they reached. When the presentation ends, ask someone to summarize the concepts on each of the flip charts or whiteboards and after the session, if appropriate, send out an abbreviated version with a follow-up memo or letter. The follow-up reinforces the concepts that the group recorded and reminds participants of their role in generating the ideas and the ensuing discussion.

EXHIBIT 6.8   Optimal flip chart placement for large group discussions.

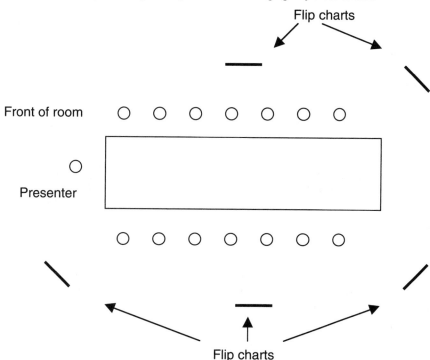

This follow-up may solidify audience buy-in on recommendations or en-hance understanding of complicated concepts.

As you can see from these tips, flip charts and whiteboards naturally in-vite active audience participation in presentations. To encourage and effi-ciently facilitate this participation, carefully plan out time allotments for each segment of the session. Err on the conservative side and allow extra time for an engaged audience's creative thinking. The amount of time necessary for audience participation will vary, depending on how often in a presenta-tion an audience is invited to participate and to what degree a presenter in-cludes them in the discussion. For example, if you have a particularly active audience, or if you ask for input at several points in a presentation, recognize that you'll need to focus your message tightly because you won't have as much time to elaborate as if you'd not opened up the presentation at all to audience participation. Additionally, you can let the audience know at each stage of the presentation what length of time they have to participate. For ex-ample, if you decide to have participants brainstorm ideas for an upcoming marketing campaign, decide how much time to allot for that particular part of the presentation and stick to that deadline. Once an audience begins par-ticipating, a presenter loses some degree of control, simply due to the time-consuming nature of fostering dialogue. If you want an in-depth discussion of an issue with plenty of input from an audience, schedule large blocks of time in a presentation to avoid stifling the free flow of ideas. To help an audience know what to expect, set the context of the discussion and participation expectations at the beginning of the presentation.

HANDOUTS

Handouts are effective visual tools because they convey important concepts from a message that audience members can take away from a session. Well-designed handouts can enhance a presentation by giving an audience a tangible, concrete image of message highlights. *Presentations* editor Tad Simons (1999) encourages presenters to consider the need for and appropriate use of handouts as a part of planning for each presentation. When researching material or completing a project, presenters can incorporate into potential visuals any information that would facilitate an audience's comprehension of the topic. In other words, don't wait until after developing the message and putting together PowerPoint slides to create a handout; create supporting material for a handout as you're planning the message! The result will be a well-prepared presenter who inevitably will have far more material to present than time allows.

Typically, handouts support one of two purposes:

- To summarize the presentation
- To illustrate one or more of the presentation's key ideas

This section discusses how and when to use each type.

Summary Handouts

Summary handouts provide a basic presentation structure for audience members both during a presentation and after they leave it. This type of handout enables an audience to *see* the message's key ideas. Two popular summary handout types are notes pages and summary takeaways.

Notes Pages

To generate audience notes pages, print slides using the PowerPoint program's three-to-a-page handout view. This print option puts three slides on the left half of each page and provides room on the right side of the page for audience members to take notes during a presentation. You'll see in Exhibit 6.9 an example of a three-to-a-page handout that I used in a recent presentation workshop.

Exhibit 6.10 shows another type of audience notes handout that I've used for presentation workshops. In this example, you can see that the presentation message is outlined with plenty of white space for presenters to use in taking notes. Additionally, a list of presentation resources is printed

EXHIBIT 6.9 **Audience notes page handout.**

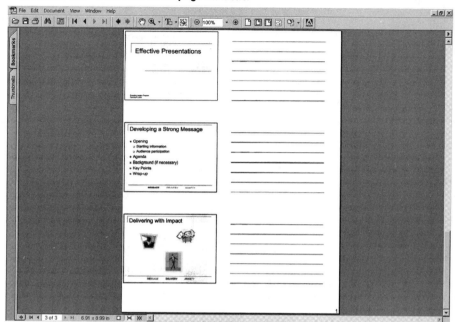

at the bottom of the handout. Audience members can take notes during the presentation and use the same handout to access electronic resources for more information after a session ends.

Some presenters prefer to pass around summary handouts before a presentation begins—audience members can "follow along" and take notes if they prefer. This handout format gives participants an outline to follow and helps them better understand the structure of a complex presentation. However, giving audience members summary handouts before a presentation begins also gives them the opportunity to read ahead. This can be problematic if a presenter needs to build a case point by point; many in the audience may skip to the final slides to review the ending recommendations before a presenter even finishes the audience connection and agenda. Each presentation situation is unique, and presenters should decide when to give an audience the handouts based on what they need to accomplish during each presentation.

Summary Takeaways

Presenters also can choose to generate summary takeaways. These handouts simply provide audience members with a basic message structure. To create this type of handout, print slides using one of two PowerPoint print options: six-to-a-page view or outline view. Like the notes pages handouts, these are summaries of the presentation. However, they're simply the printed version

EXHIBIT 6.10   Audience notes page and resources handout.

Effective Presentations

Developing a Strong Message
- Audience connection
- Agenda
- Background (if needed)
- Key points and support
- Wrap-up

Delivering with Impact
- Eye contact
- Vocal pace, tone, and volume
- Nonverbal communication

Helpful Electronic Resources for Presentations

UNC-Chapel Hill Communication Studies Oral Communication Program Home Page
http://www.unc.edu/depts/comm/

Allyn & Bacon Publishers: "Delivery Dynamics"
http://www.abacon.com/pubspeak/deliver/dynamics.html

National Communication Association Study: "How Americans Communicate"
http://www.natcom.org/research/Roper/how_americans_communicate.htm

Toastmasters: "Speaking Tips"
http://www.toastmasters.org/tips.asp

Kansas University Communication Studies Department: "Virtual Presentation Assistant"
http://www.ukans.edu/cwis/units/coms2/vpa/vpa.htm

---

of the slides themselves or an outline of the presentation. They don't contain specific details or graphics from the presentation, instead showing only the text message framework and key information.

Exhibit 6.11 shows an example of a six-to-a-page view. This particular handout gives audience members the slides. However, it doesn't leave much room for notes.

Exhibit 6.12 is an outline view. This particular option offers the basic message structure, but it is text only; it doesn't show any graphics or illustrations.

How do you decide which type of summary handout to use? I recommend giving audiences a basic outline—the notes page handout—if the purpose for a presentation is to inform; audience members can make notes

EXHIBIT 6.11 Six-to-a-page view handout.

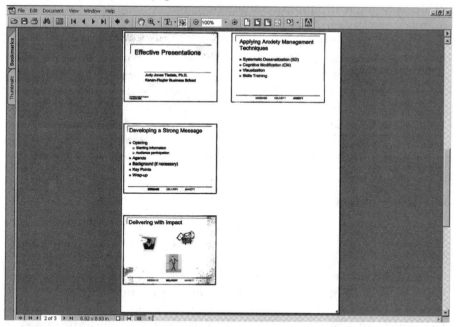

EXHIBIT 6.12 Outline view handout.

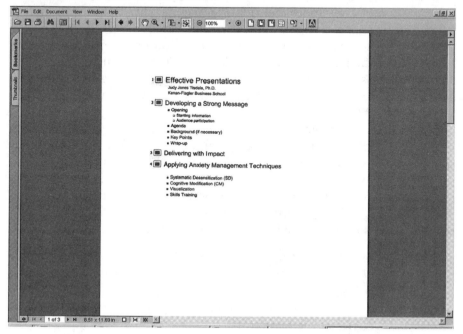

on the appropriate section as you discuss each point. If delivering a problem-solving (or complex) presentation, you probably need to reserve a summary takeaway handout until the discussion portion of the session or the Q&A. In this case, however, you should create more than just an outline of the presentation for the audience because you'll need to provide more details than a simple outline might offer. Develop an outline form and then add subpoints for the key ideas on each slide.

One more note about summary handouts—keep them short! If you compile a large packet of material for session participants to take away, they may not make time later to read all of it. So limit summary handouts to one to three pages, if possible.

Supporting Handouts

Supporting handouts illustrate information that is too complex to fit on a slide or won't show clearly enough on the screen. Exhibit 6.13 shows an example of the first page of a research project survey. An audience would probably read this material more easily as a handout than as a slide. The amount of text in this exhibit won't fit onto one PowerPoint slide, and message content doesn't call for the presenter to cover each question thoroughly. Instead, the purpose in showing this information was simply to give the audience the questions used in the project survey. To this end, a handout more effectively serves the purpose.

Exhibit 6.14 gives another example of material that would work well as a handout but not as a PowerPoint slide. On a PowerPoint slide, the text under each of the headings would be too small for an audience to see easily. Even if the audience could read it, however, there's too much information. They would be skimming the many agency programs and features of the program instead of listening to the presenter.

In small group presentations, presenters should wait until they're ready to discuss a supporting handout before giving it to the audience. And they should wait to begin speaking until everyone in the session receives a copy; otherwise, individuals may be shuffling the pages as they're passing them around, and presenters will have to talk over the rustle of paper.

Handouts can be a powerful way to send your presentation message out of the session with audience members when they leave.

1. Use handouts to give an audience a structured frame of reference for notes or to provide complex visuals that won't show up well on PowerPoint.
2. Find out how many people will attend your presentation and make a few extra copies of the handout(s).
3. Use only one or two sets of handouts to avoid overwhelming an audience with paperwork.

EXHIBIT 6.13 **Supporting handout example (Tisdale, 2001).**

Communication in Your Program

How would you rate your current students' communication skills?

Scale 1–5 *one (1) = needs significant improvement; five (5) = excellent*

Written communication skills

1   2   3   4   5

Oral presentation skills

1   2   3   4   5

What does your program do to assist students who need additonal work on oral and written communication skills? *Please check all that apply.*

_____ Require work with a tutor or teaching assistant
_____ Refer to a writing center
_____ Recommend coaching session with faculty member
_____ Bring in consultant to do workshops
_____ Recommend students to take communication course(s)
_____ Not applicable
_____ Other (*please explain*) _____

Communication in the Courses You Teach

In your course, do you assess any of the following assignments for effective or non-effective oral or written communication skills (*excluding* the final exam)? *If not, skip to question #6. Please check all that apply.*

_____ Individual oral presentations
_____ Group oral presentations
_____ Individual written assignments
　　　_____ 1–3 pages required
　　　_____ Over 3 pages required
_____ Group written assignments
　　　_____ 1–3 pages required
　　　_____ 4–7 pages required
　　　_____ Over 7 pages required
_____ Other (*please explain*) _____

EXHIBIT 6.14   Another supporting handout example.

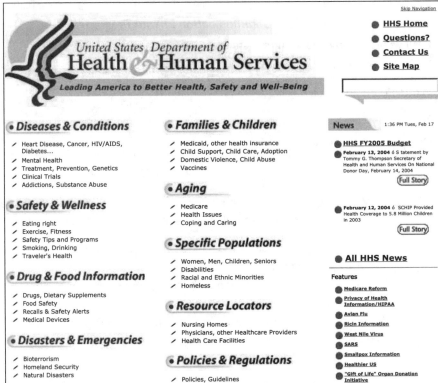

Source: U. S. Department of Health and Human Services, http://hhs.gov/.

EXERCISES Using Alternative Visuals

EXERCISE 1 Building a Slide Transparency

Using the principles of effective slide design discussed in this chapter, analyze a PowerPoint presentation you've recently delivered to determine if it would fit the conventions of a transparency presentation. (Hint—don't forget to change the style format from landscape to portrait!) If possible, make a transparency of the slides, display them on an overhead projector, and examine your results.

EXERCISE 2 Staying in Control of the Presentation

Select a PowerPoint presentation that you've recently delivered and create overhead transparencies for the slides. Videotape yourself as you deliver the presentation on an overhead projector. Use an index card to "build" points on each transparency (revealing only the part of the transparency that you wish to discuss at specific points). Watch your taped presentation and analyze yourself using the following guidelines:

Analyzing an Overhead Transparency Presentation

1. Are the slides uncluttered, sharp, and easy to read?
2. Do the slides have plenty of white space?
3. Does the presenter effectively "build" information, showing only the part of the slide being discussed at any given point?
4. Does the presenter transition smoothly from one transparency to another?
5. Does the presenter maintain good eye contact with the audience during the presentation?
6. Does the presenter appear calm and confident during the presentation?

EXERCISE 3 Using Flip Charts to Generate Audience Participation

Assume the role of team leader (four to six people per team) for a project in which your goal is to identify the qualities needed to succeed in four careers (you select the careers). Your team's goal is to develop a job description (using the qualities your team agrees on) for a position in each career. Set up a flip chart to organize the discussion and record the team's ideas. Give each person on the team the opportunity to lead key discussion points.

EXERCISE 4   Designing Summary Handouts

Select an article from *Fortune, The Wall Street Journal, Harvard Business Review,* or any business news magazine, journal, or newspaper. Using a word-processing program, write an outline of the article as a one-page handout. Condense the article into no more than three main topic headings in the outline.

EXERCISE 5   Designing Supporting Handouts

Using the same article you read for Exercise 4, create a one-page handout that concisely illustrates an important part of one of the article's main points. If possible, develop a graphic from the information instead of simply summarizing the text material.

References

Bailey, E. P. (2002). *Writing and speaking at work: A practical guide for business communication* (2nd ed.). Upper Saddle River, NJ: Prentice Hall.

Bovée, C., & Thill, J. (2000). *Business Communication Today.* (6th ed.). Upper Saddle River, NJ: Prentice Hall.

Dehaas, D. (1999). What's with the flippin' chart? [Electronic version]. *OH & S Canada, 15*(6) 52–54.

Evans, K., Hill, M., Sullivan, S., Watson, D., & Ziebell, J. (Fall 2000). NCPP team presentation for BUSI 100.

Presentations and 3M (Minnesota Mining and Manufacturing Co.) in conjunction with two independent researchers from Portland State University—Dr. Hayward Andres, Ph.D., and Dr. Candace Petersen, Ph.D. (2000). This study supports the basic results of an earlier one (1986), also completed by 3M and the University of Minnesota, on the effectiveness of multimedia visuals showing that presenters using overhead transparencies and slides were 43 percent more persuasive than those who didn't, as cited in Simons (1999).

Simons, T. (1999). Handouts that won't get trashed [Electronic version]. *Presentations, 13*(2), 47–50.

Simons, T. (2000). Multimedia or bust? *Presentations 14*(2), 39–50.

Tisdale, J. (2001). Preparing accounting students to communicate effectively in the profession. Presentation to the Association of Business Communicators, annual conference.

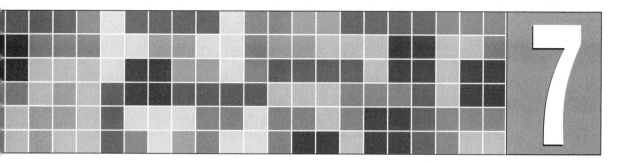

Overcoming Presentation Anxieties

PERFORMANCE GOALS

After completing this chapter, readers will be able to:

- define presentation anxiety and understand what fuels it

- use specific strategies to manage anxiety at any stage of the presentation process

- analyze presentation performance as a tool to minimize anxiety for future presentations

You've put a great deal of time into getting ready for a presentation: you know who will be in the audience, the message and visuals are polished and ready to go, and you've rehearsed several times. You're confident that you can't prepare any more without the presentation starting to sound "canned." So why are you still nervous? Why do you have that sick feeling in your stomach? Why are you still scared to get up in front of that audience? And, more important, what can you do about it?

Anyone who has experienced anxiety related to speaking in front of a group knows that this fear can create stomach butterflies at best and turn public speaking opportunities into nightmarish events at worst. Almost 40 percent of respondents to a study sponsored by the National Communication Association (1998) said that they didn't feel comfortable giving a speech or making a presentation. Even students at one of the most prestigious performing arts schools in the United States, The Juilliard School, have the opportunity to take two courses dealing with nervousness: "Overcoming Performance Anxiety" and "On the Edge: Learning to Give Peak Performances" (The Juilliard School, n.d.). Further, people in the United States rank the fear of public speaking above fear of snakes, heights, and even death (Laskowski, n.d.; Strout, 2001).

Anxiety is a common factor for many presenters; even the most accomplished speakers will, from time to time, experience some nervousness prior to speaking to a group. Experienced presenters know, however, that anxiety—in small and manageable amounts—may actually help improve a speaker's performance because it activates many of the body's internal systems that enable us to increase our attention and focus in times of stress (Gorman, 2002). In other words, anxiety—in the right dose—can help presenters prepare for and then deliver a dynamic presentation.

However, you likely wouldn't be reading this chapter if you typically experience only mild presentation anxiety. The good news is that there are methods you can use to decrease or manage nervousness. This chapter looks closely at the following topics to help speakers develop a confident approach to presentations:

- Defining presentation anxiety
- Reducing anxiety levels
- Analyzing performance to enhance confidence

We'll first examine how anxiety functions in relationship to presentations, paying particular attention to the nature of anxiety. We'll then turn to a discussion of when to expect varying levels of anxiety in a presentation and the tools and resources available to help you combat this problem.

DEFINING PRESENTATION ANXIETY

What is the anxiety that nervous presenters feel? Communication experts label it communication apprehension (CA). J.C. McCroskey (1977) defines CA as "an individual's level of fear or anxiety associated with either real or anticipated communication with another person" (as cited in Ayres & Heuett, 1997, p. 78). Note that this definition suggests that anxiety stems from real *or anticipated* interaction. McCroskey found that the anxiety experienced while awaiting a communication encounter is just as real as that felt while interacting. It makes little difference that other persons in that situation may not view the situation as threatening or that a speaker may not have actually yet been in contact with an audience. For speakers who have CA, the mere perception of the audience-presenter encounter is a threat to themselves and to their expectations of a situation, their own performance, and the desired presentation outcome.

Presentation Anxiety or Presentation Fear?

Although the terms are often used interchangeably in general conversations, mental health experts distinguish between "anxiety" and "fear." The latter involves an individual's short-term response to an *external* threat. For example, if an individual sees a car swerving into his lane on the interstate, he experiences fear if he interprets the movement as a threat to his own safety. The threat is external, and the individual reacts to it. Anxiety, on the other hand, is connected to an internal response to a perceived threat. Anxiety typically intensifies more slowly and tends to last longer than fear. Like fear, it produces physiological responses, but anxiety is influenced less by an *external* threat and more by the individual's thoughts, feelings, and images associated with the *perceived* threat (Gorman, 2002). This distinction is important because anxiety is best dealt with by using methods aimed at altering internal thought patterns, as we'll address in a later section of this chapter.

In studying anxiety, researchers also distinguish between "trait measures" and "state measures." Researchers have long used the concepts of trait and state measures, and the two responses they produce, in an attempt to identify and categorize the distinct ways individuals experience anxiety and in an attempt to measure the effectiveness of treatment alternatives (Sawyer & Behnke, 1999). Trait measures generally are considered to be a part of an individual's personality and, therefore, less likely to be changed without comprehensive and sustained efforts such as counseling or anxiety therapy (Sawyer & Behnke, 1999). State measures, on the other hand, are situational and determined in large part by what an individual is doing at any given time (Sawyer & Behnke, 1999). Both trait and state measures are *perceptual* measures of anxiety; this means that the level of anxiety is directly connected to how an individual understands a potential threat. Further, both measures (state and trait) can take either a physiological ("My hands begin shaking when I make a presentation") or a psychological ("I feel so overwhelmed when I look out at an audience") form. Because state anxiety is tied directly to situational responses, however, it's easier to modify state response patterns in minimizing CA. The strategies that we'll address later in this chapter support nervous presenters in managing state measures. Additionally, these techniques offer speakers ways to conceive control over how they understand their actions and the audience-presenter interaction in a presentation situation.

Why Do We Feel Presentation Anxiety?

Intuitively presenters know the critical importance of the ability to make clear, interesting, and cogent presentations. Performance in public speaking situations can have a significant effect on many important dimensions of an individual's life and career. Studies indicate that a direct relationship exists between speaking aptitude and public perceptions of a speaker. Researchers Kearney and McCroskey (1980) found that individuals with high CA levels may be seen as less confident and less decisive than those who aren't as anxious about verbal communication (as cited in Ayres & Heuett, 1997). Similarly, a study by Daly and Leth (1976) shows that people with high CA are less likely to be promoted than more confident speakers (as cited in Fordham & Gabbin, 1996). How someone is perceived socially and professionally impacts career advancement and has financial implications related to closing deals and increasing salary (Ayres & Heuett, 1997; Cohen, 1999; Curtis, Winsor, & Stephens, 1989; Messmer, 1999; Waner, 1995). Put quite simply, strong oral communication skills are vital to career success, and in presentation situations an audience will judge a speaker's competence and credibility by these skills. As a result, presenters naturally wish to perform as effectively as possible.

Because they recognize how much is riding on the strength of their oral communication skills, anxious speakers tend to set up unrealistic or negative objectives about what they need to accomplish during a presentation. Morton Orman (n.d.) identifies 11 causes of public speaking stress—6 of them unrealistic expectations (e.g., assuming a presentation must be perfect, trying to please everyone in an audience, or trying to control audience response). (Of the five other factors, three of them deal with preparing the message content and two with a speaker's perceptions of stress and delivery style.) For presenters to set virtually unattainable goals (such as trying to please everyone in an audience) almost guarantees failure to accomplish their objectives. As a result, presenters may feel that failure and thus approach the next presentation with a negative anticipation of the outcome.

Essentially, a presenter's anxiety starts a cycle of stress that stems from unrealistic expectations set while preparing for a presentation. This stress results in a feeling of frustration at the end of the presentation because of unrealized goals. Then the frustration carries over into preparation for the next presentation, thus recycling itself over a series of speaking sessions.

Are Some Times in a Presentation More Stressful Than Others?

Although it's tempting to feel that presentations in general create anxiety, most individuals can anticipate degrees of psychological and physiological anxiety—as well as varying levels of intensity—during specific points in the presentation process. Reviewing over two decades of presentation research, Sawyer and Behnke (1999) found specific anxiety responses in speakers at each of the traditional presentation stages: anticipatory, confrontation, adaptation, and release. They also note that anxiety is particularly evident in the first two stages. If presenters understand what nervousness pattern to expect during each of these two stages, they can begin to manage the anxiety that manifests itself before they actually step in front of an audience.

Stage 1—Anticipatory or Preparation

The preparation phase of a presentation typically includes thoughts, images, and feelings affecting a presenter at any time prior to being introduced to an audience. This stage includes the "butterflies" speakers can get just before they start speaking—as well as the anxious feelings experienced by a presenter while preparing in the days or months prior to an event itself. General opinion is that presenters experience anticipatory anxiety because they dread the moment they must stand in front of an audience. And indeed, research confirms the fact that presenters do experience greater *physiological* anxiety (sweaty palms, increased heart rate, etc.) at the time they step up to face an audience (the confrontation stage) and begin speaking than at any other time during a presentation. However, Sawyer and Behnke

(1999) found that speakers experience more *psychological* anxiety (worry, negative, or catastrophic thinking) in the anticipatory phase than in the confrontation stage. Presenters who recognize that they may be prone to excessive worrying or negative thinking prior to a presentation session itself can use behavioral or cognitive modification techniques to deal positively with the stress of an upcoming presentation.

Stage 2—Confrontation

The beginning of the confrontation stage overlaps to some extent the end of the anticipatory stage. The confrontation stage is the segment of the presentation process when a presenter arrives at the presentation site; it ends just after the speaker moves to the front of the room and starts speaking. According to research surveyed by Sawyer and Behnke (1999), physiological CA is usually at its peak during the confrontation phase. Once in front of an audience, anxious presenters could experience various physical responses, including a number of inhibited or suppressed behaviors such as monotone delivery, severely limited gestures, and little to no facial variation (Freeman, Sawyer, & Behnke, 1997). For overly anxious speakers, these traits could have the effect of making the presenter—and the presentation—appear uninteresting. Presenters who experience anxiety can use one or more calming methods to reduce this anxiety in preparing themselves to step in front of an audience.

Once well into the presentation message, presenters usually experience a lessening sense of CA. In communication research, this time period is called the "adaptation stage." While in this stage, speakers receive feedback or cues (visual, nonverbal, or verbal) from audience members, and they begin adjusting to the physical effects of anxiety. Research shows that speakers' physiological heart rates tend to slow down as a presentation proceeds, and the psychological anxiety is reduced (Sawyer & Behnke, 1999). This suggests that once speakers pass the initial anxiety "hump" in the confrontation stage, they adapt to the presentation situation. Presenters who understand these typical responses to the various points in a presentation can learn to anticipate them and deal with the anxieties at each stage in the presentation process.

REDUCING ANXIETY LEVELS

Communication experts have developed numerous strategies to help speakers begin to diffuse some of the anxiety they experience before and during presentations. This section examines the following four methods to reduce presentation anxiety:

1. Systematic desensitization
2. Cognitive modification
3. Visualization
4. Skills training

Systematic desensitization (SD) and cognitive modification (CM) are similar in recommending specific steps to combat anxiety. The essential difference between the two methods is that SD addresses what a speaker can *do* to reduce nervousness while CM focuses on how a speaker *perceives* and *feels* presentation anxiety. The third method, visualization, involves an individual repeatedly imagining himself or herself successfully presenting to an appreciative audience. And the fourth method, skills training, helps presenters focus on specific tasks in preparing for a presentation.

Systematic Desensitization

Using SD nervous presenters take small, incremental steps to experience a speaking situation while they learn to relax in the process. The theory in presentation SD is that people feel anxious in large part because they associate negative consequences with standing in front of an audience and making a presentation. To begin to modify these negative associations, M. Allen, J.E. Hunter, and W.A. Donohue, advocate using SD as a method to change "that association by exposing the speaker to the phobia and causing the speaker to involuntary associate more pleasant responses with the speaking situation" (Allen, Hunter, and Donohue, 1989, p. 58).

Using the SD method, a nervous presenter would learn a variety of relaxation strategies (e.g., controlled breathing, deep relaxation techniques, visual imaging, and reciting a simple mantra) before beginning a series of exposures to the presentation experience. These assignments might begin as a benign experience and progressively move to more intense and anxiety-provoking ones. To illustrate, an individual could start a desensitization process by watching a video of someone making a public presentation. Next, the person might attend a public presentation. Third, she might begin researching a topic for a presentation. Each step exposes the speaker a bit more to the actual experience of giving a presentation—without the immediate threat at the beginning of the SD exercises of speaking directly to a group. As the individual's anxiety increases with each progressive step, the speaker would focus on implementing the relaxation techniques learned at the beginning of the exercise. The purpose of SD is to *gradually* expose speakers to increasingly stressful situations while simultaneously assisting them in learning how to manage anxiety by remaining calm and relaxed (Allen et al., 1989; Robinson, 1997).

Cognitive Modification

CM is a method for presenters to learn how to transform negative beliefs about presentations into more positive ones. This method encourages presenters to focus on identifying and discarding irrational or unreasonable expectations about upcoming presentations and then to replace those expectations with more positive and realistic thoughts. Nervous speakers essentially develop a "coping statement" (Allen et al., 1989, p. 58). Presenters who use CM to combat presentation anxiety learn to recognize exaggerated negative beliefs about presentations and reframe them more realistically. The following examples show how presenters might use CM to overcome unrealistic thoughts about an upcoming presentation:

- *"I might trip or fall down during my presentation."* Of course it has happened in rare circumstances, but this is a worst-case scenario that most presenters never encounter. Using the CM method, presenters can recognize how unlikely this scenario actually is. Additionally, they learn to take steps to minimize the possibility of falling down during a presentation. They could dress in comfortable clothing, practice planned movements, and observe prior to a session the physical setup of the room where they'll present. This type of attitude adjustment and preventative planning helps nervous speakers develop more realistic expectations for presentations.

- *"Everyone will rip apart my ideas."* Depending on the presentation purpose and the audience attitude, this concern may or may not be a realistic one for an anxious presenter. Using CM methods, presenters can learn to accurately identify an audience's true attitude toward a topic and toward a presenter. Audiences usually want presenters to succeed in delivering a dynamic and interesting presentation. They don't enjoy seeing speakers suffer from excessive nervousness, nor do they lie in wait to gleefully harass presenters (Davidson & Kline, 1999). If a presenter chooses a topic thoughtfully, researches it adequately, spends time organizing the material and practicing the delivery, it is highly unlikely that anyone, much less "everyone," will attack the speaker or the speaker's ideas. Using the CM approach, presenters can begin to see that many of their beliefs about presentations are unreasonable if certain basic conditions are met. Once the irrational beliefs are identified and negated, presenters can replace the negative mental images or thoughts (such as, "I'll forget everything I want to say") with more positive, self-soothing thoughts (such as, "I've thoroughly prepared this presentation, and the information is valuable for my audience").

Examples of negative ideas that CM helps to modify include the following (among many others):

- "They will hate me."
- "I can't do this."
- "I have nothing to say."
- "I'll never get all of this information together."
- "The audience is just waiting for me to make a mistake or stumble over my words so they can laugh."
- "I'll forget my presentation when I stand up there."

CM helps speakers develop a series of mental thoughts to have ready if anxiety and negativity strike during a presentation. A presenter could tell himself, "I'm OK." He might figure out small mantras he could repeat to himself (maybe those learned during the desensitization process) to relax. As anxious presenters concentrate on delivering a message, it likely will be difficult to develop elaborate images to use while presenting. They are better off developing a few short, yet emotionally powerful, messages that can be used over and over, if necessary. Examples of these might include the following: "Breathe in and out," "Slow down," "I'm fine," or "I can do this."

Obviously, in persons for whom anxiety is prevalent, the typical thoughts are usually negative. CM helps a person become aware of the types of negative thoughts they associate with a particular activity (e.g., making a presentation) and then assists them in channeling those thoughts into a more positive and soothing attitude toward an upcoming presentation.

Visualization

Proven to be effective in reducing CA, visualization is a technique that helps presenters "see" themselves relaxed, thoroughly prepared, supremely confident, and eager to get in front of a friendly and receptive audience (Ayres & Hopf, 1989).

Many professional athletes use visualization techniques before a competition: Golfers picture themselves hitting the perfect shot, sprinters visualize running the fastest race, figure skaters imagine hitting all their jumps and performing a flawless routine. For individuals who use visualization to minimize presentation CA, the goal is to imagine success; this becomes the foundation for thinking positively and feeling more confident and comfortable before and during a presentation.

J. Ayres and B. Heuett (1997) found that speakers who experience low communication anxiety believe themselves more in control during a presentation situation than those who feel high anxiety. The results of their research suggest that visualization plays a strong part in reducing nervousness because speakers feel that they're more in control of themselves, a presentation, or a presentation situation. Anxious presenters, on the other hand, feel a sense of helplessness or lack of control, thus increasing anxiety because they're not sure what they can expect.

Further, nervous presenters often visualize their lack of knowledge even though they've actually put considerable time and care into working on a project; realistically, they've become quite an expert on that material. Most anxious presenters know substantially more about their material than they give themselves credit for. But, instead of recognizing their strengths and expertise in a particular area, they tend to envision themselves negatively (Ayres & Heuett, 1997).

One way presenters can begin to visualize success is to recognize themselves as experts. In other words, congratulate yourself for being asked to make a presentation. That seems like such an odd statement to make to a presenter who dreads speaking to an audience. However, individuals who don't do a good job with projects, research, or client preparation, rarely are asked to make a presentation.

Skills Training

Skills training is probably the most popular singular strategy to help presenters deal with CA. In fact, Robinson (1997) learned that 96 percent of respondents to a survey on CA treatments in college and university public speaking courses use skills training. This method encourages nervous speakers to minimize CA by refining oral communication proficiencies through education, practice, and feedback (Allen et al., 1989).

Speakers using skills training focus on learning strategies to prepare for, develop, and then deliver effective presentations. As such, the process is task oriented, encouraging presenters to follow specific actions to achieve a desired result. Proper preparation, according to the skills training method, should help speakers reduce CA. For example, a presenter who thoughtfully focuses on a topic, researches it, outlines notes, and organizes cogent content should feel confident in the thoroughness of the message. Likewise, a presenter who spends quality time rehearsing or practicing delivery techniques and using visuals should feel prepared to confront an audience.

Following are two ways you can use skills training to begin reducing presentation anxiety.

1. Prepare Your Message and Visuals

Be as prepared as possible by thoroughly developing and preparing for a presentation. Of course, three significant parts of preparation are analyzing the audience, developing a well-organized message, and creating supporting visuals. You read in Chapter 2 that audience analysis informs presenters about the various demographic, corporate, and attitudinal factors in an audience. To know before walking in to a presentation that an audience of 10 midlevel managers are receptive to hearing your ideas about cost containment helps counteract a fear that an audience will be out to discover what you don't know. And if your audience analysis reveals that individuals at a session will have a negative attitude toward your message or your company, you can (as you learned in Chapter 3) organize what you have to say in a particular way to try and defuse the negative feelings and build common ground with an audience.

Write out message content in sentence form, if this technique will help you get started. And, as you refine it to fit within the time frame that you'll have to present, you can then massage the sentences into a phrase outline. Consider this extra work a way to help you feel more comfortable with the material and thus reduce the stress associated with presentations.

Once you've written down the text version of what you wish to say and condensed it into notes format, then develop visuals to support and illustrate message content. One study (Menzel & Carrell, 1994) shows that the amount of preparation time correlates with the level of content and delivery quality. The same study also found that the amount of time that subjects spent designing visual aids makes a difference in the level of thought content. The researchers theorized that those subjects who spend time developing visual aids more effectively concretize abstract thinking and thus demonstrate a more advanced level of thought. Ultimately, the study concludes that highly anxious presenters who prepare well can minimize their presentation nervousness (Menzel & Carrell, 1994). To this end, focus on helping an audience visualize ideas through use of PowerPoint or other visuals. Use the strategies you learned in Chapters 5 and 6 to develop the best method to illustrate your ideas. You'll feel confident when you're done that you've put together the most polished version possible because you've spent so much time on the message and visuals.

Following these steps (i.e., analyzing the audience, organizing message content, and preparing visuals) will help reduce stress because you'll know that you're as prepared as possible before stepping in front of an audience. You're now ready to rehearse the presentation.

2. Practice, Practice, Practice

Obviously, any anticipatory anxiety can affect a presenter's thought process and creativity, influencing such factors as the amount of time given to the preparation of a presentation and the attention and focus applied to it. In fact, anxiety over an anticipated presentation may actually cause a presenter to reduce preparation time. Although nervousness can affect individuals in a variety of ways, studies indicate that significant levels of anxiety in the preparatory phase of developing a presentation will influence an individual to avoid preparing the presentation until as late as possible. Procrastination in working on a presentation is a classic sign that some form of anxiety is at work.

Practice giving your presentation—out loud—several times so that you'll feel confident in your delivery skills. In their study, Menzel and Carrell (1994) found that their subjects who rehearsed out loud in front of an audience appeared to have a better performance. Presenters may know their material, but no amount of reading, writing, or creating visuals can replace practicing a presentation aloud at home, in front of a colleague, or in your own office.

The most ambiguous stage of getting ready for presentation is knowing when to begin practicing it aloud. Some presenters want to have the message completely developed, the notes printed and ready, and the visuals created and loaded onto the computer before they begin practicing delivery. And as a result, they keep tinkering with the message text and the visuals until it's almost time to deliver the presentation; then they begin practicing out loud. To complicate matters, some presenters also expect their first spoken version to be perfect—after all they've been working hard on the message and the visuals!

Most of us don't speak exactly the way that we think. Consider job interviews that you've had. You may have thought long and hard about how to answer questions that interviewers might ask. And you may have solid experience to draw from in responding. But, if you've not practiced speaking your answers out loud, you probably found that you sometimes stumbled over what you wanted to say and how you said it. The next time you answered those particular questions, you likely were able to better articulate your answer.

Let's also draw a comparison between a presentation and a stage production. Few actors review their scripts silently and then jump directly into a commanding performance. Instead, they practice lines out loud with other actors to encourage and respond to them. Practicing presentations isn't all that different from rehearsing for a stage production. When to raise volume to emphasize a particular point, how to smoothly move between transitions with pauses at appropriate times, how to build information on a slide as the material is being discussed—these are all tasks that will build confidence for a presenter. The earlier you begin verbalizing a message, the more polished your delivery will be—and the higher your confidence level will be. Start practicing a presentation out loud as soon as you have a basic notes draft. Rehearse from start to finish without stopping to buff each section of the presentation before moving to the next. You'll have a better feel for the flow of the whole message if you'll practice it in its entirety.

Although researchers have shown that any one of these CA reduction techniques—systematic desensitization, cognitive modification, visualization, and skills training—can help presenters reduce anxiety, further studies evidence that no one method is more effective than a combination of methods (Allen, Hunter, and Donohue, 1989; Fordham & Gabbin, 1996; Robinson, 1997). Interestingly, when each of the methods were individually implemented and compared with one another for effectiveness, skills training alone turned out to be the least effective method for decreasing anxiety (Fordham & Gabbin, 1996). This finding suggests that although refining skills helps build a solid base for handling apprehension related to giving a presentation, anxiety will not abate simply because a presenter has developed additional skills. An anxious presenter needs methods for coping with the predictable increase in psychological and physiological states of anxiety that will inevitably occur as a speaker prepares for and then delivers a presentation.

The following practical strategies combine elements of all four coping strategies that you can use to work toward a confident presentation presence.

■ *Create a supportive climate for practicing.* Gather a group of colleagues and/or friends with whom to practice. Schedule this practice session with plenty of time to relax before and after the rehearsal. Have your group complete the presentation checklist in Exhibit 7.1 for each individual who delivers a presentation. Ask for feedback that is both supportive and constructive.

■ *Videotape your presentation practices.* This exercise helps you realize that you probably don't appear to an audience as nervous as you might feel. If you completed Exercise 5 in Chapter 4 (videotaping yourself giving a presentation and then analyzing it), you realized that the audience likely sees you as a confident, poised presenter. You may feel that your knees shake, your voice quavers, and your every nerve shows, but the audience doesn't see you that way. If you've not yet videotaped yourself presenting, do so and show the tape to friends or colleagues to ask their impression of you. Use the confidence checklist in Exhibit 7.2 to get feedback from others about your performance on the tape.

EXHIBIT 7.1   Presentation checklist.

Message Content

- How did the opening connect with the audience?

- Did the presenter give an agenda? Did the agenda have the appropriate number of key points for the time allotted?

- What was the context of the presentation?

- Did the presenter list and then provide support for each of the key points?

- How did the presenter wrap up the presentation?

Delivery Techniques

- What were the strengths of the presenter's voice (e.g., rate, tone, volume)?

- What were the weaknesses of the presenter's voice (e.g., rate, tone, volume)?

- How did the presenter move?

- How much verbal clutter did the presenter use (eg., "ah," "uhm," "like," "you know")?

- How did the presenter's notes look?

- How enthusiastic was the presenter?

- Did the presenter stay within the time limits?

Overall

- What were the key strengths of the presentation?

- What were the major weaknesses?

- What should the presenter do to correct the weaknesses?

EXHIBIT 7.2   Confidence checklist.

❏ *Posture:* Does the presenter stand erect and look comfortable and confident?

❏ *Eye contact:* Does the presenter maintain direct eye contact with individuals in the audience throughout the presentation?

❏ *Gestures:* Does the presenter gesture to emphasize points and otherwise leave hands and arms down comfortably at sides?

❏ *Voice volume:* Does the presenter have a well-modulated voice that projects easily to the back of the room?

❏ *Rate of speech:* Does the presenter speak at a measured pace so that the audience can easily understand each word?

❏ *Verbal clutter:* Does the presenter avoid unnecessary "clutter words" such as "uhm," "ah," "like," or "you know"?

❏ *Space in relation to audience:* Does the presenter interact personally with the audience, avoiding placing barriers between the presenter and the audience (e.g., consoles, lecterns)?

❏ *Comfort with visuals:* Does the presenter appear practiced in using the visuals?

❏ *Comfort with message:* Does the presenter appear assured about the quality and value of the message that's being delivered?

❏ *Enthusiasm:* How much energy and enthusiasm does the presenter appear to have about the message and the audience?

■ *Get to know individuals in your audience.* The Toastmasters organization encourages speakers to greet audience members as they arrive (Morrow, 2001). Introduce yourself and briefly interact with several people prior to a session starting. You'll find that having people in the audience whom you know will help you feel more confident than if you are speaking to a group of complete strangers. You'll have made connections with individuals.

■ *Breathe deeply.* As you're getting ready to walk into a room to meet an audience, pause to take a couple of slow, deep breaths. Visualize yourself walking into the room and making eye contact immediately with those already in the room. Just before you get up to begin the presentation, take a couple more deep breaths. Feel yourself breathing. Focus on drawing in air and then letting it out slowly.

■ *Exercise.* Even if you're not an exercise buff, take time the day before and the morning or afternoon of your presentation to walk off some of that nervous energy. If you're in a building with stairs, try walking at a brisk pace up a couple of flights and then coming back down. If the presentation is scheduled for the afternoon, take a brisk lunchtime walk. You don't need to break a sweat; the physical activity will help reduce nervousness by working off excess energy. As you're walking, visualize the positive reception you'll receive during and after the presentation. See yourself looking out confidently over the audience and commanding their attention. Congratulate yourself on being prepared!

■ *Avoid excessive caffeine and food.* If you normally have a couple cups of coffee or soda in the morning, by all means, don't change your routine. But, avoid having more than you usually do to either settle your nerves or to stimulate you. Make a point of bringing a couple of bottles of water with you that day just in case you need fluids. If your presentation is just after breakfast or lunch, eat lightly. You don't want to feel sleepy during a session, so eat a lighter-than-usual meal prior to presenting. And, if the session you're attending involves a meal, try to eat sparingly or after your presentation.

■ *Welcome your nervousness.* Mild anxiety can actually be good for presenters because it can make them more alert and boost the energy level. Even presenters who say they aren't nervous often will experience slight butterflies right before an important presentation. And they'll use that nervousness to their advantage as a stimulant to help them improve performance.

ANALYZING PERFORMANCE TO ENHANCE CONFIDENCE

As you've read in this chapter, communication experts typically break the presentation process into four stages: anticipatory, confrontation, adaptation, and release (Sawyer & Behnke, 1999). For nervous presenters who wish to manage their anxieties more effectively, there's an additional stage to work with *after* a presentation session ends—the assessment stage. Once you're in a quiet place with time to reflect, assess your performance to see if you can pinpoint any particular area that needs more work. Think about what part of the presentation you felt uncomfortable verbalizing. Answer the following questions:

- Was the opening as polished as it could be? Did you set a positive, confident tone in it to carry through into the remainder of the presentation?
- Did you feel that each of your main points were as comprehensive as they needed to be?
- Did you stay true to your notes and the points you desired to make?
- Do you think that you closed with a strong, confident call to action?

Each of these questions will help you identify specific spots in a presentation that you might find more uncomfortable than others. If the presentation was videotaped, use the confidence checklist in Exhibit 7.2 to assess your confidence level from the perspective of the audience. Once you identify any particular point in the presentation process when you feel or look more anxious, you can focus on refining that part so that you'll be more confident at that point the next time you deliver a presentation.

Break down the presentation process into specific steps and then take each step one at a time to manage the process—and your nervousness. You may not be able to completely eliminate presentation anxiety, but you *can* recognize that you have control of the process itself. And, if you carefully develop your presentation at each stage of the continuum, you will know that you've done everything possible to craft and then deliver a polished presentation.

Students often tell me when they realize they've got to give several presentations in my class, "I'm scared to death to get up in front of people," or, "I'm not good at all at talking in front of a group." And these are college students nervous about standing up in front of other students in a classroom setting. While a classroom presentation can be a scary scenario for some presenters, magnify that anxiety level for someone assigned to present to a group of strangers, executives, or colleagues—and a business deal rides on how well the presentation goes. Most presenters have good reason to feel nervous! After all, they want to do well and present themselves, their ideas, and their company in the most professional way possible. It's only natural to feel nervous about wanting to perform well.

You've read in this chapter about several ways to minimize excessive anxiety about preparing for and delivering presentations; however, just reading this chapter won't help by itself. You'll need to practice—frequently—the techniques that you find here and learn from each of your presentations. Conquering your fears or calming anxieties is a long process that takes time, but you can manage your anxiety to deliver presentations confidently.

EXERCISES   Overcoming Presentation Anxieties

EXERCISE 1   Observing Confident Presentation Models

Attend a presentation and pay close attention to how the presenter behaves:

- What does the presenter do prior to starting the presentation?
- What cues suggest the presenter is prepared and confident before the presentation starts?
- When the presenter finishes the presentation, does he or she look assuredly around the room when asking for questions?
- What does the presenter do when the presentation is over?
- What were the presenter's key strengths?
- What were the presenter's major weaknesses? And, what advice would you give the presenter to overcome these weaknesses?

EXERCISE 2   Analyzing Confident Presenters

Attend a presentation and complete the confidence checklist in Exhibit 7.2 to analyze how confident the presenter appears to be.

EXERCISE 3   Observing Your Performance as a Confident Presenter

Self

Videotape one of your presentations and complete the confidence checklist in Exhibit 7.2.

Others

Ask a colleague or friend to view a videotape of one of your recent presentations and complete the confidence checklist in Exhibit 7.2.

EXERCISE 4   Visualizing Your Success

Sit down in a quiet, comfortable place and mentally walk through a presentation from the time you enter the room until the time you leave. Think about who you know will be in the audience. Envision how you'll walk to the podium/console/front of the room. See yourself confidently beginning the audience connection, making and supporting the key points, and wrapping up. Imagine the effectiveness of the visuals you'll use to support your message. Think about how much you know about the possible questions that your audience likely will ask. Don't forget to think also about how you'll handle questions that you might not know an answer to. What will you say? Finally, see yourself shaking hands with audience members as they file out of the room after the presentation. Visualize yourself accomplishing the purpose you set out to do when you took on this assignment. Good job!

EXERCISE 5   Setting Goals to Reduce Anxiety

Research shows that the most effective way to combat presentation anxiety is to combine several communication anxiety (CA) methods of coping. To map out your own plan to reduce nervousness, use the techniques you learned about in this chapter to detail how you plan to apply two or more methods. In the following table, write out two specific steps that you plan to take in working toward minimizing your presentation anxiety.

Method to Reduce Anxiety	Specific Steps to Take
Systematic desensitization (SD)	1. 2.
Cognitive modification (CM)	1. 2.
Visualization	1. 2.
Skills training	1. 2.

References

Allen, M., Hunter, J. E., & Donohue, W. A. (1989). Meta-analysis of self-report data on the effectiveness of public speaking anxiety treatment techniques. *Communication Education, 38*(1), 54–76.

Ayres, J., & Heuett, B. L. (1997). The relationship between visual imagery and public speaking apprehension [Electronic version]. *Communication Reports, 10*(1), 87–94.

Ayres, J., & Hopf, T. S. (1989). Visualization: Is it more than extra-attention? *Communication Education, 38*(1), 1–5.

Cohen, A. (1999). The right stuff. *Sales and Marketing Management, 151,* 15.

Curtis, D. B., Winsor, J. L., & Stephens, R. D. (1989). National preferences in business and communication education. *Communication Education, 38*(1), 6–14.

Daly, J. A., & Leth, S. (1976). Communication apprehension and the personnel selection decision. Paper presented at the annual convention of the International Communication Association, Portland, OR.

Davidson, W., & Kline, S. (1999). Ace your presentations [Electronic version]. *Journal of Accountancy, 187*(3), 61–63.

Fordham, D. R., & Gabbin, A. L. (1996). Skills versus apprehension: Empirical evidence on oral communication [Electronic version]. *Business Communication Quarterly, 59*(3), 88–97.

Freeman, T., Sawyer, C. R. & Behnke, R.R. (1997). Behavioral inhibition and the attribution of public speaking state anxiety. *Communication Education, 46,* 175–187.

Gorman, C. (2002, June 10). The science of anxiety. *Time,* 46–54.

Heuett, B. L. (1997). The relationship between visual imagery and public speaking apprehension [Electronic Version]. *Communication Reports, 10*(1).

The Juilliard School. (n.d.). Course descriptions: Performance practice. Retrieved May 29, 2002, from http://julliard.edu/evening/courses_performance.html.

Kearney, P., & McCroskey, J. C. (1980). Relationships among teacher communication style, trait and state communication apprehension and teacher effectiveness. In D. Nimmo (Ed.), *Communication Yearbook* 4 (pp. 533–551). New Brunswick, NJ: Transaction Books.

Laskowski, L. (n.d.). Overcoming speaking anxiety in meetings & presentations. Retrieved July 2, 2002, from www.speaking.com/articles_html/LennyLaskowski_532.html

McCroskey, J. C. (1977). Oral communication apprehension: A summary of recent theory and research. *Human Communications Research, 4,* 78–96.

Menzel, K. E., & Carrell, L. J. (1994). The relationship between preparation and peformance in public speaking. *Communication Education, 43*(1), 17–26.

Messmer, M. (1999). Skills for a new millennium [Electronic version]. *Strategic Finance, 81*(2), 10–12.

Morrow, E. P. (2001). One of America's top financial writers explains making better presentations. *Financial Services Advisor, 144*(3), 27–31.

National Communication Association. (1998). How Americans communicate. Retrieved April 1, 2002, from www.natcom.org/research/Roper/how_americans communicate_htm

Orman, M. C. (n.d.). How to conquer public speaking fear. Retrieved June 19, 2002, from www.stresscure.com/jobstress/speak.html

Robinson, T. E., II (1997). Communication apprehension and the basic public speaking course: A national survey of in class treatment techniques. *Communication Education, 46*(3), 188–197.

Sawyer, C. R., and Behnke, R. R. (1999). State anxiety patterns for public speaking and the behavior inhibition system [Electronic version]. *Communication Reports, 12*(1), 33–41.

Strout, E. (2001). The show must go on [Electronic version]. *Sales and Marketing Management, 153*(11), 52–59.

Waner, K. K. (1995). Business communication competencies needed by employees as perceived by business faculty and business professionals. *Business Communication Quarterly, 58*(4), 51–56.

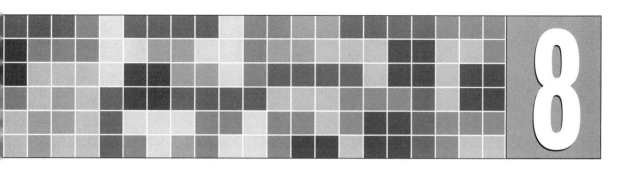

Handling Q&A
(Question-and-Answer Session)

PERFORMANCE GOALS

After completing this chapter, readers will be able to:

- research potential questions and prepare to answer them
- recognize different types of questions and respond accordingly
- apply effective delivery techniques when answering questions

Effective planning for the Q&A (question-and-answer) session is critical for a successful presentation. The final impression an audience will have of a presenter is directly tied to what the presenter says—and how he or she says it—toward the end of a presentation and in the Q&A session. Additionally, research indicates that audiences consistently recall presentation openings and closings more than any other part of an oral message (Bovée & Thill, 2000; Kiechel, 1987).

Presenters typically prepare long hours for a presentation, putting in significant amounts of time crafting a message, practicing delivery, and designing complex graphics to illustrate points. After such intensive planning, they're ready to deliver the message to an audience. The brief—but vitally important—Q&A after a presentation, however, appears to some presenters to be entirely separate from the presentation itself. I once heard a diligent professional say that she'd spent hours planning for a 30-minute presentation. She researched her audience, knew the material, and crafted well-designed visuals. Yet she told me that when she finished and asked for questions from the audience, she hoped no one would ask anything.

What makes the Q&A session such a challenge for presenters? Ken Haseley (2001) attributes the trepidation with which speakers approach the end of a presentation to a fear of losing control of the session to the audience. After all, speakers who ask an audience to hold questions until the end of a presentation "have the floor" and control the tempo, flow, and direction from start to finish. The Q&A session, however, invites an audience to participate. Presenters who aren't comfortable in the fluid exchange of ideas with an audience during a Q&A may feel nervous about moving away from the more scripted presentation material. They may worry about what people in the audience might ask. . . and what if someone asks something they don't know how to answer?

By anticipating and planning for questions, presenters can prepare as carefully for a Q&A session as for a presentation itself. Of course, that's not to say that presenters can anticipate all possible questions that an audience may ask. Nor will an audience expect a presenter to address all potential questions in a short period of time. Nevertheless, Chapter 8 will help presenters prepare as efficiently as possible for what to expect when they tell an audience that they'll be delighted to answer questions. This chapter covers the following topics:

- Preparing for questions
- Anticipating different question types
- Addressing questions
- Using effective delivery techniques

To master these strategies is to position yourself as confident, professional, and poised in a Q&A session. Your confidence and credibility while "thinking on your feet" as an audience asks questions demonstrates how well you've prepared to present a message to that particular audience.

PREPARING FOR QUESTIONS

The art of a Q&A session is much like fielding questions in job interviews—the best preparation is to anticipate potential questions and plan how to structure answers. Someone interviewing for a job, for example, should spend time reviewing material on the résumé because an interviewer likely will ask questions about the information listed on it. To prepare, a recruit needs to think about what experiences on the résumé best match up with the skills an interviewer might be looking for. If a job involves significant collaborative work, for example, a recruit can anticipate questions about teamwork skills. Or, if a company's goal is to hire someone who has substantial self-motivation, a recruit should expect a few questions about entrepreneurial experiences.

The same premise about planning for interview questions holds true for presentation Q&A as well. Speakers should consider the presentation purpose, individuals in the audience, and the topic itself to anticipate what questions audience members might ask. Or, if a speaker knows that the purpose of a presentation is to convince a group to act on a recommendation, she should take into consideration what objections or concerns individuals might have. Presenters need to address specific objections during a presentation or expect questions in the Q&A spurred by objections to the topic. If an audience analysis indicates a few audience members traditionally want more data than can possibly be provided in the time span of a presentation, presenters should prepare to answer such in-depth questions and have additional data available when the questions are raised.

To start planning for a Q&A session, answer the following two questions as you're developing presentation content:

1. *What has been excluded from the presentation content?* Of course, presenters can't say everything there is to know about any given topic. Audiences don't expect presenters to cover all details within a limited time frame. Speakers may have spent months on a market research project, for example, and only have 30 to 45 minutes to explain it to an audience. You read in Chapter 3 how to limit the scope of a topic to two or three key ideas. As you filter out information that you won't cover within the allotted time, put this collateral material in a special folder. The information in the folder isn't unimportant; rather, it doesn't

fit within the time or the topic scope of that particular presentation. Reviewing the contents of the folder just prior to the presentation session will remind you about important points left out of the message—points that someone may ask about. Additionally, the recognition that you've got a lot more to talk about than what you covered in a presentation will help you welcome an opportunity to expand on ideas. *Make a list of questions that someone might ask about information that you didn't include in the presentation message.*

2. *What questions will people who disagree with your points likely ask?* Presenters will find it impossible to deliver persuasive messages without some people being, at best, resistant to their ideas. Some may even be outright hostile. And in informative messages, some audience members might be skeptical of the information or a speaker's intentions because they may believe the message will result in changes that won't benefit them. So don't realistically expect a contented, satisfied audience that will be ready at the close of a presentation to adopt your way of thinking without question. But the presenter-audience relationship during a Q&A session isn't an adversarial one either—instead, consider it an extended opportunity to share more information with an audience. A Q&A session is a time for you to provide more information than you could during the presentation. *Make a list of questions that someone might ask if they disagreed with your recommendations or data.*

Categorize question topics—and review areas in a presentation that may need more support. Once you've developed potential audience questions based on what you've left out of a presentation or what audience members might object to, supplement these with other likely questions. Diane Diresta and Pamela Leigh (1996) suggest that presenters organize three lists of questions:

1. Questions that you expect and that you believe you already know the answers to
2. Questions that you expect and that you don't feel confident yet in answering
3. Questions that challenge you or your topic, or "all the questions that you dread." (p. 21)

Diresta and Leigh recommend that presenters practice the answers to the first list, research answers to the second, and plan how to respond to those in the third. Essentially, question lists give presenters an outline to use in preparing specific answers to each question.

Once you've jotted down all the possible questions to anticipate, take time to then write down—in phrases—the answers you'll use in response. There's no need to write complete sentences because this exercise is simply to help you begin organizing your thoughts. Anticipating the questions and considering how to answer them is a good exercise to prepare for a presentation Q&A session. It's simply not enough, however, to list the questions and sketch out possible responses—actually practicing answers out loud is the key element to producing polished, confident answers.

As with interview answers and presentation delivery techniques, some-times what presenters *think* won't necessarily come across as polished when they *verbalize* a response for the first time. To most effectively prepare, prac-tice fielding questions privately and then again later in front of a colleague or two. Try a mock Q&A session by having a colleague ask questions from your list in a random order.

There's no substitute or shortcut to preparing for the Q&A session. An-ticipate specific questions prior to a session and prepare to answer them by practicing—out loud—how you'll respond. This intensive presentation prepa-ration will give you more confidence in how to handle questions that you'll likely get in a Q&A. Additionally, it will minimize the stress that you may feel in answering the one or two questions that might surprise you.

ANTICIPATING DIFFERENT QUESTION TYPES

The majority of questions that an audience will ask generally fall into four main categories: queries, clarification, confirmation, and challenge. Fol-lowing are some of the types of questions to expect from each category and how you can respond to each type. Additionally, at the end of this section, I've briefly addressed a situation that may arise in some Q&A sessions—audience members who ask questions that aren't really questions—I call these "self-validation questions."

Query Questions

Query questions are often simply requests for more information. A presenter or idea intrigued someone in an audience who wants to know more than what a pre-senter addressed: Perhaps a person asking a question wants to understand more about the context or background of a message. Or, an individual wishes to explore a thread of a topic that a presenter didn't have time to address. Ba-sically, an audience member asking a query question wants to learn more about an issue related to the ideas expressed in the presentation. You'll rarely find a hidden agenda or negative attitude behind this type of question.

Following are a few examples of some common query-type questions:

- What is the full name of the acronym you used, HELOC?
- How do you see our company's strategy on cost containment fitting in with the larger industry trends?
- Could you expand on what you believe will be the impact of our re-cent board decisions on our policy of customer-driven service?

You can see from the language and tone of these examples that the ques-tioners simply want additional information. Individuals asking query ques-tions view the presenter as an expert and wish to learn more.

Consider query questions an opportunity to talk more about a topic that you already know well, to use some information you may have filed away while preparing for a presentation because you recognized you couldn't cover it during the time you had available. Because a questioner wants to learn from you and your experience, you can discuss information about the topic that didn't fit into the presentation due to time or scope limitations. I'm always delighted, for example, when someone asks after a short workshop on presentations about how to handle a Q&A session. Because of time constraints, I'm often not able to talk about strategies for a Q&A session unless it comes up during the actual Q&A!

Clarification Questions

Clarification questions generally are requests for more information or support about a key point made in the presentation. Because audience members aren't able to go back and re-read information, as they can with a written document, someone may ask a clarification question so that a presenter will repeat information or elaborate more on a specific point. Presenters may spend days, weeks, even months working on material for a presentation; however, audience members may be hearing the information details for the first time. Generally, clarification questions target issues that presenters have briefly addressed in a presentation. But either a presenter didn't flesh out the details to the degree that an audience wants or an audience needs to hear more to better understand the recommendation or ideas.

Here are some sample clarification questions:

- "You mentioned _____ in your second main point. Can you talk a bit more about that?"
- "Would you go through the steps in _____ for us once more?"
- "What were your resources for the graphic that showed _____ ?"

As is the case with the query questions, the language and tone of clarification questions indicate that the audience is interested in the material that was presented. Clarification questions are neutral or friendly in attitude toward the material and the presenter.

To respond to clarification questions, simply restate for the rest of the audience a summary of the part(s) of the presentation that the questioner asked about. Be patient and gracious, even if you believe that you already thoroughly covered the material requested. People filter information in different ways, and you may need to explain a point slightly differently in responding to a question than the way you did when addressing the same issue within the presentation. Take care, however, to avoid saying, "As I stated _____ . . ." This may embarrass a questioner, indirectly scolding him or her for not listening during a presentation. Instead, repeat or expand on the information an audience member asks about. And if the situation seems appropriate, put the slide for the point in question back up on the screen and rephrase what you said when you originally showed the slide.

Confirmation Questions

Confirmation questions often don't come in the form of a question. In this type of question, audience members want to make a statement about one or more of a speaker's points to reemphasize key ideas or to further flesh out what a presenter has said. To illustrate, perhaps a topic touches on an agenda that a particular audience member has been advocating for some time in the company. Or, perhaps a presentation was so convincing that the presenter "sold" the audience on the recommendation, and someone wants to express enthusiasm for the ideas. If a confirmation question actually does come in the form of a question, it typically calls for a closed-ended response; a speaker could answer simply "yes" or "no" and then repeat specific information to drive home the point to the audience.

Following are a few examples of confirmation questions:

- "So you're saying that we should consider implementing a formal email policy to help the company avoid potential liability issues?"
- "We should be able to walk out of here with the tools you've given us and begin selling this product immediately, right?"
- "As I'm hearing it here, we'll benefit from the new electronic billing system by decreasing the amount of time we spend preparing, sending, and handling our current paper system."

Notice that the last bulleted item isn't in the form of a question but does ask for the presenter to affirm the statement. If a confirmation question supports the ideas presented, a speaker can gauge from the audience's reaction to the question if the questioner's ideas need to be restated—or if a simple nod "yes" will suffice. Or, a presenter could put back up the slide that the questioner references and reemphasize the point with a visual.

Confirmation questions typically come from audience members who have a positive attitude toward the topic; they agree with the presenter and want to either show that they've understood the point or they want to show others in the audience that they agree with that particular issue.

Challenge Questions

Challenge questions are those that indicate the questioner has concerns with the material or (in some cases) with the presenter. If you are presenting material that you know may impact the audience negatively, expect challenge questions. For example, if a presenter is talking with a group of salespeople and explaining a new evaluation system that will increase goals, he can expect challenge questions from some of these people; after all, they're not going to be happy that their goals are going up. Or, a speaker making a pitch to a client who might have had a less than positive experience in the past with the product or service being sold can anticipate that the client will have some hard questions. And unfortunately, sometimes challenge questions can be explicitly hostile. If a presenter is unfamiliar with the corporate politics of an audience, he may be caught inadvertently in a clash between two political factions. The politics would be revealed in the form of challenge questions about presentation content.

In general, challenge questions tend to exhibit a negative language and tone toward the presenter and/or the topic and will focus on what's *not* in a presentation. The examples below show challenge questions.

> "I'm **concerned** that you're **underestimating** the numbers in your forecast data. . . ."

> "You **don't** take into account our position on _____. How do you account for that?"

> "The company seems to be wanting to **run off** the older workers with this policy. Why is this?"

Note the words in bold font. The questioner may place emphasis on certain words to show a disagreement with the material. In addition to the negative language in the question, it's likely that the questions also carry an angry or forceful tone.

The best way to respond to resistance or challenge questions is to first diffuse your own defensiveness. Someone asking challenge questions typically isn't attacking the presenter but presentation content or an issue in general. Even if a questioner is attacking the presenter, however, it's critical for a speaker to maintain professionalism and avoid being defensive. Rephrase the question in more positive language and then answer it. For example, to answer the question, "The company seems to be wanting to **run off** the older workers with this policy. Why is this?" you might respond, "Our company values all workers, and I think I hear you asking what criteria the company used to develop the new policy?" Push past the negative language to pinpoint exactly what the questioner wants to know.

If you reasonably expect challenge questions due to the nature of your presentation content, Diresta and Leigh (1996) recommend using a note card strategy in the Q&A. This method of answering questions involves having audience members write their questions on note cards during a presentation. Presenters can collect cards at a break or at the end of the session and select questions to respond to. This approach gives speakers a brief space of time to review questions and rephrase them in a more positive tone.

Bob Lucas (personal communication, December 2001), who works for a major government department, says that his group frequently uses the note card Q&A strategy when presenting for regional workshops about regulations. Because these workshops are open to the public and often address controversial topics, the presenters typically expect some resistance from various audience members. To most effectively answer questions in a positive fashion, this group announces the Q&A structure prior to the presentation and collects the question cards during breaks. This strategy neutralizes any potential negativity by giving the presenters the opportunity to rephrase questions with more positive language and tone before responding.

Self-Validation Questions

Self-validation questions typically aren't really questions at all. Instead, questioners use them as an opportunity to take the floor and air opinions about the topic. Often, self-validation questions are long, sometimes in two or three parts, and in the form of a statement. Sometimes these questioners barely mention the topic and launch instead into their own agenda. Unless you know the questioner and the corporate situation, there's no way to understand the motivation behind self-validation questions. For example, a questioner may be someone new to the company trying to show off knowledge in an area related to the topic. A questioner may be someone who wants to participate in the session to show that he or she is important to the meeting, department, or company. Or, a presentation may have touched on a hot topic in the company, and a questioner is processing out loud the issue and the presentation material for the audience.

Consider self-validation questions to be either neutral or resistant. However, keep in mind that a presenter may simply be the catalyst for this question that really addresses a bigger topic already being discussed in the company. The best way to respond to self-validation questions is to clarify what the questioner is really asking about the presentation material. It very well may be that the questioner doesn't have a question for the presenter but for the audience. However, audiences expect presenters to sift through the potential question meanings and try to identify them. So, paraphrase in a concise fashion the statement a questioner makes and wrap it up in the form of what you think the question might be. Then ask a clarification question back to the questioner to see if you've understood what the questioner is trying to ask.

ADDRESSING QUESTIONS

Setting Expectations

It's always good practice to let an audience know how you plan to handle questions. Some firms, for example, may expect associates to ask questions during presentations; others may have a tradition of waiting to ask questions until the end of a session. Cue an audience early in a presentation about how you'd prefer to structure the Q&A to minimize interruptions if you plan on answering questions at the end. Or, if you want to handle questions throughout a session, let audience members know your expectation that they need to be more participatory with questions during the presentation itself. Share this information with an audience immediately following a presentation agenda and just before beginning the context (or background).

Either option for fielding questions (during the presentation or at the end) can be effective in the right circumstance. However, keep in mind the following two factors when planning the Q&A component:

- *Time.* if you've only a short amount of presentation time, ask an audience to hold questions until the end of the session. With limited time to provide a specific amount of information, you'll need to reserve the majority of a presentation to convey the necessary information.
- *Audience culture.* If your audience has rigid ideas about what it expects from a presenter, you'll need to be adaptable to that group's expectations. For example, if an audience is accustomed to waiting until the end of a presentation to ask questions, it may be difficult for audience members to change the pattern and ask questions during presentations—even if they're encouraged to do so.

You'll likely find, however, that audiences will be responsive to your request—as long as you let them know what to expect.

The following outlines list the benefits and drawbacks for each way to structure a Q&A session.

Q&A During a Presentation

Benefits

- Promotes a more interactive exchange with audience because presenter elicits participation while discussing the material
- Encourages a more informal relationship between audience and presenter
- Enhances a creative, problem-solving environment

Challenges

- Could take up too much time early in presentation if presenter addresses questions about material planned for later in the session
- Could force a presenter to go into more depth than he or she anticipated about points an audience wishes to discuss
- Could trip up presenters who may be uncomfortable moving information out of order or who might not realize until too late that they're spending too much time on an early point. As a result, presenters may be unable to finish the remainder of their presentation in the allotted time

Strategy

- If you decide to respond to questions during a presentation, pare down the key points. Build in more free time to fully answer questions during a presentation and don't try to pack as many points into the allowed time.

Q&A at the End of a Presentation

Benefits

- Effective way to wrap up a presentation and make sure an audience leaves with the key information
- Enables speakers to set out a clearly defined section in which to address questions; they then complete the presentation before opening up the floor to the audience
- Helps presenters stick to their time limit and cover all necessary points

Challenges

- Doesn't offer opportunity for audience members to ask questions while topic is fresh
- May prevent some audience members from asking questions because they're concerned a Q&A segment will cause the session to run longer than scheduled

Strategy

- Diffuse concerns that a presentation will go over the session limit by including in the call for questions a time span that you've allotted for Q&A. For example, "We've got about five minutes left, and I'd like to invite any questions about the material that I've covered." Then, keep an eye on the time and let an audience know when there's time for only one more question. This strategy helps an audience know that the speaker appreciates time constraints while keeping open the presentation session to handle questions.

Restating Questions

It's a good idea to restate a question if some audience members might not have heard it well. This ensures that everyone in the room understands what a questioner wants to know. Restating a question also helps a presenter in the following ways:

- Reframes the question if it's off topic and the presenter needs to tie the question more closely to the presentation purpose
- Validates the questioner by acknowledging the individual's spoken words
- Gives the presenter a brief space of time to think quickly how about to respond, as well as a brief time to gauge audience reaction to the question
- Clarifies the question if the presenter isn't exactly sure what the questioner wants to know

Of course, it's not necessary to restate all questions. If a question is asked clearly enough so that everyone in the room hears it, there's no need to restate it. Similarly, if a presenter understands the question and/or doesn't need a short space of time to frame an answer, there's no need to rephrase it.

Handling Questions Without an Immediate Answer

What do you do if someone asks a question and you don't know the answer? Many presenters fear the Q&A session because of this very scenario; after all, no professional wants to have to say, "I don't know." Yet, chances are, if you make presentations regularly, it will happen from time to time. In this day of rapidly evolving business practices, presenters simply can't know everything. And for the most part, audiences don't expect presenters to have all the answers on the spot. What they do expect, however, is for the presenter to get an answer for them.

If asked a question that you don't know the answer to, here are a few possible responses:

"I wish that I'd had time to look into that during my research. I can check that and send on some information to you within _____ time."

"I hadn't considered that option/perspective/possibility when I was preparing my presentation for you. I'll look into that and send the information to you within _____ time."

"We don't know how this will affect our _____ yet because we've not tried this strategy before. However, based on similar experiences other companies have had, we can speculate that _____."

In all three of these responses, the presenter acknowledges that there's no immediate answer. But notice in the first two bulleted responses that the presenter commits to getting information, if possible. If, however, a presenter agrees to follow up with audience members on specific issues, it's important to do so within the time frame given. Meeting that commitment reinforces presenter credibility.

Another option for presenters if asked a question that they can't answer immediately is asking an audience to be a resource. If, for example, you know that someone in an audience might be able to talk about a specific topic (and if the situation is conducive for this strategy), open the floor to audience members. Ask the audience for suggestions and moderate a brief discussion of the varying answers. Be confident enough in your own preparation to know that you might not be able to handle all questions and let the audience participate as "experts" in the Q&A session.

USING EFFECTIVE Q&A DELIVERY TECHNIQUES

Effective delivery techniques are just as important during a Q&A session as they are during the presentation proper. An audience constantly

checks a presenter's credibility against what she's saying, how she's saying it, and how she presents herself and her material. Thus, when a presenter ends a presentation by clicking to the black slide (or turning off the overhead projector) and asking for questions, all eyes in the audience turn to the presenter.

As you learned in Chapter 4, research has found that 65 to 90 percent of what a speaker communicates to an audience is nonverbal (McKay & Rosa, 2000). And Mehrabian (1971) postulates that an audience relies on less than 10 percent of the spoken word to determine a presenter's message meaning. Therefore, in a Q&A session, how a presenter manages nonverbal communication—volume, eye contact, and body movements—conveys a significant amount of information to an audience.

Volume

Continue to maintain strong volume when inviting questions. If presenters allow their volume to drop when they ask for questions, audiences may get the impression that they really don't want anyone to ask questions. A soft voice at this closing point in a presentation suggests the presenter lacks confidence. When you finish your concluding sentence in the wrap-up, take a breath and wait one or two seconds to use silence in emphasizing the change from the main part of the presentation into the Q&A. Then, as one of my colleagues, Susan Irons, likes to say, **boldly** invite the audience to ask questions. When answering questions, keep that volume strong; don't limit voice projection to wherever the questioner is sitting; make sure that everyone in the room can hear you clearly.

Eye Contact

During a Q&A session, look directly at individuals when they ask questions and concentrate intently on what they ask. Pay close attention to questioners' tone and nonverbal communication cues. Tone and nonverbal signals assist presenters in determining what type of question they're being asked so that they can then frame their answers accordingly. For example, someone with a warm, friendly tone who smiles when asking a question likely is asking a confirmation or clarification type of question. On the other hand, someone who uses a louder, hard tone combined with raised eyebrows and "closed" body posture may be asking a challenge question.

In particular, be sure to listen to the entire question and avoid interrupting before a questioner finishes. Then, when answering, start by looking at the questioner before making eye contact with the rest of the audience. Don't exclude other members of an audience just because one person asked a question. By watching their nonverbal cues, you'll learn valuable information from other audience members about how they feel about a question or what they think about a particular topic. Additionally, one question may elicit follow-up questions from other audience members, and consistent eye contact with the entire audience allows presenters to be more responsive to these follow-up questions.

Nonverbal Communication

Exhibit as much confidence in a Q&A session as in a presentation. Your body language should signal to audience members the message that you're interested in their questions. If, for example, a presenter fiddles with computer equipment or presentation materials during the Q&A session, an audience may get the impression that the presenter doesn't really care much for answering questions. If a presenter crosses his arms protectively in front of him or moves behind some physical object in the room, the audience may assume he's uncomfortable taking questions.

Instead of turning control over to the audience, demonstrate a readiness to answer questions. Stand squared to the audience with both arms in a natural position at your sides. Smile and let your nonverbal signals tell the audience that you're ready to answer their questions. Look intently at a questioner and nod your head while listening. Smile while answering if it's appropriate. This suggests comfort with the audience and the content material. I even like to walk a step or two toward a questioner, if possible, just to focus more intently on that individual and what that person is asking. Then, as I rephrase the question to confirm the meaning or begin my answer, I step back away from the questioner to open up my area of vision in order to include the entire audience.

Silence

Once a presenter asks for questions, *give audience members time to respond.* Make the invitation and simply look around at the audience. Ideally, several people will respond simultaneously. If not, wait 10 to 15 seconds to give individuals time to formulate their questions before closing the session. However, don't be discouraged if an audience doesn't have any questions. You could have thoroughly presented the material, and the audience might not have questions at that time.

A second or two of silence also can work well after restating a question or a concept before answering. Rather than rambling for a few sentences (essentially talking your way into an answer), pause to gather your thoughts and then begin a cogent, concise answer. A brief silence can have a positive effect because it refocuses an audience on the presenter and what the presenter is about to say.

TIME LIMIT RESTRICTIONS

I'd be remiss if I wrapped up a section on Q&A and didn't include a brief section about sticking strictly to the time limit during a Q&A session (if answering questions at the end of a presentation). Leave 3 to 5 minutes in a 20-minute presentation for questions, more in a longer one. You should reserve time to answer a few detailed questions. *And, keep an eye on the time!* When you notice about 30 seconds left in the Q&A session, begin wrapping it up by letting the audience know that the Q&A is coming to a close. Here are some possible ways to do this.

"We've only got a short time left, but I'd be glad to stick around after the presentation to answer additional questions."

"We've got less than a minute left, but I'll pass out my business cards; you're welcome to email additional questions to me."

"If you have additional questions, please send them to your direct supervisor who can get them to me. I'll be glad to send out a question-and-answer summary to everyone who is here."

Ideally, a Q&A session should end, at minimum, a minute or so prior to a presentation deadline.

Exhibit 8.1 summarizes key points about Q & A sessions.

EXHIBIT 8.1   Keys to Q&A sessions.

Plan Ahead

- Prepare for all potential questions.
  - List questions about material that you excluded from the presentation.
  - List questions about material that you know an audience may disagree with.
- Anticipate the types of questions that might be asked.
  - Query, Clarification, Confirmation, Challenge
- Decide when you want to answer questions (during or after a presentation).

Pay Attention

- Look directly at an individual asking a question.
- Listen intently to the entire question.
- Avoid handling presentation materials, computer equipment, or your notes while listening to questions and while answering.

Process the Question

- Answer the question that was asked and respond with specifics.
- Take time to reframe a question if you feel that it's a challenge question or if it's confusing; also, restate a question if you believe the audience might not have heard the question clearly.
- Keep your volume as strong and confident when answering questions as you did during the presentation.
- Maintain eye contact with the entire audience as you're answering each question (beginning with the person who asked the question).
- Feel comfortable pausing a second or two before answering a question in order to process how to frame an answer before speaking.

EXERCISES   Handling Q&A

EXERCISE 1   What Might They Ask Me?

To prepare for an upcoming presentation, complete the Q&A checklist in Exhibit 8.2.

EXHIBIT 8.2   Q&A checklist.

When do I want to answer questions?

_____   During a presentation
_____   After a presentation

What questions might an audience ask about material that I had to leave out of the presentation in order to stay within the scope of time or topic?

1.

2.

3.

4.

What areas of the presentation are more complex than others?

1.

2.

3.

4.

Based on my audience analysis, what areas of the presentation do I know that audience members might disagree with or be resistant to?

1.

2.

3.

4.

EXERCISE 2   How Will I Respond to What They Ask Me?

Draft an outline with bulleted responses to the list of questions you developed for Exercise 1.

EXERCISE 3   How Will I Come Across When They Ask Me?

Once you've completed Exercise 2, have a colleague randomly ask you questions from the list you developed for Exercise 1. Practice smoothing out the answers to the questions until you're comfortable with your responses. Ask your colleague to give feedback on your nonverbal communication cues.

EXERCISE 4   Assessing a Q&A Session

Attend a presentation and answer the following questions:

- How did the presenter ask for questions? What was your impression of the presenter's confidence and credibility at this point in the presentation?
- What were the presenter's nonverbal communication signals as he or she responded to questions (facial expressions, gestures, posture, stance, movement, tone, etc.)? Were they effective in portraying the presenter as a confident, competent professional? Why or why not?
- What did the presenter do and say if he or she didn't know an answer to one of the questions?

EXERCISE 5   Recognizing Question Types

Attend a different presentation than you did for Exercise 4. At the end of this presentation, listen carefully to the questions and try to write them down exactly as they're asked. After the presentation, categorize the questions based on what you learned in this chapter about how to recognize the different question types (Query, Clarification, Confirmation, Challenge, Self-Validation).

References

Bovée, C. L., & Thill, J. V. (2000). *Business Communication Today* (6th ed.). Upper Saddle River, NJ: Prentice Hall.

Diresta, D., & Leigh, P. (1996). Grace under pressure: Managing the Q&A. *Training and Development, 50*(5), 21–23.

Guffey, M.E. (1997). *Business Communication: Process & Product* (2nd ed.). South-Western College Publishing.

Haseley, K. (2001). Build bridges to make your Q&A session successful. *Presentations, 15*(11), 66.

Kiechel, W., III. (1987, June 8). How to give a speech. *Fortune, 115*(12), 179–182.

McKay, M., & Rosa, E. (2000). *The accountant's guide to professional communication: Writing and speaking the language of business.* New York: Harcourt.

Mehrabian, A. (1971). *Silent Messages.* Belmont, CA: Wadsworth, p. 44. Cited in Guffey (1997), p. 45.

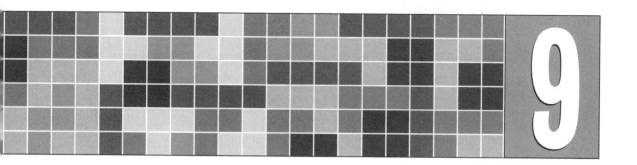

Presenting as a Team

PERFORMANCE GOALS

After completing this chapter, readers will be able to:

- identify and sharpen individual presentation strengths and challenges to mesh smoothly with team goals

- divide presentation tasks efficiently, including offering feedback and coaching during practice sessions

- convey professionalism and confidence before and during a presentation

Team presentations aren't all that different from individual presentations. Both follow the typical stages of the presentation process:

- Identify the presentation objective
- Analyze the audience
- Develop a message organized to accomplish the presentation goal
- Practice delivery skills
- Give the presentation
- Assess the effectiveness of the experience

Because more people are involved in team presentations, however, this type of presentation has unique benefits and challenges. On the one hand, responsibilities or tasks can be divided so that all team members share the workload fairly equitably. And presenters can rely on others' skills to supplement areas in which some team members may lack experience or strength. Further, individuals on a team can creatively build on each other's ideas so that the team develops a significantly better product than an individual could create. On the other hand, an audience will judge the effectiveness of a team presentation based on the whole—all presenters—not necessarily just on the strongest presenter. How a team executes when delivering a presentation colors an audience's perspective of team members and the credibility of the team's message. Clearly, a cohesive team presentation requires more than simply stitching together each individual's contribution.

Effective teams will be more resourceful and time efficient on a complex project than any one person could possibly be. A synergistic team will divide tasks, leverage each team member's skills, and end up with a product result that will surpass the creative energy of one individual. This chapter addresses the following concepts to maximize team dynamics for a presentation:

- Individuals make up teams
- Team strategies preparing for a presentation
- Team strategies during a presentation

These effective presentation teamwork concepts offer specific ideas for speakers to refine their contributions to a team as well as strategies to make a team more efficient and a presentation more unified.

INDIVIDUALS MAKE UP TEAMS

The success of any team is rooted in the combined contributions of its members. As my colleague Heidi Schultz is fond of saying, "Strong teams are made up of strong individuals." So, how can you prepare yourself to be a strong individual team member? Start by assessing the skills you have to offer:

- Presenter strengths and challenges
- Presenter work patterns

After you've read this chapter, complete the strengths and challenges assessment in Exhibit 9.1 and then develop an action plan to increase your effectiveness as a presenter. You can use the goals sheet in Exhibit 9.2 to address challenge areas. Those assessment and goal-setting steps will support you in refining your individual performance so that you can be as productive as possible in team presentation situations. Both of these exhibits are discussed in more detail below.

Presenter Strengths and Challenges

Think about the many tasks required to develop an effective presentation: research, analysis, organization, visuals development, practice, and assessment (just to name the primary ones). Although presenters may be exceptional in some areas and competent in others, it would be difficult for one individual to excel in all of these categories. Some presenters might enjoy doing research for presentations, for example, but would prefer to let others stand in front of a group to share that information. Others might be technology wizards and have a creative bent for helping audiences conceptualize complex information with a few well-designed graphics. Some people are more comfortable in the unstructured Q&A session, and some feel more at ease with notes and visuals.

While presenters may have preferences for and strengths in various presentation components, it's important to be as well-rounded as possible in each area in order to support a team effort. To polish individual skills, take the following steps:

1. Identify areas to work on
2. Map out a plan to begin improving these areas

EXHIBIT 9.1   Strengths and challenges assessment.

Presentation Component	Strength	Consistent	Challenge
Clearly understanding a presentation's purpose and goal—and able to state the goal succinctly			
Perceiving audience commonalities and differences based on prior experience and on audience analysis			
Thoroughly researching background information			
Organizing and prioritizing large amounts of material into concise segments			
Developing a clear, well-organized message with language appropriate to the audience			
Using technology to create electronic and hard-copy visuals			
Feeling comfortable delivering a presentation to a group			
Handling the Q&A session			
Following up after the presentation on any unanswered questions or requests for material			

EXHIBIT 9.2   Presentation goals sheet.

1. The presentation area that I want to focus on polishing is (fill in with one of the presentation components in Exhibit 9.1):

2. I will work on refining this area by taking the following three steps (be as specific as possible):

   a.

   b.

   c.

3. I will know I'm successful in cultivating this presentation area by (be as specific as possible):

EXHIBIT 9.3   Sample completed goals sheet.

Presentation Goals Sheet

1. The presentation area that I want to focus on polishing is *feeling more confident in my delivery because I know that I talk too rapidly.*

2. I will work on refining this area by taking the following steps:

   a. *Consciously enunciate each word during practices and presentations*

   b. *Time myself during each practice session and gauge my pace to speak 125 to 150 words per minute*

   c. *Videotape myself to later listen to how well I'm slowing down my pace*

   d. *Solicit feedback from a colleague who will watch the tape and talk with me about my pace*

3. I will know I'm successful in cultivating this presentation area *by hearing for myself that I'm speaking clearly and distinctly—and by receiving positive feedback from my colleague who is assisting me. Also, by meeting the 125 to 150 words per minute guideline.*

Exhibit 9.1 shows a strengths and challenges assessment chart. Presenters can use this chart to assess their skills at various steps in the presentation process to determine whether they're particularly strong or need to develop one of these areas. If they're proficient in an area (it's neither a strength nor a challenge), they'll mark the "Consistent" box. Ideally, presenters will focus first on improving a particular skill so that they can move the "Challenge" marks in Exhibit 9.1 (if any) to the "Consistent" boxes. Once they feel their skills are proficient (or if they don't have any marks initially in the "Challenge" column), presenters can then target specific areas and plan strategies to move performance from the "Consistent" level to the "Strength" level.

You'll see in Exhibit 9.2 a presentation goals sheet to support strengthening skills in specific areas. When setting goals, presenters need to be as specific as possible in listing the steps to take toward reaching a particular goal. Additionally, they must have a clear understanding of how to know when they're successful in reaching the goal—what is the ideal end result? Exhibit 9.3 illustrates a detailed example of a completed goals sheet.

Of course, strong presenters set aside time regularly to rate their performance in these categories because they recognize that their skills aren't static. They know that it's an evolving process and strive to develop their skills in each presentation component as much as possible. Audience feedback assessments, of course, provide one measure of performance appraisal;

self-reflection offers another. Just as athletes view tapes of their competitions to break down performance patterns in order to maintain top form, so presenters should objectively analyze their performance—both during a presentation and in the presentation planning stages.

Presenter Work Patterns

In addition to assessing a presenter's individual strengths and potential roles on a team project, it's critical to further reflect on how each team member's work ethic and habits might differ from (and complement) those of colleagues. If, for example, one team member's most productive time to work is early morning, the team needs to know this so that they can plan accordingly, if possible. Thus, if that particular presenter is on a team with several people who happen to work better during the late afternoon hours, these team members will understand that the "early bird" presenter might not be as creative or energetic during late-day meetings. Additionally, that presenter should understand why teammates aren't excited about planning meetings during early morning hours.

Another work habit to consider is how team members meet deadlines. Some presenters prefer to complete tasks as early before a deadline as possible so that they have plenty of time to review and revise material. Some like scheduling tasks and sticking to deadlines in order to complete a project within a specific amount of time. And some feel more creative and energetic working against a deadline. Consider the illustration below of the balancing act team members must negotiate in working with each other's sense of urgency about deadlines.

> Laurie prefers to work with specific, clear deadlines so that the project is finished ahead of schedule; on the other hand, Chris relishes the adrenaline surge that comes with working madly on a project at the last minute.

If Laurie and Chris don't understand and compensate for how each works best, they'll likely experience difficulties or conflicts developing a project or presentation. Clarifying how people prefer to work—and appreciating that others may work differently—can minimize potential team miscommunication when a deadline looms.

TEAM STRATEGIES PREPARING FOR A PRESENTATION

Once you've committed to a team presentation project, immediately begin—as a team—planning a strategy to complete it. There's no substitute or shortcut for deciding at the beginning of the process who will handle

EXHIBIT 9.4   **Presentation management chart.**

Task	Deadline	Team Member
Develop audience connection, background, and wrap-up	September 23	Sally, Shane
Develop key points and handout	September 29	Vin, Gus
Develop PowerPoint slides	October 3	Vin
Review audience connection, background, and wrap-up	October 15	Gus
Review key points and handout	October 15–18	Sally
Review PowerPoint slides	October 15–18	Shane
Practice presentation	October 20, 8:30 A.M. October 23, 8:30 A.M.	All team members

each task. One way to divide duties is to complete a presentation management chart. Use this chart to break down tasks so that each individual on the team knows what everyone is responsible for; this clearly delineates responsibilities and minimizes the risk of anyone duplicating tasks. Exhibit 9.4 shows an example of a completed presentation management chart for a four-person team.

Notice in this example that the presentation development stages are spelled out so that each team member is responsible for a particular component of the presentation. Further, the chart identifies which team member will review another team member's work. This ensures the team will have the opportunity for "fresh eyes" to review each segment of the presentation before they rehearse. Additionally, this revision process helps to give a cohesive "voice" to the presentation. Of course, every team presentation situation will be different. As a result, the specific tasks for the chart will vary, depending on what a team needs to accomplish. You'll find in Exhibit 9.5 a sample presentation management chart to use in planning team presentation responsibilities. Use the blank rows to add additional tasks.

Practicing and Giving Constructive Feedback

It can be tempting for team members to "wing it" for a presentation because of the difficulty in coordinating several schedules for practice sessions

EXHIBIT 9.5   Presentation management chart.

Task	Deadline	Team Member
Develop audience connection, background, and wrap-up		
Develop key points and handout		
Develop PowerPoint slides		
Review audience connection, background, and wrap-up		
Review key points and handout		
Review PowerPoint slides		
Practice presentation		
(Other)		

(Neuborne, 2002). And some presenters may believe that team presentations aren't as difficult as individual presentations; after all, an audience's attention will be divided among the team members, thus diluting the focus on individuals, right? Wrong! Practicing team presentations is critical if presenters want to give the impression that their message is seamless and organized (Flett, 1998). Ideally, a team presentation's visuals and message should appear as if one person coordinated them, and the transitions between speakers should be smooth and subtle.

Group rehearsals help team members know what areas of a message, delivery, or visuals they need to polish up before delivering a presentation. Additionally, practice sessions help teams stick within the time frame they're given for a presentation by allowing them the opportunity to time each segment and rehearse transitions between presenters.

Just like individual presentation run-throughs, the first few "dry run" team practices don't sound like they eventually will after several rehearsals. Practice a complete run-through—without stopping for any reason—at least three times before the actual session. The first time your team practices, time the presentation to know how long or short the message is in relation to the time expectation. Typically, presentations will run either too short or far too long on the first practice run. Learning early where content needs to be added or cut helps a team decide where to focus efforts. Individual team members also may realize during the first run-through that they need to polish specific sections of the message or specific delivery skills. Likewise, a team will also benefit from an early rehearsal by seeing how presentation visuals mesh with the message. The team can then determine if a presentation needs more graphics to underscore key points or a few additional slides for added emphasis.

Don't be overly concerned about polishing up individual parts of a presentation during the first practice. Think of the initial rehearsal as a trial to determine, in the big picture, what works well and what areas require more work. The second and third times through a team practice session, offer feedback to individuals on the team to help them refine their sections. (Exercise 9.5 in this chapter offers a "target practice" exercise for teams to support each other in polishing delivery skills.) At this stage, team members should know how they plan to coordinate the message and delivery with their visuals. Thus, in final practice, the team can focus on refining delivery, presenter transitions, and timing.

For many people, presentations are cause enough for anxiety because they know that they'll be in front of an audience who will evaluate them. So to have fellow presenters critiquing their delivery style during a presentation practice can be discouraging and nerve-racking. However, feedback during team practice sessions is an opportunity for substantive one-on-one coaching to raise the level of individual delivery skills. Set the stage early that you expect teammates to give you constructive feedback throughout a presentation-building experience; when you get to the practice sessions, the team should use the same feedback strategies. By this point, it is hoped that your team will have the rapport and trust that's necessary for candid discussion of delivery techniques—what works and what doesn't.

Exhibit 9.6 lists some guidelines for teams to use in giving constructive feedback. As your team rehearses, try some "target practice." This involves each presenter sharing with the team one weak delivery skill he or she wants to focus on during the practice. Presenters will concentrate on strengthening these particular areas, and the team will coach each presenter on the effectiveness of the effort. For example, if one presenter knows she talks too quickly, she can work on slowing down her delivery during the practice. If team members believe that she still needs to slow down her speaking pace, they can have her deliver one of her key points again and try to improve her pace. And if she is still talking too rapidly, team members can have her deliver just a portion of one of her points again to try to help her get the desired pace. The presenter and her teammates "target" a specific skill that the presenter needs to polish. This gives the presenter time during a team session to practice a skill and receive immediate and individualized feedback on the effort. Teammates are valuable coaching resources during practices if the team takes time to refine each member's presentation skills.

EXHIBIT 9.6   Presenter and team feedback guidelines.

Presenter Guidelines

1. Accept feedback as constructive—not destructive. Your teammates want your part of a presentation to be as strong as possible, so they're making suggestions based on what they believe will improve your delivery.

2. Accept feedback as *suggestions*—not demands. You ultimately have the choice to accept, reject, or modify the suggestions that teammates offer you. Don't change a part of your presentation or the way that you deliver material just because a team-mate suggested that you do so. If you're uncomfortable with a suggestion, solicit feedback from other team members to gain consensus. Even so, however, ultimately you're the one "on stage" during your part of any presentation. You have to be comfortable with what you're presenting and how you deliver the message.

3. Accept criticism as one perspective that an audience might have. Recognize that your team members during a presentation practice are acting as "stand-ins" for the audience, and they'll hear or see what the audience will hear or see during your part of a presentation.

Team Member Guidelines

1. Phrase your feedback as constructively as possible. For example, avoid saying, "You have to slow down!" Instead, give feedback in the form of specifics about how *you perceive* the behavior: "When you were talking about point #2, I had a difficult time understanding because you seemed to be talking quickly in that part. Can you try that part again for us just a bit slower?"

2. Don't expect each team member to present just like you do. There are many effective presentation styles, and yours is simply one of them. Instead, focus feedback on basic presentation principles to help colleagues understand how an audience might hear or see a particular part of a presentation.

3. Accept the fact that colleagues may modify or reject your suggestions. Remember that you are giving only one part of a presentation, and team members have to be comfortable giving their respective parts.

TEAM STRATEGIES DURING A PRESENTATION

Even though this section of the chapter is subtitled "during a presentation," it doesn't simply address what happens when the first presenter begins speaking. Teams often spend substantial amounts of quality time analyzing an audience and practicing delivery skills. However, attention must also be paid to the image a team creates before a presentation begins as well as during a presentation. Additionally, teams must carefully plan

and rehearse how they'll transition between speakers so that their presentation is as seamless as possible. This section addresses the following issues:

- Starting professionally
- Transitioning between speakers

Starting Professionally

As team members enter a room or move to the front to start a presentation, audiences begin assessing presenters' nonverbal communication signals. Thus, team members have the opportunity to establish credibility and professionalism before the first presenter begins speaking.

Many sessions start with presenters, either on a panel with other presenters or as the main speakers, seated in the room with the audience. It's easy for an individual preparing to give a presentation to focus and exhibit quiet, confident preparedness just before getting up to speak. With three to five presenters on a team, however, this can be a different story.

Sometimes presenters on a team don't realize that they're a "visual aid" while they're waiting their turn to deliver their part of the message. Unfortunately, this lack of awareness could result in behavior that distracts audience attention from a team member who may be speaking. Or it could present the wrong impression of a team's credibility. A few teams that I've coached, for example, appeared disorganized at the outset because two or three of the presenters clustered around the computer to load or open the

EXHIBIT 9.7   Team presentation room setup.

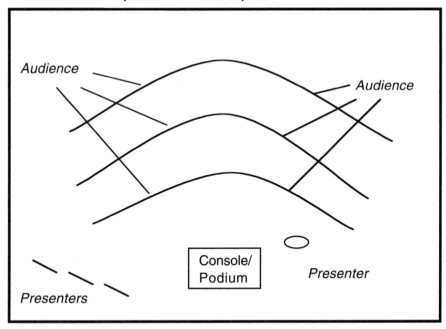

presentation, while the remainder of the team stood at the front of the room waiting for their teammates to bring up the visuals on the screen.

To help teams see themselves and their every movement and facial expression as audience members might, I often videotape team presentation practices. Without telling them, I start the videotaping two or three minutes before they're ready to begin the presentation. Invariably when we view the tape together, they comment that an audience might think that the team appears unfocused.

To look as prepared and professional as possible, each team member should know exactly what to do as the team readies to begin a presentation. I recommend that one team member load the presentation on the computer system (or set up the overhead transparency projector) while others set up their chairs (if not already set up) and sit waiting, ready for the presentation to start. Those seated can then look alertly at the audience to appear interested and to gauge their nonverbal communication cues before the presentation begins. The seated presenters need to have their own material ready for their turn—even the last presenter on the team—so that they don't have to shuffle papers while another presenter is speaking.

If possible, slant the presenters' chairs toward the front corner of the audience. Exhibit 9.7 shows an example of an ideal room set-up for a four-member team presentation. Notice that there are only three chairs for this

EXHIBIT 9.8   **Team presentation conference room setup.**

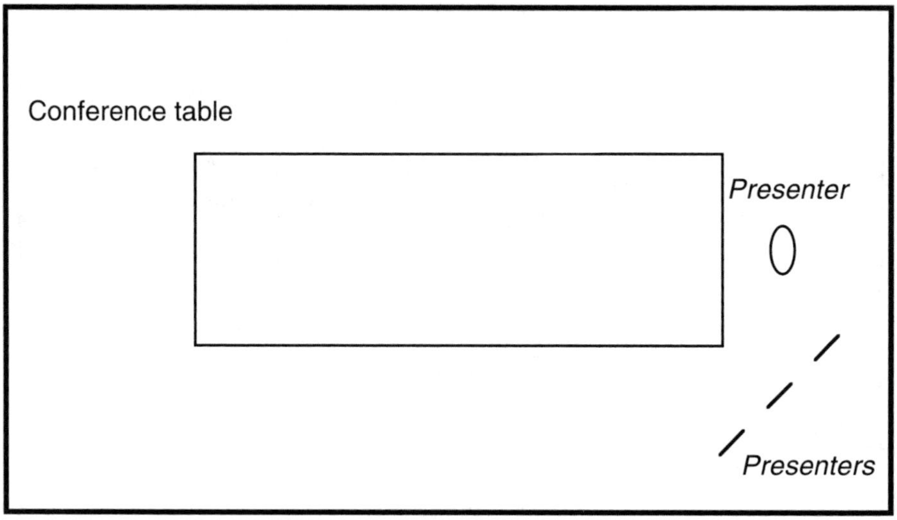

four-person team. At no time during a team presentation will all presenters be seated, so teams need only have enough chairs for the presenters awaiting their turn to step to the front of the room. Whenever a speaker finishes, that individual will take the chair of the next presenter in turn.

The example in Exhibit 9.8 shows a setup for a team presentation around a conference table (if presenters aren't already sitting together around the front corner of the table). In this example and in the one before it, presenters position themselves so that they're able to easily scan the audience to see how individuals might be receiving the presentation. The seated presenters should make a point of looking at the audience for nonverbal feedback or at the presenter to support the points that the presenter makes. An audience's attention will waver, and, at various points, audience members may look away from the presenter or the visuals at the other presenters. Seated presenters should not be yawning, slouching, or talking among themselves when the audience looks at them. In other words, they shouldn't become more interesting than the individual who is presenting. Team members also should avoid looking back at the slides because this could steer the audience's attention in a different direction from where the presenter is leading.

Of course, there will be situations in which the slant seating model won't work well. The following are just a few of the most typical examples:

- If your team has more than four or five people
- If the room's physical environment is too small
- If the audience is small (fewer than 10)

In any of these cases, discuss with teammates ahead of the presentation session how to handle where the waiting presenters should be, depending on the physical environment or the team situation.

Presenters waiting their turn shouldn't stand during a team presentation because they can be too much of a distraction for the audience. Most people are uncomfortable standing in front of an audience if they're not doing anything, and there's too much of a temptation to fidget. Instead, those waiting to present should sit relaxed until time for their segment.

Transitioning Between Speakers

An additional technique that teams can use to make a presentation more cohesive is developing smooth transitions between speakers. This is an area that requires careful advanced planning so that the various sections of a presentation appear the seamless work of an organized team.

Typically, the first presenter doesn't need to introduce individuals on the team at the outset. Instead, the person who opens the presentation session itself (most business meetings will have someone kick off the meeting and introduce speakers to the audience) will comment on the meeting purpose and perhaps the presenting team in general. For situations in which the presenters may already work closely with those in the audience, one of the presenters may take this role.

There is an exception to relying on someone else to introduce your team—if a team needs to develop strong credibility because of the presentation purpose, the session's goal is directly connected with who the presenters are in relationship to their audience. In these situations, presenter credibility may be the key to gaining an audience's confidence. To develop this, the opening presenter should consider introducing each speaker by name and area of expertise before beginning the session. This enhanced introduction emphasizes credentials and serves the presentation purpose particularly well in a session with a skeptical or hostile audience.

For most presentations, however, the first presenter should introduce himself or herself and simply begin the presentation. This reinforces for the audience who the opening presenter is, even if the person who introduced the team also introduced the first speaker. When the first presenter concludes his section of the presentation, he will introduce the next speaker and offer a very brief description of what that next speaker will cover. For example, if Sally opens a presentation, she'll transition to Josiah's part of the presentation by saying, "Next, Josiah Jackson will give you a context for our recommendations." A transitional sentence such as this serves several purposes. First, the transitional word "Next" lets the audience know that the team is shifting into a different part of the presentation message. Second, Sally specifies which presenter will be coming to the front. Finally, Sally tells the audience members what they can expect Josiah to discuss. These transitional steps help audiences move easily from one segment of a presentation to another. When Josiah finishes his part of the presentation, he'll do the same with the next presenter. Thus, each presenter introduces the speaker and topic that follow.

One delivery tip to use in making transitions: talk to the audience when introducing the next speaker. Inexperienced presenters, relieved that their section of the presentation is over, often will turn to the person that they're introducing and speak to that individual. Make a point of looking at the audience when introducing the next speaker—and then turn to go sit down.

Finally, let's address who should change the slides during a transition in a PowerPoint presentation. Should the presenter who just finished a section click to the next presenter's slide, or should the presenter coming up to the front change the slide? Depending on how your team practiced and what you're trying to accomplish, either method can be fine. I prefer that a presenter coming up to begin her part of a presentation click to change the slide because it emphasizes the fact that this presenter is moving into a new section of the presentation. Either way, however, the transition should look planned and polished to an audience.

EXERCISES   Presenting as a Team

EXERCISE 1   Assessment of My Strengths and Challenges

Complete the strengths and challenges assessment in Exhibit 9.1. Select five presentation components that you indicated were a challenge for you. If you didn't mark at least five challenge areas, select enough areas that you marked "consistent" until you have selected five total. From your selection of five presentation components, select the top three that you'd like to focus on in refining your presentation skills. Then, complete—in detail—the goals sheet in Exhibit 9.2 for each of these components.

EXERCISE 2   Here's How Our Team Works

If you're working on a team project from which you'll eventually deliver a presentation, have each member of the team complete the work habit checklist in Exhibit 9.9. In a 30- to 45-minute meeting, compare each individual's work preferences with other team members' preferences. Be sure to talk about how team members could be flexible in working with differing habits. If you're not

EXHIBIT 9.9   Work habit checklist.

1. My most productive time of the day is:
   _____ In the early morning
   _____ In the midmorning
   _____ In the afternoon
   _____ In the evening
   _____ In the late night

2. I prefer to meet:
   _____ Frequently in person
   _____ Infrequently in person with substantial sharing of material via email or other electronic methods
   _____ Infrequently via teleconference or videoconference with substantial sharing of material through email or other electronic methods

3. My feelings about deadlines are:
   _____ I prefer to finish projects several days early
   _____ I prefer to schedule my time so that I meet the deadline exactly
   _____ I'm more creative the closer I get to the deadline
   _____ I don't worry about deadlines because the work always gets done

4. I typically take one or more of the following roles on a team:
   _____ Leader
   _____ Organizer
   _____ Quality control manager
   _____ Time manager
   _____ Detail person
   _____ Big picture person
   _____ Management perspective
   _____ Client perspective

5. My most positive team experiences have been (explain what—specifically—made them positive experiences):

   My most negative team experiences have been (explain what—specifically—made them negative experiences):

currently involved with a team project, complete the list on your own and think about how your habits differed from team members' habits on a recently completed project. What work habits supported the team goal? Were there conflicts? How could these conflicts be resolved?

EXERCISE 3   Plan Who Will Complete Each Presentation Task

Using the presentation management chart in Exhibit 9.5, have members on a team project break down all tasks involved with an upcoming presentation and sign up to take responsibility for each task. Be sure to have each team member assigned to review another team member's work. If you're not currently working on a team project that you anticipate will lead to a presentation, complete the chart for a recent team presentation. Consider how effectively the team did or didn't allot responsibility for each component of the presentation.

EXERCISE 4   Let's See How We Look and Sound

Generate a 20- to 30-minute team presentation based on a group project that you've been working on. Schedule an hour to meet for a special practice session once the team has developed the presentation message and visuals. If possible, try to rehearse the presentation a couple of times individually before getting together for this special practice session. Make sure the PowerPoint slides and handouts are polished before the team meets as well. When the team starts the special session, videotape yourselves going through the entire presentation—without stopping for discussion. Consider it a "dress rehearsal." Be sure to record the presentation from start to finish to determine an approximate time frame. Use the team presentation practice checklist in Exhibit 9.10 to assess the presentation's effectiveness.

EXERCISE 5   Target Practice

Schedule a one-hour practice session for an upcoming team presentation. Follow these steps to refine a specific delivery skill:

1. At the start of the session, team members should identify one delivery skill to focus on during the session (e.g., talking more slowly, gesturing with purpose, maintaining eye contact with audience members).
2. Videotape the team practice.
3. As a team, watch the first presenter's segment and then give positive and constructive feedback on the skill the presenter seeks to polish. If the presenter still needs to practice that particular skill (e.g., still talking too

EXHIBIT 9.10 Team presentation practice checklist.

Timing

Actual presentation time _____   Time allowed _____

1. What areas do we need to trim (if any)?

2. What areas do we need to expand with more detail (if any)?

Message

1. Is the audience connection effective?

2. Do we provide a clear agenda of our key points early in the presentation?

3. Do we thoroughly support our key points?

4. Do we close with a call to action, a recommendation, or a summary of key points?

Delivery

1. Does each speaker transition smoothly to the next speaker (telling the audience who will be stepping up next and what that presenter will cover)?

2. Does the speaker maintain eye contact with the audience when transitioning?

3. Does each speaker appear confident with each section of the presentation?

4. Does each speaker maintain strong volume? Eye contact? Appropriate pace? Enthusiasm for the topic?

Visuals

1. Are all visuals coordinated with each other so that they appear prepared by one person?

2. Do the visuals support or illustrate our message?

quickly), ask the presenter to stand at the front of the room and deliver 30 to 60 seconds of his or her part of the presentation, focusing on effectively applying the constructive feedback. If the presenter needs still more practice, repeat the 60-second exercise once more.

4. Repeat step 3 with each presenter.

The purpose of this exercise is for presenters to "target" specific delivery skills to work on and receive immediate feedback on the effectiveness of their practice in a supportive environment.

References

Keene, M. (1993). *Effective professional and technical writing* (2nd ed.). Lexington, Massachusetts: D. C. Heath & Company.

Neuborne, E. (2002). Tag-team pitches: group presentations are a different ball game. Here's how to play [Electronic version]. *Sales & Marketing Management, 154*(3), 57.

Flett, N. (1998). Ensure you're all on the same team [Electronic version]. *Management, 45*(2), 14.

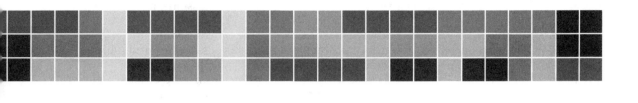

Index

Presenters:
 "born," 3
 as a team, 207–226 (*see also* Team presentations)
 attitude toward, 30–32
 credibility of, 20, 21, 23, 31, 36
 formal training for, 2–3
 gestures and, 94–97
 learning from accomplished, 9–10
 nervous, 11 (*see also* Presentation anxiety)
 nonverbal cues and, *see* Nonverbal cues
 roles of, 27–28
 status of, 23
 strengths and challenges, 209–213
 use of space and, 97–99
 voice and, *see* Voice
 work patterns, 214, 223
Problem solving, 152
 presentation pattern, 64–72
Projection, voice, 79–81 (*see also* Voice)
Purpose, 58, 65
 identification of, 36
 of a presentation, 14–16, 17
 secondary, 18

Q&A, 3, 187–204
 addressing the questions, 195–198
 anticipating question types, 191–195
 challenge questions, 193–195
 checklist, 203
 clarification questions and, 192
 confirmation questions and, 193
 delivery during, 198–199
 handling questions with no immediate answer, 198
 keys to sessions, 202
 nonverbal communication during, 200–201

 preparing for questions, 127, 189–191
 query questions and, 191–192
 restating questions and, 197–198
 self-validation questions and, 195
 setting expectations, 195–196
 time restrictions and, 201
Query questions, 191–192
Questions (*see also* Q&A):
 addressing, 195–198
 anticipating types of, 191–195
 challenge, 193–195
 clarification, 192
 confirmation, 193
 preparing for, 127, 189–191
 query, 191–192
 restating, 197–198
 self-validation, 195
 without immediate answer, 198

Rate, 83–86
 confidence and, 179
 exercise regarding, 105
Recommendations, key, 70, 72
Research, on corporations, 24–26
Room:
 acoustics, 81
 eye contact and, 91
 setup for team presentation, 219–220

Sans serif type vs. serif type, 116–118
Self-validation questions, 195
Serif type vs. sans serif type, 116–118
Setting:
 room acoustics and, 81
 type of for presentation, 33–34
Shared goal, 69–70, 71
Silence, during Q&A, 201
Six to a page view handout, 158, 159

Six x six rule, 112
Skills:
 assessment of presenting, 3
 oral communication, 2
Skills training, anxiety and, 174–180
Slide design:
 color use, 118–121
 contrast, 118–121
 dim feature, 126
 enhancement of slides, 127–137 (*see also* Graphics; Visuals)
 fonts, 116–118
 four by six rule, 112, 115
 graphs and, 130–131
 hyperlinks, 136–137
 information structure, 121–127 (*see also* Information structure)
 motion and sound, 134–136
 phrase check, 115
 planned builds, 125–126
 slide sorter view, 115
 tables and, 130
 text, 112–116
 use of white space, 112
 using bullet points, 112–116
 using phrases instead of sentences, 112, 115
 watermarks, 120–121, 122
Slides (*see also* PowerPoint):
 agenda, 122–124
 design, *see* Slide design
 enhancement of, 127–137 (*see also* Graphics; Slide design; Visuals)
 four x six rule, 112, 115
 graphic enhancement of, 127–137 (*see also* Graphics; Slide design; Visuals)
 information on, *see* Information structure
 PowerPoint, *see* PowerPoint
 six x six rule, 112
 titles, 122–124
 transitions, 125